WILLIAM S.
BURROUGHS &
THE CULT OF
ROCK 'N' ROLL

William S. Burroughs & the Cult of Rock 'n' Roll

Casey Rae

University of Texas Press

AUSTIN

Requests for permission to reproduce material from this work should be sent to:
Permissions
University of Texas Press
P.O. Box 7819
Austin, TX 78713-7819
utpress.utexas.edu/rp-form

⊗The paper used in this book meets the minimum requirements of ANSI/NISO Z39.48-1992 (R1997) (Permanence of Paper).

Library of Congress Cataloging-in-Publication Data

Names: Rae, Casey, author.
Title: William S. Burroughs and the cult of rock 'n' roll / Casey Rae.
Description: Austin : University of Texas Press, 2019. |
Includes bibliographical references and index.
Identifiers: LCCN 2018035621
   ISBN 978-1-4773-1650-4 (cloth : alk. paper)
   ISBN 978-1-4773-1866-9 (library e-book)
   ISBN 978-1-4773-1867-6 (non-library e-book)
Subjects: LCSH: Burroughs, William S., 1914-1997. |
   Burroughs, William S., 1914–1997—Friends and associates. |
   Rock musicians.
Classification: LCC PS3552.U75 Z833 2018 | DDC 813/.54—dc23
LC record available at https://lccn.loc.gov/2018035621

doi:10.7560/316504

For Sandy, among the stars

Contents

WILLIAM S.
BURROUGHS &
THE CULT OF
ROCK 'N' ROLL

Introduction

*Burroughs' career is counted
out in transformations.
There is no one Burroughs.*

VICTOR BOCKRIS

In 1995, toward the end of his life, William S. Burroughs posed for a picture by Kate Simon, who had worked with him over a period of twenty years. The octogenarian author is seen smoking a joint beneath a large black-and-white screen with big block text that screams LIFE IS A KILLER. Burroughs' celebrity—or notoriety—was primarily earned as the writer of such groundbreaking novels as *Junkie*, *Naked Lunch*, *The Wild Boys*, and *Cities of the Red Night*, along with countless articles, essays, and interviews. He also turned heads in the fine arts world with his infamous shotgun paintings—which he made by blasting both barrels at a can of spray paint positioned near a plywood canvas affixed with collage. At age eighty-one, Burroughs was a living icon who had inspired countless younger artists—especially musicians—over four decades of creative, psychological, and pharmacological exploration.

The most transgressive of the Beat writers, Burroughs was also something of a clandestine agent in the development of rock 'n' roll—a spectral figure who haunted the cultural underground and helped usher it into the mainstream. His direct impact on musical artists over a half century is immense but largely unexplored. From the Beatles, to punk, to today's remix scene, Burroughs helped accelerate an evolution in sound that continues to reverberate across continents and eras. This book tells the story of his personal connection to musicians and how his influence continues to echo more than twenty years after his death.

Burroughs still had plenty of spark at his final photo shoot, holding the pose for an extended period so Simon could properly frame him beneath a print made by his dear friend John Giorno. "I thought the screen was beautiful," she remembered. "He was smoking a joint. This was the last shot I took of him. . . . It's something; life is a killer." A potent statement, sharp and impossible to ignore, like a switchblade to the stomach. And true to boot. *Born to Die* isn't just the name of the second Lana Del Rey album: it is part of humanity's source code, which according to Burroughs was written onto our fleshy systems by an unseen and unperceivable operator that he called Control. "All species are doomed from conception like all individuals," he said.

Burroughs spent his life researching and experimenting with ways to transform himself and the world around him. He did so through his writing as well as his work with audio—both of which inspired artists from Bob Dylan to Kurt Cobain—helping pave the way for today's sample- and remix-based music. It's strange to think of this Jazz Age relic, whose gentlemanly manners belied an uncompromising intellect, having an impact on so many different genres. Still, there is little doubt that the music of the twentieth century and beyond owes much to Burroughs' methods and worldview.

Burroughs explored intense inner and outer landscapes and reported back his findings, typing up his reports with remarkable discipline, day in and day out. This commitment, in addition to his immense talent and intellect, makes him a rare creative visionary. But what did Burroughs see through his deeply scarred lens? Pure, insatiable need. Instead of running away, however, he examined it up close. Drugs, the occult, psychic home surgery—any and all of it was worth experiencing and documenting. Like the musicians he inspired, Burroughs was a fearless and intrepid reporter who not only cataloged his adventures, but used them as raw material to initiate real change in the world around him. In doing so, he opened up new creative vistas to others, who in turn reshaped culture using techniques that he helped pioneer.

Today, Burroughs the icon captivates imaginations as much as

Burroughs the author. He expended great effort to depersonalize his work using cut-ups—a technique whereby pre-existing text, film, or audio is sliced up and rearranged—yet his biography has become as legendary as even his most celebrated novels. Here was a homosexual drug addict, born in the Gilded Age, who killed his wife in a drunken game of William Tell and wrote infamous prose featuring orgasmic executions, shape-shifting aliens, and all manner of addicts, sadists, and creepy crawlies. But there exists a real person within the legend, a man who exhibited genuine kindness and hospitality to those who knew him, including many of the musicians discussed in this book.

In many ways, Burroughs is a cipher, a puzzle to decode. Like a multifaceted prism or mirror, Burroughs reflects different things to different people depending on their own interests or agendas. To some, Burroughs is a junkie priest offering hardboiled wisdom from the narcotic underground. To others, he is a dark magus whose occult philosophies paved the way for today's DIY sorcerers. Still others—especially recording artists and songwriters—find inspiration in his creative methods, including cut-up text and tape-splicing. That there are so many different ways to engage with Burroughs' work and worldview is key to the perpetuation of his influence. It allows other artists to take his vision forward, often in mutated form. Over time, this gravelly voiced son of midwestern privilege has become like a space-borne virus from one of his books, hopping from host to host, medium to medium, each strain transforming culture in profound, though sometimes obscure, ways. This is just how he would have wanted it.

Burroughs is a highly significant figure in the world of music, even if he professed little knowledge about the form. It's not hard to see how his writing—exploding with disquieting, even ghastly imagery—might serve as fodder for music genres like punk, heavy metal, and industrial. To be sure, it is within these subcultures that most present-day Burroughs acolytes are found. But his anti-Establishment attitude and unconventional personal habits also found favor with such artists as Paul McCartney, Bob Dylan, the

Rolling Stones, Lou Reed, Frank Zappa, Iggy Pop, Patti Smith, Laurie Anderson, and countless other musical innovators. The Beatles even put him on the cover of *Sgt. Pepper's Lonely Hearts Club Band* alongside the likes of Carl Jung, Lenny Bruce, Karl Marx, and Oscar Wilde. Once you start looking, Burroughs is everywhere. It's like a game of "Where's Waldo?" with a killer soundtrack. But instead of a chipper youth in a striped sweater, we're spying a wan junkie in an old fedora.

His influence extends beyond the work itself to the actual methods used to create it. Burroughs' focus on recombinant media—that is, cut-up text, "found sound," and tape-splicing—would become the lingua franca of experimental audio production in the 1990s and continues to be today. He first began working with cut-ups alongside painter Brion Gysin in 1950s Paris. The original method involved slicing up prewritten text from one or more sources into quadrants and rearranging the pieces at random. Later experiments involved machine-based cut-ups devised by Burroughs' lover Ian Sommerville, an early computer programmer. Going forward, Burroughs would embrace random elements in almost all of his work, especially his audio experiments, some of which were conducted on tape recorders provided by Paul McCartney in a flat owned by Ringo Starr. These operations inspired the Beatles to include found sound and tape cut-ups on seminal recordings like *Sgt. Pepper* and *The White Album*, ushering in a new dawn for recorded sound.

It's hard to imagine sample- and remix-based music without Burroughs, or at least without the artists he inspired—David Bowie, Throbbing Gristle, and Coil among them. Hip-hop and electronic acts like Michael Franti, DJ Spooky, and Justin Warfield embrace Burroughsian ideas in their work, and a few were lucky enough to have collaborated with him. Arena conquerors U2 used video cut-ups on massive global tours and sought Burroughs out for their 1997 video for "The Last Night on Earth"—his last filmed appearance. Countless bands got their monikers from Burroughs' novels or incorporated his phrases in song titles and lyrics. Steppenwolf, who are credited with bringing the term "heavy metal" to music, borrowed the phrase from Burroughs. Then there's Steely Dan, who famously took their name from a state-of-the-art dildo in *Naked Lunch*. And there are others—such as the Soft Machine, Nova Mob, Wild Boys, and the Mugwumps—to name but a few. Iggy Pop and Patti Smith lifted lines directly from Burroughs and weren't shy about letting the world know. At one point, synth-poppers Duran Duran attempted to make a full-length film based on their video for "Wild Boys," a song that took its inspiration from a Burroughs novel of the same name. More recently, psychedelic rockers Howlin Rain borrowed the title for a song that bandleader Ethan Miller described as an homage to Burroughs. "There is little that we find astonishing about the present American landscape in all its chaos and turmoil that wasn't uttered in a fearsome, frothing monotone of absolute contempt by Burroughs a long, long time ago," Miller told *Relix Magazine*.

Burroughs was an intrepid investigator of the paranormal and maintained an active interest in what we would today call fringe science. He held sway over occult-minded artists like Genesis P-Orridge of Throbbing Gristle, Chris Stein of Blondie, and John Balance and Peter Christopherson of Coil. Jimmy Page, lead guitarist and magus-in-chief of Led Zeppelin, spent time with Burroughs discussing music's supernatural potential and the connection between Zeppelin's thunder and the Master Musicians of Joujouka—a tribe of Moroccan musicians Burroughs referred to as "a 4,000 year-old rock 'n' roll band." Although he professed little firsthand knowledge of musical composition, Burroughs understood how performance could be used to affect reality. He delighted in Patti Smith's shamanic stagecraft, and the two became good friends. "He's up there with the Pope," Smith said of Burroughs. Bob Dylan practically chased him down for a meeting that took place at a Greenwich Village café in early 1965. Not long after, the studious folkie would reemerge at the Newport Folk Festival as a wild-eyed visionary backed by a raucously heretical electric band.

David Bowie used cut-ups in his work, from the 1974 album *Diamond Dogs* to *Blackstar*, released days before his death in 2016.

Bowie called cut-ups "a form of Western Tarot" and throughout his career credited Burroughs with helping to advance his own art and aesthetic. Erstwhile Bowie associate Lou Reed was a Burroughs obsessive going back to his days with the Velvet Underground. Reed didn't go for cut-ups, but he did borrow a great deal from earlier Burroughs books like *Junkie*, with its matter-of-fact portrayal of the ravages of addiction and sardonic observations of street life. Both Bowie and Reed spent time with Burroughs in the 1970s, scenes that will be recounted here along with analyses of the recordings influenced by him.

Burroughs spent much of his time abroad, living in Mexico, Morocco, Paris, and London, and making frequent trips back to New York City, where he moved in the mid-1970s. After a couple of downtown apartments, he settled into a windowless former YMCA locker room affectionately known as "the Bunker." The hideout sat just a couple of streets over from the legendary club CBGB in the seedy Bowery neighborhood. Here Burroughs played host to the denizens of the emerging punk scene, including Patti Smith, Chris Stein and Debbie Harry of Blondie, Joe Strummer of the Clash, and Richard Hell of the Voidoids, to name a few. Though Burroughs more or less rejected the "godfather of punk" title bestowed on him affectionately by the press, he did find the new generation more interesting than the hippies. He even sent the Sex Pistols a letter of support when they took heat for "God Save the Queen," their monarchy-bashing single from 1977. "I've always said that England doesn't stand a chance until you have 20,000 people saying 'Bugger the Queen!'" Burroughs enthused.

In 1978 a coterie of musicians, writers, and performance artists came together to celebrate Burroughs' return to the United States at the Nova Convention, held at the Entermedia Theater in New York. Frank Zappa read one of the more notorious bits from *Naked Lunch*, the "Talking Asshole" routine; Smith, suffering from pneumonia, nonetheless delivered a righteous reading backed by her loyal axman Lenny Kaye; Laurie Anderson brought an experimental edge to the proceedings with pitch-shifted vocals and sparse electronics;

and Philip Glass melted minds with his then-new composition "Einstein on the Beach." The after-party boasted performances by Suicide, Blondie, the B-52s, and King Crimson guitarist Robert Fripp.

Punk begat industrial music, including the groundbreaking sonic assaults of Throbbing Gristle and Psychic TV—two bands led by "occulture" doyen Genesis P-Orridge. One would be hard-pressed to find a more persistent evangelist of the Burroughs world-view than P-Orridge, who has a great many stories and observations about the emerging industrial scene and Burroughs' covert role in shaping it. P-Orridge is the link between Burroughs and the tech-enabled "chaos magicians" who began colonizing the weird wide web at the advent of dial-up. Burroughs did not live to see the Internet become the force for creative, social, economic, cultural, and political disruption that it is today. But he would no doubt have recognized it for what it is: a cut-up. Today we are positively bombarded with fragmentary sounds and images, recombined and often weaponized to serve one agenda or another. What do we call it when one of these "small units of information" holds brief sway over our consciousness? We say it "went viral." Somewhere in space-time, the old man twists his thin lips into something resembling a smile.

Burroughs continued to impact the world of music after he moved to Lawrence, Kansas, in 1981. His early spoken-word and tape-splicing experiments were collected on *Nothing Here Now But the Recordings*, originally released on Throbbing Gristle's label, Industrial Records, in 1981. That same year saw a joint album featuring Burroughs, performance poet John Giorno, and experimental musician Laurie Anderson called *You're the Guy I Want to Share My Money With*—Anderson's first official release. Not long after, Burroughs appeared on records alongside artists like Nick Cave, Tom Waits, Butthole Surfers, Swans, and David Byrne.

The 1990s saw Burroughs, then in his late seventies, become even more of a hero to the music world. He wrote the text for *The Black Rider*—a theatrical collaboration with Robert Wilson and Tom Waits—which was also released as a Waits solo record. On it, Burroughs can be heard singing the standard "T'ain't No Sin" in his creaky drawl. A "magical fable" that borrows from Faust and echoes Burroughs' accidental shooting of his wife, *The Black Rider* is still performed around the world to critical acclaim. The spoken-word album *Dead City Radio* appeared in 1990 and included background music by Donald Fagen of Steely Dan, Sonic Youth, and John Cale. Once again, it contains Burroughs' singing, this time on a charming version of the Marlene Dietrich warhorse "Falling in Love Again."

In the '90s, Burroughs didn't travel much anymore, but plenty of notables came to him. The final decade of his life saw him hosting the likes of Kurt Cobain, Sonic Youth, and members of R.E.M. and Ministry at his red bungalow in Lawrence. In 1992, bassist and producer Bill Laswell released *The Western Lands*, based on Burroughs' book of the same name. That same year, Ministry sampled Burroughs in the song "Just One Fix"; he also appeared in the video. Burroughs collaborated with the Disposable Heroes of Hiphoprisy for *Spare Ass Annie and Other Tales*, released in 1993. Burroughs and Cobain released a record together, *The "Priest" They Called Him*, shortly before Cobain's suicide in 1994. In 1996, Burroughs teamed up with R.E.M. for a cover of their song "Star Me Kitten" and time-traveled back to the 1960s for a bizarre mash-up with the Doors, "Is Everybody In?."

Today, Burroughs' sway over the music scene is somewhat less pronounced. And yet his influence is often the most persuasive when his presence is hardest to detect: they didn't call him "El Hombre Invisible" for nothing. Music is actually just the tip of the iceberg. Burroughs' impact on a range of popular media—including films, comics, video games, and other literature—is equally immense. He predicted a future where minds would be literally infected by "very small units of sound and image" distributed en masse and electronically, which we see in today's meme wars on social media and at certain message boards like 4Chan, where hordes of young, mostly male raconteurs engage in ceaseless rage attacks against tolerance and reason. "Storm the citadels of the Enlightenment," Burroughs once wrote. It is rapidly becoming a truism that on the Internet, "Nothing is true; everything is permitted," to borrow one of his favorite turns of phrase. The stories captured in these pages demonstrate that Burroughs not only foresaw but may even have helped initiate our increasingly chaotic present and uncertain future. Still, the most enthusiastic ambassadors of his worldview happen to be musicians. Those appearing in this book serve as a Rosetta stone for understanding key aspects of Burroughs' work that predicted so much about our current society and may have more to reveal about where we are going.

This book is about music, musicians, and William S. Burroughs. It is also an account of the social, political, and technological transformations that have transpired since Burroughs committed to "writing his way out" of his own personal traumas—many of which were self-inflicted. The musicians who gravitate to Burroughs have a lot in common with one another, even if they come from highly divergent backgrounds. All of them burn with a desire to break out of the ordinary, to escape social or institutional conditioning. Many struggle with impulse control. No doubt some of them just wanted to hang out with the Pope of Dope, but his most intrepid devotees made waves using the author's techniques and aims. Their adventures are recounted here, interwoven with Burroughs' own biography. In this way, a broad range of concepts, ideas, methods, obsessions, and outcomes are explored, connecting everything from EDM to hip-hop to punk to heavy metal to drug culture to the occult to media to technological dystopia.

As the author of this book, I can tell you plainly that even I had no idea when I began my research just how many fascinating—and deadly relevant—intersections are found in the Burroughsverse. But remember, this is just one facet of the mirror—a collection of impressions from the world of music, which in turn informs and shapes the broader culture. The real-world interactions between Burroughs and musicians described in this book were hilarious, confounding, and life-altering, just like the best of his writing. Burroughs said the only reason to write is "to make it happen." The artists within these pages all changed society in ways large and small. Like Burroughs, they are world travelers, experimenters, addicts, chameleons, influencers, and soothsayers. As were Burroughs', their bold excursions on the fringes of creativity—even sanity—serve to broaden our own horizons and inspire worthwhile expression across many media.

If this were just a collection of vignettes of Burroughs hanging out with rock stars, it would be plenty entertaining. But there is much more to the story. I see this book as a tribute to all great artists who push the limits, even when their efforts come at considerable cost. And everything has a cost, because everything is a hustle. Sex, drugs, religion, politics, finance, technology . . . we're all marks in some pusher's game. They all aim to make us dependent on sundry products, experiences, ideologies. And we're always hungry to score—forever hunting for some small distraction from the pains of our own existence. It's no fault of our own. According to Burroughs, our flesh is already infected with the prewritten script: we are the soft machines upon which the "algebra of need" is encoded.

*   *   *

There are quite a few Burroughs biographies on the market, many of them worthwhile. One of the first, Ted Morgan's *Literary Outlaw: The Life and Times of William S. Burroughs*, is based on interviews with the author and his associates. The more recent *Call Me Burroughs: A Life*, by Barry Miles, is a doorstop that doesn't skimp on the details. Other books cover more esoteric ground, such as *Scientologist! William S. Burroughs and the Weird Cult*, by David Willis, or *The Magical Universe of William S. Burroughs*, by Matthew Levi Stevens. Victor Bockris deserves credit for capturing many fascinating conversations between Burroughs and the art stars of the 1970s in *With William Burroughs: A Report from the Bunker*. This book is not meant to replace those works but rather to supplement them with additional insights and analyses specific to the world of music. However, it is necessary to delve into Burroughs' biography in order to establish the themes that connect it to the musicians' stories in this book. Our tale for the most part unfolds chronologically, though it occasionally skips around on the "time track," to borrow a Burroughs phrase. The reason for this is because Burroughs' personal history begins well before the advent of rock 'n' roll. Readers will encounter the bulk of his biography in the first couple of chapters, after which his life trajectory begins to line up with the music-centric material. If you're already familiar with his life story, you will no doubt discover additional ideas to consider. And if you're new to Burroughs, don't be surprised if you're hooked right out of the gate—his story is incredibly compelling.

I remember my first shot of William S. Burroughs. It was 1988, when I was a freshman in high school following around a pair of upperclassmen who were in a cover band that played the school dances. They were, and remain, cooler than that description suggests. And I'm not just saying that because they let a precocious motormouth follow them around. These kids were enthusiastic explorers of art and culture, from Dylan to Dada. They expanded my literary horizons and helped turn me into a half-decent guitarist and recording geek. Frankly, I was lucky. Hoping for any glimpse of a world beyond my no-horse New England town, and encouraged by my older peers, I consumed primo VHS fare like *Repo Man* (directed by Burroughs enthusiast Alex Cox) and listened to Sonic Youth back when they only played noise. Sandwiched between the Vonnegut and the Brautigan on a friend's bookshelf was *Naked Lunch*, published thirty years earlier—an infinity to a sixteen-year-old. Yet the words were like a live wire jacked straight into my still-developing cerebral cortex. I had been infected.

An early reader, I had already torn through the gothic literature at home, polishing off the likes of Bram Stoker, Edgar Allan Poe, H. G. Wells, and Jules Verne. Fervid peeks at the topmost shelf, where Anaïs Nin and Henry Miller were rightfully paired, offered a window into a more lascivious world. But nothing, not even H. P. Lovecraft—Burroughs' cosmic horror doppelganger—could have prepared me for *Naked Lunch*, with its alternately horrifying and hilarious visions of drug abuse, carnality, and monsters both human and insectoid.

These days, kids can get their hands on all manner of subversive media at the flick of a fingertip. Back in the '80s and decades prior, it took real effort. First off, things cost money. You couldn't just download a song, movie, or, God forbid, a book for free on the Internet. It took a lot of mowed lawns and shoveled driveways to purchase even the relatively small number of Cure albums available at the time. (I speak from experience.) My interest in Burroughs was reinforced by other media, especially music. I remember hearing about Kurt Cobain's audio collaboration with Burroughs, the 10-inch single *The "Priest" They Called Him* back in 1993, and driving a town over to the only decent record store to see if they had it. They didn't, but I made damned sure that the record store I managed a handful of years later did. By the mid-1990s, I had read most, if not all, of Burroughs' novels and whatever nonfiction I could get my hands on. I recall being particularly taken by *The Job*, which grew out of a series of interviews conducted by Daniel Odier in the 1960s, when Burroughs was living in England. It was less of a Q&A than a stream-of-consciousness rant in which Burroughs put forward the notion that language is literally a virus that infected the human larynx early in the development of our species. This virus caused a mutation in the biological animal that, in turn, remapped our mental circuitry. Whether this idea had any basis in evolutionary theory was unimportant: it was wildly entertaining, as was the author's syntax—spare, but with its own weird meter, sort of like Charlie Watts' drumming in the Stones. Later on, when I heard one of his taped readings, it only amplified these qualities, clearing further space for this high strangeness to flower in my mind. For me, as a creative person, Burroughs inspired a kind of fearlessness, an urge to experiment, and a sense that no matter how alienated I felt, I wasn't alone. There were others out there.

Creative people need other creative people, as is clear from the stories in this book. Many young artists endure intense personal struggles, often related to feeling like outsiders of some kind. This is probably why small groups of artists form bonds; it's a survival strategy, a kind of social insurance in an antagonistic world that tends not to tolerate freethinking. This is as true now as it was in the 1940s, when Burroughs was a young man in New York, where he felt the pangs of romantic rejection, developed his unique approach to composing scenes, and got hopelessly hooked on heroin. As a member of what came to be known as the Beats, Burroughs—along with Jack Kerouac, Allen Ginsberg, and a motley cast of supporting players—upended American literature and seeded a counterculture that persists to this day. Not long after came rock 'n' roll, which boasts its own pantheon of renegades and outsiders. Even when their audiences number in the thousands or millions, rock stars tend to operate in small tribes. A band is a tribe. A substitute family. Because with a few exceptions, artists tend not to have great histories with their original ones.

Burroughs' circle, relatively small but highly engaged, enabled him to float new ideas and conduct experiments of the metaphysical and pharmacological kind. His friends helped him complete his masterwork, *Naked Lunch*—a product of "team editing" by Ginsberg and Kerouac, who both looked up to him for many of the same reasons that musicians did later. Burroughs might not have deliberately sought his status as the godfather of punk, but he is nonetheless the ultimate antihero, someone who refused to be conditioned by Establishment norms. To be sure, some of his disciples may have been indulging a lifestyle crush, at least at first. But even that is interesting. What kind of person gravitates to a guy who shot his own wife? What kind of person admires an unrepentant addict? Who would want to hang out with a weird old junkie who lives in a windowless Bowery basement? As it turns out, quite a few. And I probably have all of their records.

As someone who carries the "Burroughs gene"—that is, who has taken more than a passing interest in his life and work—I remain drawn to his fierce intellect and black humor, as well as his refusal to conform. But there's more to it than vicarious thrill-seeking. The more one reads Burroughs, listens to his recordings, or examines his interviews, the further one is drawn in. Burroughs occupies his own universe: an area beyond known space-time coordinates where he serves as both sovereign and ambassador. To travel with Burroughs is to see the world you thought you knew get cut up and reassembled in strange, funny, and sometimes frightening forms. Burroughs isn't just the ticket: he's the locomotive and the tracks, the rocket and the launchpad. Of course, you'll never understand William S. Burroughs by reading *about* him. Just like you'll never understand a record by looking at it. You have to sample the wares, kid. Good thing there's plenty to go around: interviews, essays, videos, albums, and of course, books, to which I am honored to add my own. Now go ahead and get yourself hooked.

Nirvana the Hard Way

There's something wrong with that boy.
He frowns for no good reason.

WILLIAM S. BURROUGHS, following
a meeting with Kurt Cobain in 1993

El Hombre Invisible

By the dawn of the 1980s, decades abroad and several years of holding court among the New York City underground had brought William S. Burroughs to a place of exhaustion and, once again, addiction. He no longer felt the wanderlust that had propelled him through South America, North Africa, and Europe, and informed books like *Naked Lunch*, *The Soft Machine*, and *The Wild Boys*. Now in his sixties, it was time for Burroughs to get clean and go home. But where was that exactly? Surely not Saint Louis, where he was born and experienced a privileged childhood as the favored son of a midwestern family of diminishing industrial wealth. By then his parents were deceased, along with his own son, William S. Burroughs Jr., who died in 1981 from cirrhosis of the liver at the age of thirty-three. James Grauerholz—Burroughs' steadfast literary secretary, business manager, and friend—would be his closest family in his final years. Concerned for Burroughs' health, Grauerholz encouraged the author to move to his own hometown of Lawrence, Kansas. Burroughs had been to most places worth visiting, and plenty that weren't, and Lawrence seemed nice, if quiet. And that was good. Lawrence was the kind of town where the jackboots wouldn't storm in if he wanted to shoot guns at, say, a can of spray paint placed before a piece of plywood. This was the formula behind shotgun painting, a creative habit Burroughs took up in his later years that also helped pay the bills; he did remarkably well in the fine arts market. Another interest was animals, specifically those of the feline variety. When asked what was attractive about the sleepy college town, Burroughs quipped that Lawrence provided the opportunity to "go shooting and keep cats."[1]

The sixty-seven-year-old Burroughs was freshly signed to a seven-book deal with Viking Press when he arrived in Lawrence in December 1981. In the preceding years he'd given numerous public readings of his work around the world, cementing his reputation among a new generation of artists within the rock, punk, and new wave scenes. But at home in his modest red bungalow, he was just William. "Burroughs was very comfortable because the rest of the town just let him be," said Phillip Heying, a local photographer who befriended the aging author and served among a small but dedicated crew of locals who took turns making Burroughs dinner and assisting with chores and errands.[2]

Many years earlier, while living abroad, Burroughs had earned the nickname "El Hombre Invisible" from locals who noted his skill at not being noticed—no small feat for a stiff-limbed white guy on the streets of Tangier. By then he had had plenty of practice dodging authorities, which may be why he believed invisibility was a technique one could learn. The magician revealed his secrets—well, this one at least—in *The Adding Machine*, a collection of essays first published in 1985. "The original version of this exercise was taught me by an old Mafia Don in Columbus, Ohio: seeing everyone in the street before he sees you," Burroughs wrote. "I have even managed to get past a whole block of guides and shoeshine boys in Tangier this way, thus earning my Moroccan moniker."[3]

In 1950s North Africa, Burroughs chased drugs, sex, and literary immortality to the sound of reed pipes and drums played by musical mystics. His best-known work, *Naked Lunch*, was largely written in this heady environment. It would be published in Paris in 1959, while Burroughs was staying at the infamous Beat Hotel in the city's Latin Quarter. He haunted London in the 1960s, rubbing elbows with the Beatles and the Rolling Stones and singing the praises of the "aphomorphine cure" that helped him kick heroin, however briefly. The next stop was New York's Bowery neighborhood, where he commandeered a converted YMCA locker room affectionately known as "the Bunker" in the mid to late 1970s. They were productive years, but Burroughs' underground celebrity had gone from an entertaining distraction to a sycophantic drag. As Blondie cofounder Chris Stein says, "I think he got to a point at the Bunker where every time he left the house some guy was coming up to him with a manuscript."[4]

Even if he didn't leave the house, odds were he'd end up having dinner with the likes of Mick Jagger, Lou Reed, or Joe Strummer, to name a few of the well-known guests who visited Burroughs at the Bunker. But that didn't pay the soon-to-be-raised rent, which his latest junk habit was already eating into. Given these realities, relocating to Lawrence seemed like the smart choice. Burroughs' ties to New York remained strong, however, and he would return in later years for social occasions, commendations, and the occasional gig. One major event was his seventieth birthday party in 1984, held at a nightclub called Limelight—a former church that welcomed a congregation of notables looking to rub elbows with the iconic author. Madonna and Lou Reed were there, as well as Philip Glass, Jim Carroll, Lydia Lunch, and rising star Sting, accompanied by then-bandmate Andy Summers. When Burroughs heard that "the police" were at the party, he became concerned, telling a friend, "I don't know if you're holding but someone told me those two guys over there are cops."[5] The fête was fun, and the company interesting, but in New York everyone always wanted something.

This was refreshingly not the case in Lawrence. It wasn't long before Burroughs had established a routine that included writing, target shooting, methadone schedules, and feline feedings. Months stretched into years under the canopy of elm and honey locust trees that decked the city's wide sidewalks and Gothic Revival architecture. Townsfolk did not view Burroughs as a druggy firebrand, but as a congenial, if eccentric, old man, which is just what he had become. Lawrence poet Jim McCrary, who befriended Burroughs in his final years, recalled an obliging figure with proper midwestern manners. "He was a nice guy. You know like, if you came to his house, and you hung around and you left, he would always walk out on the porch and wait until you got into your car. If he drove you home, he would wait until you got into your door."[6] After years of globe-trotting, Burroughs had finally settled down.

Although his social obligations were fewer than in New York, Burroughs maintained a well-populated calendar with visits from old friends and colleagues, including Allen Ginsberg, Keith Haring, Norman Mailer, Timothy Leary, and Hunter S. Thompson. Admirers from the music world—such as Nirvana's Kurt Cobain, Michael Stipe of R.E.M., Thurston Moore of Sonic Youth, and Al Jourgensen of Ministry—also paid their respects. Blondie's Chris Stein, who spent several weeks in Lawrence in the mid-1980s while recuperating from an illness, first met the old man in 1970s New York. The two remained friends until Burroughs' death in 1997. "I always thought he was a really sweet guy," Stein says. "Just a very nice person. I like guns, you know, so we had that in common."[7] In the early evenings Burroughs would go shooting in a nearby cornfield with friends. Later Stein would head out to a local punk club, the Outhouse, on his own. "It was so outlaw and fringe because the club was only accessible at the end of a dirt road, and it was literally a cement bunker," Stein recalls. "I don't know if they stole the electricity, but it was coming off this lamp post or something like that, and all these punk bands would come through there and play."[8] Those bands included the likes of Bad Brains, Circle Jerks, Meat Puppets, and a soon to be massive trio from Seattle called Nirvana. That band's leader, Kurt Cobain, was a Burroughs obsessive of whom the older writer was genuinely fond.

Teen Spirit and Other Viruses

It is hard to overstate the impact Nirvana's 1991 breakthrough, *Nevermind,* had on popular music as well as the lives of the young men who wrote and recorded it. Cobain, bassist Krist Novoselic, and drummer Dave Grohl blew the opening bugle for alternative rock while defining its Seattle-centric subgenre, grunge. In a music landscape dominated by hair bands and cookie-cutter dance-pop, *Nevermind* was one of those rare impact objects that are directly responsible for the extinction of an entire species—in this case, hairsprayed and spandexed strutters like Poison, who pranced and pouted their way into the mainstream in the 1980s. *Nevermind* was responsible for a massive restructuring of the music business, which had previously bet big on glam metal. Now label execs parachuted into local scenes ready to sign anyone with a goatee and a pawnshop guitar. "Everyone was a little shocked," said Janet Billig Rich, who once managed 1990s alternative music megastars such as Nirvana, Smashing Pumpkins, and Hole. "Everything got really easy because it was this economy—Nirvana became an economy."[9]

Nirvana's popularity was epidemic. *Nevermind* achieved diamond sales status and knocked Michael Jackson from his position at the top of the charts. The band's videos aired incessantly on MTV, and their backstage brouhaha with Guns N' Roses at the 1992 Video Music Awards became the stuff of legend.[10] It had been a while since anyone had this kind of culture-changing impact, but it had happened before. Elvis Presley's pelvic thrusts during his 1956 performance on *The Ed Sullivan Show* had brought a new carnality to popular music. The Beatles' 1964 appearance on the same program cemented rock 'n' roll as the international language of youth. Since then, music—perhaps more than any other popular media—has matured into a massive global business.

Commoditized as it may be, no one would argue against music's power to move the masses, even in today's so-called distraction economy. In 2014, hip-hop producer Pharrell inspired millions in every corner of the world to make fan videos for his song "Happy." The track exploded on YouTube, a site whose global reach and influence has come to define "viral." These days record labels, movie studios, artists, and political candidates all seek to capitalize on contagion. This is the modern media hustle, where you're either a pusher or a mark. Burroughs died nearly a decade before YouTube was a glimmer in its developers' eyes, but he was a lifelong student of influence; specifically, how the virus of word and sound can shape the destiny of humankind. As he explained in 1986:

> My general theory since 1971 has been that the Word is literally a virus, and that it has not been recognized as such because it has achieved a state of relatively stable symbiosis with its human host; that is to say, the Word Virus (the Other Half) has established itself so firmly as an accepted part of the human organism that it can now sneer at gangster viruses like smallpox and turn them in to the Pasteur Institute. But the Word clearly bears the single identifying feature of virus: it is an organism with no internal function other than to replicate itself.[11]

In the Burroughs worldview, language is a mechanism of what the author called Control with a capital C: an insidious force that limits human freedom and potential. Words produce mental triggers that we can sometimes intuit but never entirely comprehend, making us highly susceptible to influence. But there's an upside: language can also be used to liberate by short-circuiting preprogrammed ideas and associations. Burroughs believed humanity is held back by constraints imposed by hostile external forces that express themselves in our reality as various aspects of the Establishment. Using fragments of word, sound, and image, reordered and weaponized, Burroughs sought to dismantle Control and its systems. His stance inspired other artists across generations and genres to use similar methods to rattle the status quo in ways that even he could not anticipate. You'll get to know them, and their connections to Burroughs, as his story unfolds.

Burroughs saw reality as hostile, malleable, and possessed of hidden potential that could be actualized through a kind of occult media arts. Though primarily known as the author of such groundbreaking novels as *Junkie* (1953), *Naked Lunch* (1959), *The Soft Machine* (1961), and *The Wild Boys* (1971), Burroughs was also enthusiastic about audiotape, which he believed could be used to gum up the space-time continuum by playing back prerecorded sounds in random juxtaposition. Burroughs' tape experiments have been compiled on such albums as *Call Me Burroughs* (1965), *Nothing Here Now But the Recordings* (1981), and *Break Through in Grey Room* (1986)—all of which have made an impact on the musicians discussed in this book.

In his writing, recordings, films, and paintings, Burroughs sought to subvert habitual thought processes and logic structures. He has few peers in literature, though James Joyce and Thomas Pynchon are similar in that their own authorial feats are both dissociative and evocative. Still, neither of them is as far out as Burroughs, which probably comes down to the purpose behind his writing. Burroughs was convinced that humankind is at the threshold of an evolutionary breakthrough that will allow the species to travel space and time unhindered. In his view, this next and final stage of human development requires a mutation that will only become possible when we overcome the tyranny of Word—that is, language itself—which Burroughs asserted was deeply encoded into our individual biological units. These are the "soft machines" upon which Control's script is emblazoned; Burroughs' work was an attempt to circumvent the invisible authority that conditions human experience.

It sounds pretty crazy, but he didn't come up with it entirely on his own. Burroughs' "language as virus" premise owes something to metaphysical syllogist Alfred Korzybski, whose theory of general semantics argues that humans' central nervous systems have been evolutionarily shaped by language to the extent that it defines our perceptual reality.[12] The only way forward is to expand our scope of comprehension—to stop confusing the map (words) with the territory (perception). Burroughs' philosophy also has commonalities with that of William Blake—the English poet, printmaker, and mystic whose proto-psychedelic visions concerned warring gods of liberation and subordination.[13] In Blake's cosmology, the authoritarian deity Urizen compels conformity through the Book of Brass, the source code of mass influence. This is similar to Burroughs' own conceptions of Control—that insidious force which limits human freedom and potential through various manipulations, including mass media. The goal of any serious artist, in his view, is to break down the mechanisms of Control by hacking into and disrupting its core programs using the selfsame tools: words, sounds, and images.

Burroughs saw Control as the by-product of a space-borne mutation that colonized human larynxes millennia ago and continues to perpetuate itself through language, infecting individuals for no purpose other than viral replication—in which case Pharrell's "Happy" might have been engineered by Control to produce spasmodic gyrations like those of the purple-assed baboons frequently referred to in Burroughs' work. (Exhibit A: "Roosevelt After Inauguration," a scathing satire of American politics in which the entire Supreme Court is taken over by debased simians.)[14] To Burroughs, all forms of Control are to be rejected. "Authority figures are seen for what they are: dead empty masks manipulated by computers," he croaks on *Seven Souls*, a 1989 release by the band Material. "And what is behind the computers? Remote control, of course. Look at the prison you are in—we are all in—this is a penal colony that is now a death camp."[15]

Radio-Friendly Unit Shifter

For Kurt Cobain, the music business was a particularly grueling prison. Artists with hits as big as "Smells Like Teen Spirit" are expected to crisscross continents on tours that can last two, even three years. It's an exhausting lifestyle, to say the least, especially if you've got a raging heroin addiction and need to score to avoid feeling horribly ill. Even without a junk habit, success—or any form of notoriety, really—can be stressful. Cobain adored Burroughs' breakthrough work, *Naked Lunch*, though he may have been unaware of the onslaught its author endured for having written it—including a high-stakes obscenity trial and public misunderstanding regarding its portrayal of addiction. If Cobain did know the story behind the book's publication, it no doubt deepened the connection he felt. He could also tell that Burroughs wasn't entirely comfortable in his own skin. Such a condition screamed for self-medication, and both men preferred opiates. It's possible that Burroughs made junk seem cool enough for Cobain to try; then again, he could have easily gotten strung out on his own. In the Pacific Northwest of Cobain's era, heroin was more prevalent than sunshine.

Before junk, Cobain had music. At times it felt like it was all he had. Music helped Cobain deal with his parents' traumatic divorce at age nine; it also helped him through miserable days at school, lessening somewhat his deep feelings of isolation. If music had the power to do that, maybe it could save him from working in a gas station or, worse, in the woods. So Cobain improbably decided to be a rock star. For his fourteenth birthday, his uncle gifted him a used electric guitar, which he used to "write his way out," to borrow a Burroughs phrase.[16] Burroughs himself imagined growing up to be an author who lived in exotic locations and indulged strange vices. He claimed that the purpose of writing is "to make it happen," and for him, it did. Likewise, Cobain poured his angst and animosities into song, transforming himself from bullied malcontent to the hero of bullied malcontents the world over. And yet it was a case of be careful what you wish for—you might just get it.

Cobain's rock 'n' roll dreams came true, but the reality was like a waking nightmare. The more people went nuts for Nirvana, the more claustrophobic he felt. His addiction deepened along with his sense of estrangement. Cobain attempted to justify his habit among colleagues and in the media, claiming that he self-medicated to ameliorate an undiagnosed stomach ailment. His pain may have been real, as was the relief that junk temporarily provided. But he was soon profoundly addicted, which only exacerbated his suffering.

Cobain's personal turmoil was authentically channeled on *Nevermind*, which served as the soundtrack to a flannel-draped movement that briefly defined 1990s music culture. It took only one shot—the bipolar rave-up "Smells Like Teen Spirit"—and the kids were hooked. Cobain's status as a depressive martyr has since been maintained by successive waves of young people who ape his look and attitude. At this point, his legend is far taller than the amount of music he left behind; Nirvana T-shirts are worn by everyone from the kid bagging your groceries to Justin Bieber. Trends come and go, but Nirvana still scans as hip and subversive, for the most part due to Cobain's uncompromising attitude. People continue to be drawn to Burroughs along the same lines. Often the attraction is superficial: the author's icon is at least as compelling as his output (not that the two can be meaningfully separated). A select few, like Cobain, become completely hooked.

Nirvana flipped the music industry on its ear, but there were other pacesetting acts in the late 1980s and '90s who primed the pump for the alternative revolution. R.E.M., from Athens, Georgia, and Ministry, from Chicago, both rejected the dominant sounds of the day and were rewarded with varying amounts of mainstream success. In 1991, the year that *Nevermind* was released, R.E.M. issued their second major label album, *Out of Time*. Propelled by the hit song and video "Losing My Religion," the album topped the sales charts in both the United States and the United Kingdom. Singer Michael Stipe also made a trek to Lawrence to visit Burroughs, and the band collaborated with him on a cover of their song "Star Me Kitten" in 1996, one year before the author's death. Ministry front man Al Jourgensen became friends with Burroughs in his later years and even convinced him to appear in the video for the band's 1992 punishing industrial metal track "Just One Fix." Other artists, like Sonic Youth and U2, also made direct connections with Burroughs in the final decade of his life; their stories will be told in subsequent chapters.

In contrast to his friend Allen Ginsberg, who ofttimes embraced popular culture, Burroughs had little interest in the contemporary scene. That didn't mean he couldn't appreciate the rock 'n' roll lifestyle. "He didn't know much about music, but he did know about the stage," James Grauerholz says.[17] "And he knew about backstage. And he knew something about life in the caravan, going down the road to the next theater." So did the acts on the original Lollapalooza tour in 1991, which brought punk, goth, metal, industrial, and gangster rap together under the new banner of alternative. In its initial run, the traveling festival boasted an anything-goes spirit that was soon exorcised by commercial forces. These days, Lollapalooza is a single-site honeypot for marketers at which bands also happen to play. (Control really should think about investing in a music festival.)

Also released in 1991 was David Cronenberg's film adaptation of *Naked Lunch*. That movie took considerable liberties with the source material but nevertheless infected a whole new generation of would-be subversives with the Burroughs bug. The author himself was aware of his growing influence, though he had limited interest in serving it. "He was a mirror in which others would see themselves reflected in his work," Grauerholz says. "He didn't create his icon, but he certainly knew how to dress for a photo shoot."[18] There are numerous pictures of the author with well-known musicians such as Patti Smith, Mick Jagger, David Bowie, and Cobain, to name just a few. Despite being old enough to be their grandfather, Burroughs doesn't look out of place in a single one of them.

Come as You Are

Nirvana's serrated riffs and pockmarked melodies had little competition in the 1990s singles charts, especially compared to acts like Paula Abdul and Bryan Adams. The band's songs packed plenty of catchy hooks, but their attitude was punk all the way. Nirvana's debut in 1989, *Bleach*, had made them instant heroes in the underground when it was released by indie kingmakers Sub Pop Records. Yet the band's searing club performances and support from college radio failed to move the mainstream needle. Cobain and Co. made their play for the big leagues when Nirvana signed to Geffen Records for their next release, *Nevermind*. The gambit worked, and the remainder of Cobain's short life would be spent negotiating his sudden and overwhelming success. Everyone now seemed to want something from the art-obsessed kid who never felt wanted.

Like Burroughs, who happily received accolades but spurned expectations, Cobain sought validation even as he bristled at fame. Of course, Burroughs' experience of success was very different from Cobain's. For much of his life, the writer was an enigma in exile, El Hombre Invisible. By contrast, Cobain felt the spotlight acutely, with the demands of his audience and handlers resulting in a persistent feeling of walls closing in. Those closest to Cobain did their best to banish thoughts about him not being long for this world, a view he likely shared. Burroughs' friends felt similarly at certain points in the author's life. It's why James Grauerholz brought him to Kansas—to keep him away from temptations that would otherwise do him in.

In the fall of 1993, Cobain saw Burroughs as something more than a dispenser of obscure junkie wisdom. By virtue of the fact that he'd survived, the wan seventy-nine-year-old offered a glimmer of hope to the cherubic superstar. Here was someone who had experienced the ravages of addiction and notoriety, and come out the other side, integrity intact. "It was, 'Okay, I'm in this situation but I can last, I can get through,'" says Alex MacLeod, Nirvana's tour manager and Cobain's close friend.[19] A year before their Kansas meeting, Cobain sought out Burroughs to work on a project that he described in his personal journal. "I've collaborated with one of my only Idols William Burroughs and I couldn't feel cooler," Cobain wrote.[20] Their collaboration, *The "Priest" They Called Him*, was released in 1993 on a 10-inch vinyl picture disc, which today fetches premium prices in the collectors' market. The two-song set features Cobain's junk-sick guitar weaving webs of feedback around Burroughs' laconic croak to arresting effect. Though the pair would later meet in person, their parts were recorded separately: Burroughs' at Red House Studios in Lawrence in September 1992, and Cobain's two months later, in November, at Laundry Room Studios in Seattle.

The "Priest" They Called Him had roots in a previous collaboration with filmmaker Gus Van Sant called *Burroughs: The Elvis of Letters*. Released in 1985 on Tim/Kerr Records, the EP features Burroughs' spoken vignettes backed by Van Sant on guitar, bass, and drum machine. Surprisingly tuneful, it demonstrates, if nothing else, that the director might have made a serious go at indie rock. The label behind the Van Sant record was co-run by the recently departed Thor Lindsay, who played an instigating role in the Cobain-Burroughs project. "Thor was the one who said, 'Maybe we should do something with Kurt,'" Grauerholz recalls. "And he was actually the middleman. That's how we did the tape swaps before the actual meeting."[21]

The combination of Cobain's guitar novas and Burroughs' tremulous rasp taps a vein of unease. Taken together, the musical mangling of "Silent Night" and the track "Anacreon in Heaven" tell a grim tale of a junkie priest trying to score on Christmas Eve. Burroughs' spoken parts were taken from *Exterminator!*—a short story collection originally published in 1973. With its abrasive sound and bleak subject matter, the record failed to light up the Christmas sales charts. Still, it is an enduring testament to Burroughs' cross-generational appeal. It also highlights the author's unparalleled ability to convey the grimness of addiction. "Then it hit him like heavy silent snow," Burroughs wearily utters. "All the gray junk yesterdays. He sat there and received the immaculate fix. And since he was himself a priest, there was no need to call one."[22]

Around this time Cobain was anguishing over Nirvana's second effort for Geffen Records, the sludgy and depressive *In Utero*. The label almost refused to release the album due to concerns over commerciality, which was a serious blow to the songwriter's confidence. Bright spots were few in Cobain's world in those days, and Burroughs featured in at least two of them—the trip to Lawrence and their earlier collaboration. Cobain loved *The "Priest" They Called Him* because it was so out there and abrasive—the kind of thing that could only be released on an independent label. There was no way *this* music would find favor with the jocks he castigated with lyrics like: He's the one / Who likes all our pretty songs / And he likes to sing along / And he likes to shoot his gun / But he don't know what it means.[23]

Cobain's fascination with Burroughs had begun years earlier.

The author's entire universe stood in stark contrast to the everyday world of the banker, the schoolteacher, or the laid-off logger. Burroughs' exotic escapades in far-flung places like Morocco looked irresistible to a young man on a go-nowhere track. Cobain initially discovered Burroughs as a teenager, furtively reading dog-eared library copies of *Naked Lunch* and *Junkie* in between ditching class and experimenting with drugs and alcohol. It wasn't just a lifestyle crush; he was also taken by author's pioneering work with cut-ups—a technique Burroughs developed in collaboration with visual artist Brion Gysin in a Paris hotel in 1958. The method is simple: take some text and slice it into quarters with scissors or a razor blade, then randomly reassemble the pieces. Burroughs believed cut-ups were a more accurate portrayal of reality, if not a by-product of our very existence. "Consciousness is a cut-up," he explained in a 1986 collection of essays, *The Adding Machine*. "As soon as you walk down the street, or look out the window, turn a page, turn on the TV—your awareness is being cut," he said. "That sign in the shop window, that car passing by, the sound of the radio. . . . Life *is* a cut-up."[24]

In an interview shortly after "Smells Like Teen Spirit" catapulted Nirvana into the mainstream, Cobain referred to Burroughs as his favorite author and called the cut-up approach "revolutionary." On the 1991 European tour for *Nevermind*, his sole piece of luggage was a small bag containing *Naked Lunch*, which he had recently rediscovered at a used bookshop in London.[25] Cobain was such a fan that he asked Burroughs to appear as a crucifixion victim in the video for "Heart-Shaped Box." In a 1993 letter to Burroughs, Cobain came across as sincere and respectful. "I wanted you to know that this request is not based on a desire to exploit you in any way," he wrote. "I realize that stories in the press regarding my drug use may make you think that this request comes from a desire to parallel our lives. Let me assure you that this is not the case. As a fan and student of your work, I would cherish the opportunity to work directly with you."[26] In his personal journals, Cobain described his vision for the video:

William and I sitting across from one another at a table (black and white) lots of Blinding Sun from the windows behind us holding hands staring into each other's eyes. He gropes me from behind and falls dead on top of me. Medical footage of sperm flowing through penis. A ghost vapor comes out of his chest and groin area and enters my Body.[27]

Burroughs declined the offer—he would not be depicted as dying on film—but he did give Cobain a standing invite to visit him in Lawrence. On a sunny day in October 1993, Cobain—just three days into the American tour for *In Utero*—arrived at Burroughs' home at 1927 Learnard Avenue. With a population of nearly 70,000, Lawrence was far larger than the Aberdeen, Washington, of Cobain's youth, where there were more trees than people. Cobain was already familiar with the city, having performed there with his band shortly before they broke into the mainstream. His Lawrence visit offered brief respite from the treadmill-like existence of a superstar who at that time wanted to be anything but. Exhausted, addicted, and struggling with the unasked-for appointment as the "voice of a generation," Cobain desperately needed the breather.

Tour manager Alex MacLeod drove Cobain to meet the old man following Nirvana's performance at Memorial Hall in Kansas City. "I called his room, and he's already ready to go," MacLeod says. "I recognize this is completely different than any other day, because there's no prodding. There's no 'Come *on*, you're killing me here.'"[28] Cobain was not the kind of person to telegraph elation at the best of times; in the depths of narcotic numbness and depression, he was even more remote. But this day was different. "He was quite excited, and he was nervous," MacLeod recalls. "He was meeting someone who he had an immense respect for as a writer. Burroughs was this artist who covered so many mediums, and it's what Kurt wanted to be. He saw himself as someone who could create in different mediums, as he did with his paintings, drawings, his writing, music, and everything else."

Giddy with anticipation, but trying his best to be cool, Cobain stepped along the narrow walkway leading to the cozy porch of Burroughs' home. "William opened the door and greeted Kurt," MacLeod describes. "I mean, he was a real gentleman. We went through and sat down, talked, and tea was made. Then the two of them went off and talked and did the whole tour—you know, the typewriter and the rest—the two of them wandering around the house together and then outside." Their rapport was genuine. "William made him feel at ease very quickly. There was definitely a connection on an artistic level. I think William saw a lot more in him than Kurt even realized."

Burroughs recognized a deeply troubled soul. "As we were about to leave the room, William said to me, 'Your friend hasn't learned his limitations, and he's not going to make it if he continues,'" MacLeod remembers.

> I think he saw himself at a certain point in his own life maybe, or someone who was very similar in many ways. At a certain point he could have gone in one direction, and it all would have been lost. With Kurt, he saw this kid moving in that direction very quickly. It was meaningful the way William interacted with him and how he welcomed Kurt and myself into his home and kind of guided him around his world. I think William understood his position. . . . It's maybe why he voiced his concern.

Scentless Apprentice

Thirty-five years and two months prior, in July 1958, Burroughs had found himself face-to-face with an older artist he greatly admired, Louis-Ferdinand Céline. Alongside his lifelong friend and one-time romantic obsession Allen Ginsberg, Burroughs journeyed to Meudon, a suburb of Paris where Céline and his bevy of dogs resided. Céline's home, like Burroughs' later Lawrence spread, was painted red and set back from the road. By this point Céline, who was also a physician, was living a solitary life, muttering and cursing about whoever had crossed him recently or in the distant past. Burroughs and Ginsberg were greeted by ferocious barking until a lanky and disheveled figure appeared and cajoled the dogs into something resembling calm. Of the animals, Céline remarked, "I just take them with me to the Post Office to protect me from the Jews."[29] Despite his prejudices, Céline was regarded as a titan of French letters, and his misanthropic yet blackly humorous prose delighted Burroughs and Ginsberg.

The trio settled in for conversation in a manicured spot of yard outside the house. Céline prattled at length about those who had slighted him, his experiences of prison, and how the neighbors were trying to poison his dogs. When the conversation shifted to his work as a physician, Céline expressed a cynical kind of job satisfaction, saying, "Sick people are less frightening than well ones." To which Burroughs retorted, "And dead people are less frightening than live ones."[30] When asked about literary contemporaries, Céline didn't hesitate to dismiss other writers and countrymen such as Jean Genet, Jean-Paul Sartre, and Henri Michaux as "just another little fish in the literary pond."[31]

Burroughs and Ginsberg departed with the sense that Céline, while brilliant, had little time for anyone but himself—least of all a pair of young writers from an insurgent American literary movement. They nevertheless enjoyed their visit, which they found both amusing and legitimizing. It's possible that Burroughs' tolerance for the younger artists who later came to pay their respects was informed by his own experiences with figures like Céline. Then again, it might have just been good manners.

He Likes to Shoot His Guns

Cobain's meeting with Burroughs lasted a handful of hours, during which the two exchanged presents. Burroughs gave Cobain a painting he'd made, and the musician gifted the author a signed biography of Leadbelly, whom Cobain claimed he'd discovered from reading an interview with Burroughs. He also presented a large decorative knife that was more art piece than weapon, which Burroughs later gave to his Lawrence friend Wayne Propst.[32] Cobain gamely explored Burroughs' orgone accumulator—a coffin-like box built from a design by Austrian psychoanalyst Wilhelm Reich that was meant to capture a potent yet elusive energy called orgone. Inside this unhandsome plywood apparatus, Burroughs would bathe in the "universal life force" first posited by Reich in 1939. A pariah of the medical establishment, Reich died in prison in 1957, sent there by the US Food and Drug Administration for committing "fraud of first magnitude," including claims that the device cured cancer.[33] For his part, Burroughs often said that the orgone accumulator was a substitute for orgasms (which might make sense given that the junkie libido is next to nonexistent). Still, the box was not without its risks. "Warning—misuse of the Orgone Accumulator may lead to symptoms of orgone overdose. Leave the vicinity of the accumulator and call the Doctor immediately" read the label posted on Reich's personal contraption.[34]

Cobain entered the box and posed for a photo with a rare grin breaking across his face. Maybe it was the orgone. MacLeod has another theory. "The focus wasn't him," he says. "He was obviously happy. He was invigorated. He's smiling. And you know, that didn't happen too often at that point." On the ride back to meet the tour, Cobain was chattier than usual, even effusive. "He was talking about the pieces of art he'd seen, the orgone accumulator and the rest," MacLeod remembers. Cobain was deeply touched that Burroughs had accepted him as a fellow artist. "I think he was kind of in awe that he was treated as an equal by this person he had perceived as being, you know ... elevated."

Burroughs' impressions of Cobain were touchingly earnest. As he later recalled, "Cobain was very shy, very polite, and obviously enjoyed the fact that I wasn't awestruck at meeting him. There was something about him, fragile and engagingly lost. He smoked cigarettes but didn't drink. There were no drugs. I never showed him my gun collection."[35]

Burroughs was a lifelong firearms enthusiast who felt stymied by handgun restrictions in New York City, where he lived from 1974 to 1981. In Lawrence he was able to build a small arsenal that included several shotguns, a Colt .45, and a .38 Special. Thurston Moore, then the vocalist and guitarist for New York City noise-rock heroes Sonic Youth, met Burroughs in the early '90s: "I recall sitting in his living room and he had a number of *Guns and Ammo* magazines laying about, and he was only very interested in talking about shooting and knifing.... I asked him if he had a Beretta and he said: 'Ah, that's a ladies' pocket-purse gun. I like guns that shoot and knives that cut.'"[36]

Burroughs' only real competition in the literary legend/firearms freak department was Hunter S. Thompson, who in the mid-1990s drove down from his Woody Creek, Colorado, compound—his candy-apple red 1971 Chevy Impala loaded with drugs, guns, and ammo—for two days of blasting at targets with Burroughs. Between sessions, the famously gonzo Thompson raised hell throughout Lawrence, but he dialed it back considerably in the presence of the older author. As Jim McCrary later said, "We managed the final few blocks to William's house. And then something amazing happened. Dr. Thompson switched gears. The minute he walked into the house his demeanor, his energy, his self became as quiet and attentive as a student before the master."[37] Thompson gave Burroughs a one-of-a-kind .454 caliber pistol. "It did back him up at least five feet," McCrary said. "When the smoke cleared there was a rivulet of blood trickling down William's thumb and wrist. 'Son of a bitch bit me,' he giggled."

Burroughs' relationship to guns—he was an avid shooter but never hunted—was greatly complicated by the tragic killing of his wife, Joan Vollmer. Though the incident was ruled an accident, the rest of the author's life was spent privately interrogating his role in her death. Vollmer, a poet and fellow drug user, was Burroughs' constant companion in the years leading up to his emergence as a writer. She was also a key player in the early Beat movement, albeit behind the scenes. Her flat on 100th and Broadway in New York was a gathering place for the emerging heroes of the new literature, including Allen Ginsberg, Jack Kerouac, and Neal Cassady. The Beat movement was very much a boys' club, but Vollmer was respected for her razor-sharp wit, which intertwined with Burroughs' dyspeptic asides to such an extent that outsiders had a hard time keeping up with their repartee. The poet and street hustler Herbert Huncke, who gave Burroughs his first heroin fix and coined the term "Beat," claimed the two of them were "very witty with a terrific bite, almost vitriolic with their sarcasm. They could carry on these extremely witty conversations. . . . I couldn't always understand them, and it used to make me feel sort of humiliated because I obviously did not know what they were talking about."[38] As Kerouac—author of *On the Road*, *Dharma Bums*, and *Desolation Angels*—put it, "She loved that man madly, but in a delirious way of some kind."[39]

On the evening of September 6, 1951, Burroughs, thirty-seven, and Vollmer, twenty-seven, were three sheets to the wind at their friend John Healey's apartment on 122 Monterrey in Mexico City, above a bar popular with Burroughs and the coterie of expats at Mexico City College, where he studied Mayan archaeology. The late summer heat was oppressive, as was the sour mood that had settled over the festivities. Vollmer was nearly as drunk her husband; the Benzedrine she'd been popping for years was difficult to obtain south of the border, so she relied on swigs of tequila for the majority of her waking hours.

As daytime bled into a thick and humid evening, Vollmer compulsively rolled an empty glass tumbler between her palms while making the occasional snide remark about Burroughs' recent "honeymoon" in the South American jungle with his then–romantic obsession, Lewis Marker, a twenty-one-year-old American boy from Jacksonville, Florida. His attempted fling with Marker hadn't been the only reason for the trip. Burroughs was in pursuit of a botanical hallucinogen called *yage*, which he describes in the novel *Queer*, written between 1951 and 1953 but not published until 1985. "He had these different properties in east Texas and south Texas, and it is immediately concurrent with the sale of these properties that he turns to Lewis and said, 'Hey, let's go on a trip to South America and take this *yage* stuff,'" James Grauerholz says. "Because he had money. He said, 'I'll stash the old lady and the kids and you and me will go, and we'll find it.' Well, they didn't, as you can see at the end of *Queer*."[40]

The romantic part of the trip didn't go very well either. Marker was a reluctant sexual partner, identifying primarily as heterosexual. Nevertheless, Burroughs wouldn't drop the idea of taking the family, Marker included, to Ecuador, where they'd live off the land. On the night of her death, Vollmer, having endured Burroughs' failed farming efforts in Texas and legal troubles in New Orleans, verbally dismissed the plan in front of Marker and his school pal from Jacksonville, Eddie Woods, the only other witness. "I think it's about time for our William Tell routine," Burroughs is said to have replied. According to witness accounts, Vollmer then positioned the shot glass atop her unkempt hair, which was thinning due to a combination of stress, a recent bout of polio, and the long-term effects of alcohol and amphetamine addiction. Burroughs, known to friends as a crack marksman, steadied his aim and fired. Vollmer slunk to the floor, a single bullet hole in the left side of her forehead.

Something in the Way

The story of how Burroughs, Vollmer, her daughter from a previous marriage, and their infant son, William S. Burroughs Jr., ended up in Mexico City is one of desperation, criminality, and plain bad luck. In November 1946 the family had ditched New York City for south Texas, where Burroughs made what would turn out to be an ill-fated foray into vegetable and marijuana farming. He had recently kicked the heroin habit that had precipitated the family's flight from New York under a cloud of legal hassles and psychological strain; Burroughs had been pegged for prescription forgery, and Vollmer had recently been released from Bellevue Hospital, where she'd been placed under observation for erratic behavior. Burroughs' escape to Texas was in some ways an attempt to prove to his parents that he could provide for his family without their monthly allowance of around $200 (a tidy sum that he continued to accept until age fifty). For their part, the long-suffering Laura and Mortimer ("Mote")

Burroughs were thrilled to see their son turn his back on hard drugs and petty crime.

The family settled into the ramshackle spread along with their fast-talking hustler of a farmhand, Herbert Huncke, who also played the role of nanny and drug courier. Biographer Ted Morgan wrote about Burroughs and Vollmer's relationship following extensive interviews with Huncke in the 1980s:

> They slept in separate rooms, and there seemed to be no physical contact between them. One night when [Huncke] was trying to sleep he heard Joan knock on Burroughs' door. When the door opened, Huncke heard her say, "All I want is to lie in your arms a little while." . . . Once they were walking in the woods and Joan was tiring from carrying Julie and Huncke said "Why don't you fuckin' help her," and Burroughs responded that the Spartans knew how to deal with the excess baggage of female infants by throwing them off cliffs. . . . [Huncke felt] that kind of sardonic humor was Burroughs' way of coping with emotions, but [he] never got used to it. On the other hand, if anyone criticized Joan, Burroughs came to her defense. When Huncke said that she was a little extravagant in her shopping, Burroughs said, "Well, after all, she wants to see that we're fed properly." He never said anything about her benzedrine habit.

By October the marijuana crop was ready. This was to be Burroughs' big financial windfall. He persuaded Vollmer and Huncke to head back to New York City so they could find buyers for the pot that they had stuffed into mason jars and loaded into duffel bags. With the trusty jeep packed with what Burroughs assumed was primo tea, he and Huncke drove straight through to New York, with Vollmer and the kids traveling separately by train. But Burroughs had forgotten an essential step in the cultivation of marijuana: the curing process. Turns out all that pot had next to no value as an intoxicant, a fact that Burroughs discovered when he tried to find his first buyer. Making matters worse, Burroughs and Huncke arrived in New York to find that Vollmer and the kids had been picked up by police at Grand Central Station on suspicion that she was about to abandon them. Vollmer was once again being held at Bellevue for observation, but Burroughs was able to spring her by showing off his Harvard Club membership and making vague intimations of social standing.[41]

Unable to find buyers for the botched crop, Burroughs kicked around the city for a few weeks, picking up another junk habit and trying to avoid the cops. His time in New York—originally as one of the criminals, oddballs, and dropouts hovering around Vollmer's apartment, and now as a desperate addict with two kids—would later be chronicled in *Junkie*, a terse, reportorial novel that would captivate artists from Lou Reed to Hüsker Dü. Burroughs was always drawn to the seedier side of life. As a young man, he was smitten with the switchblade slang of *You Can't Win*, the autobiography of 1920s hobo burglar Jack Black. The book's drug depictions mirror Burroughs' own accounts of addiction. "It was the small, still hours of the night that got me," Black wrote. "Opium, the Judas of drugs, that kisses and betrays, had a good grip on me, and I prepared to break it."[42]

In addition to the killing of Vollmer, Burroughs' criminal history included prescription forgery, petty theft, possession of narcotics, and simply being a gay man in America decades before *Lawrence v. Texas*, the landmark 2003 Supreme Court ruling that struck down the nation's last remaining sodomy laws. In some ways his behavior can be seen as an attempt to transform himself into something other than an upper-middle-class nobody, even if the attention received was negative. Many of his hijinks were harmless. Burroughs liked to rope his friends into routines—a form of playacting that often featured characters and situations that would later turn up in his work. He was obsessed with capturing these routines, which he saw as a potent means of making things happen in the real world. They were a way to record his fantasies, obsessions, and animosities— the cornerstones of his work—when no other means were available. Also, they were great fun. Regular participants included Columbia

University freshman Ginsberg and the ruggedly handsome Kerouac, a former college football star and onetime merchant marine. Burroughs, Ginsberg, and Kerouac formed the triumvirate that would transform American literature and inspire a revolution in youth culture. But even before a single book or poem was published, there was trouble.

It was 1944, the final stretch of World War II—a tense time in America given that Allied victory was hardly guaranteed. Nevertheless, life went on, especially in New York. The city was aflame with passion and plight. There was jazz in the clubs, junk in the streets, and GIs looking for a good time before they shipped out. Lucien Carr, the precocious Puck of Burroughs' social set, was a nineteen-year-old college student in an intense friendship with David Kammerer—a teacher from Saint Louis who had earlier grown infatuated with the young man, going so far as to follow him to New York. The two were close friends, but Carr had become increasingly put off by Kammerer's persistent sexual advances. On August 13, their dynamic turned deadly. Stumbling drunkenly along the shores of Riverside Park in the early morning hours, Carr fatally stabbed Kammerer, hastily dumping the body in the Hudson. Panicked, the young man turned to his closest friends, Kerouac and Burroughs. Kerouac stood watch as Carr buried the murder weapon and was later arrested as a material witness to the crime. Burroughs, too, was picked up after Carr went to his apartment and handed him a pack of Kammerer's bloody cigarettes. Burroughs promptly flushed them down the toilet, advising Carr to find a good lawyer and turn himself in. Carr eventually went to the district attorney and made a confession. He served two years for second-degree murder and largely kept his nose clean upon release.

Many years later, in 2013, the Carr-Kammerer affair was made into a not very good movie, *Kill Your Darlings*, the best part of which is Ben Foster's low-key portrayal of Burroughs. Overall, the tale is reminiscent of the 1990s Norwegian black metal scene, in which a member of the group Mayhem murdered a bandmate in an impulse killing with homophobic overtones—another ugly incident that is being made into a movie. For whatever reason, people are fascinated by the violent shared histories of small cliques whose leaders have artistic ambitions. At the very least, it explains the ongoing fascination with Charles Manson.

By January 1948, Burroughs had more than a few reasons to want to leave the traps and temptations of New York City. The killing of Kammerer weighed heavily on everyone in their social circle. And Burroughs had picked up a raging junk habit that he desperately wanted to kick. Rehab clinics were few and far between, and most were brutal. The junkie's choice for recovery at the time was the notorious "federal narcotics farm" in Lexington, Kentucky, where patients could get their fill of opiates in exchange for signing on to an experimental drug program run by the US government. Burroughs first attempted to wean himself off heroin while driving to Texas, where he intended to get back to the farm life. He had previously attempted a self-administered cure, but that didn't take, so Burroughs made a beeline for Kentucky and the strangest rehab facility in North America.

The Clinical Research Center of the US Public Health Service Hospital in Lexington opened its doors to neuropsychiatric patients in 1935, after which it became a top-secret CIA facility where drugs like LSD were tested on hapless patients.[43] Junkies were provided whatever they wanted so long as they consented to be dosed with industrial-grade psychostimulants, which the spooks believed held the key to programmable assassins and the flipping of enemy agents.[44] Burroughs did not take part in that program, choosing instead the regular ten-day regimen of dose reduction. Lexington was a popular rehab facility for musicians as well; jazz musicians Chet Baker and Sonny Rollins also cleaned up at the facility. Burroughs' time at Lexington is matter-of-factly chronicled in *Junkie*, where he describes the effects of heroin addiction and recovery:

> Junk turns the user into a plant. Plants do not feel pain since pain has no function in a stationary organism. Junk is a pain killer. A plant has no libido in the human or animal sense. Junk replaces

the sex drive. Seeding is the sex of the plant and the function of opium is to delay seeding.

Perhaps the intense discomfort of withdrawal is the transition from plant back to animal, from a painless, sexless, timeless state back to sex and pain and time, from death back to life.

Having broken free from the grip of junk, Burroughs and his family next put down stakes in New Orleans. He was rid of the Texas farm by June 23, 1948, at which point he was already living with Vollmer and the kids in a rooming house at 111 Transcontinental Drive. Shortly thereafter they settled across the river in Algiers, in a house at 509 Wagner Street purchased with financial assistance from his parents. Burroughs' time was largely spent drinking and chasing young men. He managed to keep off heroin, however, mostly because he wasn't able to decode the rules of the New Orleans junk scene. Sex was easier to come by. "In the French Quarter there are several queer bars so full every night the fags spill out onto the sidewalk," he said.[45]

Eventually, he managed to get himself strung out with the help of local addict Joe Ricks (referred to as "Pat" in *Junkie*). Early in 1949, Jack Kerouac visited and found Burroughs in such a state of disarray that he split after about a week, having had his fill of the household's slovenliness. He was also put off by Vollmer's woebegone appearance: sallow eyes, puffy face, and beset with a limp from her polio bout. By April, Burroughs found himself in trouble with the law yet again, getting arrested when his strung-out associates were busted driving his car, prompting a search of the Wagner Street house, where cops found contraband and a few handguns. Burroughs' parents once again bailed him out, but he'd already grown tired of what he perceived to be draconian law enforcement in America. Vollmer described the situation in a letter to Kerouac dated April 13, 1949:

I don't know where we'll go—probably either a cruise somewhere or a trip to Texas to begin with—After that, providing Bill beats the case, it's harder to say. New Orleans seems pretty much out of the question, as a second similar offense, by Louisiana law, would constitute a second felony and automatically draw 7 years in the State pen. Texas is almost as bad, as a second drunken driving conviction there would add up to about the same deal. N.Y. is almost certainly out—largely because of family objections. . . . It makes things rather difficult for Bill; as for me, I don't care where I live, so long as it's with him.

Vollmer and the kids ended up following Burroughs to Mexico. In the months before her death she slipped further into alcoholism, her once alluring face aged well beyond her twenty-seven years. Burroughs had already initiated his ill-fated romance with Lewis Marker and started raising hell at area watering holes. His troubled wife tended to their children to the best of her ability between gulps of tequila.

By the spring of 1951, Burroughs had taken his *loco* schtick too far on more than one occasion, even having his firearm taken away by a Mexican cop for brandishing it drunkenly at bar patrons. It seems that Burroughs was more out-of-control on booze than junk. Could it be that the William Tell incident would not have happened had he been strung out?

There were ominous clouds on the horizon well before the fatal evening. Lucien Carr showed up with Allen Ginsberg in August, and some believe that Vollmer filed for divorce after a brief fling with Carr. But Burroughs and Vollmer quickly reconciled, and he stuck to the claim that he and Joan suffered no real marital strife—that is, besides the fact that he was a homosexual drug addict and she an alcoholic with lingering health problems as a result of Benzedrine abuse. Still, the connection they had at the outset of their relationship—that telepathy Vollmer so affectionately noted—remained intact right up to her death.

Carr's visit, which took place while Burroughs was on his jungle adventure with Marker, was as much a provocation as a reunion. The behavior he describes in Howard Brookner's *Burroughs: The*

Movie (1983) is as irresponsible as any involving rock 'n' roll animals like Lou Reed or Jim Morrison. "Joan and I were drinking and driving so heavily that at one point we could only make the car go if I lay on the floor and pushed on the gas pedal, while she used her one good leg to work the brake and clutch," Carr said. "It was a pretty hairy trip, but Joan and I thought it was great fun. Allen I don't think did, and surely the kids didn't." Ginsberg recalled that Carr "was going around these hairpin turns and she was urging him on saying, 'How fast can this heap go?'—while me and the kids were cowering in the back."

It is tempting to see Vollmer's behavior with Carr as a death wish, one of a finite series that ended with a shot from her husband's pistol. It is a view that Ginsberg advanced as a way of making sense of the killing: "I always thought that she had kind of challenged [Burroughs] into it . . . that she was, in a sense, using him to get her off the earth, because I think she was in a great deal of pain."[46] Burroughs did not accept Ginsberg's rationalization, telling biographer Morgan in the 1980s, "I'll never quite understand what happened. Allen was always making it out as a suicide on her part, that she was taunting me to do this, and I do not accept that cop-out. Not at all. Not at all."

Loss can drive people to embrace all kinds of questionable ideas. Look no further than obsessive Kurt Cobain fans who truly believe Courtney Love hired someone to kill him. It is perhaps unsurprising that Burroughs' friends, lovers, colleagues, biographers, and readers would attempt to divine meaning from a cruelly senseless act. And yet, for all the speculation, we are no closer to truly understanding the underlying motivation—if any—behind Burroughs' shooting of the woman who by all accounts was his ally and partner.

In 1953, Burroughs wrote to Ginsberg, addressing an odd moment with his childhood friend Kells Elvins, who was also kicking around Mexico City around the time of the tragedy. "Did I tell you Kells' dream the night of Joan's death?" Burroughs wrote. "This was before he knew, of course. I was cooking something in a pot, and he asked what I was cooking and I said 'Brains!' and opened the pot, showing what looked like 'a lot of white worms.'" The extent of Burroughs' culpability eluded him. As he said to Ginsberg in the same letter:

One more point. The idea of shooting a glass off her head had never entered my mind consciously, until—out of the blue, as far as I can recall—(I was very drunk, of course), I said: "It's about time for our William Tell act. Put a glass on your head, Joan." Note all those precautions, as though I had to do it, like the original William Tell. Why, instead of being so careful, not give up on the idea? Why indeed? In my present state of mind, I am afraid to go too deep into the matter. I aimed carefully at six feet for the very top of the glass.

All Apologies

Chaos and confusion greeted the aftermath. Burroughs changed his story at least four times, and the newspapers had a field day. Burroughs' brother Mort Jr. came down and irritated all his friends. The slick lawyer representing his case, Bernabé Jurado, was well suited to Mexico City's culture of bribery and graft. Did Burroughs' parents pay to get him off the hook? James Grauerholz concludes that while Burroughs' parents likely spent considerable cash to influence everyone from ballistics experts to arraignment officials, it didn't necessarily impact the verdict.[47] Burroughs' sentencing falls within a range common not only in Mexico, but also in many parts of the United States. Still, a two-year suspended sentence seems light given the severity of the crime. That doesn't mean Burroughs didn't suffer for his actions. In fact, he continued to be haunted by Joan's death right up until his own. On July 27, 1997, just five days before his passing, he referenced Joan in his journal. His regrets are plain: "Why who where when can I say—Tears are worthless unless genuine, tears from the soul and the guts, tears that ache and wrench and hurt and tear. Tears for what was—"[48]

In being charged with manslaughter in absentia, Burroughs

dodged serious punishment that might have deprived the world of a powerful literary voice. And yet his complicity in Vollmer's death is inescapable, even if the act was unintentional. But what if intention doesn't matter? Burroughs was still guilty of committing the action. "In the magical universe there are no coincidences and *there are no accidents*," he said.[49] A bullet leaves the chamber and narrowly misses its target. The tape machine replays the loop: forward, backward; backward, forward. The bullet re-enters the chamber from the barrel end. A gaunt man cocks his eye and takes aim. Again, the reel clatters, the scene unfolds. Backward. Forward. The gun is steadied. The woman turns her head. A shot rings out.

Kurt Cobain's life was punctuated by shots—a procession of needles, then a single blast from a hastily obtained firearm. In a grim foreshadowing of his own end, Cobain's last photo session in Paris depicted him with a handgun to his mouth, which was apparently his own idea. The pictures, captured in February 1994, sit uncomfortably with those from April 5, 1994, when the world glimpsed Cobain's sneakered foot peeking out from the greenhouse of his Lake Washington home, his life cut short by what investigators concluded was a self-inflicted shotgun wound to the head.

Would Cobain have made different choices had he not encountered Burroughs? *Junkie*—originally published in 1953 under the pseudonym William Lee—remains the gold standard for heroin reportage. The book and its author have been accused of glamorizing addiction, a charge Burroughs consistently rejected. As friend and collaborator Victor Bockris says, "He imagined a way of living that he tried to pass on in his books, and he tried to live it as closely as he could."[50] Cobain copped to Burroughs being among his inspirations for trying heroin: "Maybe when I was a kid, when I was reading some of his books, I may have got the wrong impression. I might have thought at that time that it might be kind of cool to do drugs. I can't put the blame on that influence but it's a mixture of rock 'n' roll in general—you know, the Keith Richards thing and Iggy Pop and all these other people who did drugs."[51]

In an attempt to fathom his own motivations for using, Burroughs explored "the algebra of need," his term for the myriad equations of dependency. "The questions, of course, could be asked: Why did you ever try narcotics?" he wrote in *Junkie*. "Why did you continue using it long enough to become an addict? You become a narcotics addict because you do not have strong motivations in the other direction."

Cobain had "motivations in the other direction," his wife and infant daughter among them, but for whatever reason, they weren't enough. It's easy to blame childhood trauma, addiction, and the pressures of fame for his decision, which isn't entirely spelled out in the sweet and rambling suicide note he left. There is little use wondering where his talents might have taken him had he remained above ground. We will never know. Burroughs managed to survive, producing a mountain of work that has captured the imaginations of artists well before and well after Cobain. But who is the man behind the icon? Does the character that Kurt Cobain, Patti Smith, David Bowie, Lou Reed, Thurston Moore, and many more admired have anything in common with the real William S. Burroughs?

Burroughs' relationship to music was like a centipede trapped in amber—that is to say, frozen in time. When compiling the soundtrack for *Burroughs: The Movie*, Grauerholz wanted to feature songs that Burroughs knew and enjoyed. He worked with Hank O' Neal—an accomplished music producer, author, photographer, and one-time CIA agent—to assemble the material. O'Neal ended up making a couple of cassette tapes for Burroughs for his own use. "We used to listen to them on the trip to the methadone clinic," Grauerholz says. The cassettes featured popular artists of yesteryear, including Wendall Hall and Max Morath. "These cold, gray mornings . . . he's just woken up and sniffling. We'd listen to these tapes, and it would come up to something from the 1920s, like, 'Please don't be angry, 'cause I was only teasing yooooou.' And that was originally a 78. He had a Victrola. He really was a creature of the nineteenth century."[52]

With tastes like these, Burroughs was not Nirvana's target

demographic. Still, he maintained a soft spot for the band's leader. For Cobain's twenty-seventh birthday on February 20, 1994, Burroughs sent a photo of Kurt inside the orgone accumulator affixed to a painting he had made himself. A note in cramped handwriting read: "For Kurt, all best on 27th birthday and many, many more. From William S. Burroughs." Less than two months later, the young star was dead. In the wake of the tragedy, Burroughs reflected on their meeting and Cobain's choice to end his life. "The thing I remember about him is the deathly grey complexion of his cheeks," he remarked. "It wasn't an act of will for Kurt to kill himself. As far as I was concerned, he was dead already."[53] As Christopher Sandford describes in the biography *Kurt Cobain*, Burroughs, troubled by the musician's violent end, attempted to find meaning in Kurt's lyrics: "There was surely poignancy in the sight of the 80-year-old author, himself no stranger to tragedy, scouring Cobain's songs for clues to his suicide. In the event he found only the 'general despair' he had already noted during their one meeting." Cobain's suicide note demonstrates his intense feelings of empathy: "There's good in all of us and I think I simply love people too much, so much that it makes me feel too fucking sad."

Burroughs' own exit would not come for three more years. He made his final journal entry on July 30, 1997—just three days before he died from complications following a heart attack. This last testament bears some similarities to Cobain's: "There is no final enough of wisdom, experience—any fucking thing. No Holy Grail, No Final Satori, no solution. Just conflict. Only thing that can resolve conflict is love, like I felt for Fletch and Ruski, Spooner, and Calico. Pure love. What I feel for my cats past and present. Love? What is it? Most natural painkiller what there is. LOVE."

Subterranean Homesick Burroughs

Since music is registered with the whole body it can serve as a means of communication between one organism and another.... Agent attends a concert and receives his instructions.

WILLIAM S. BURROUGHS, *The Western Lands*

Simple Twist of Fate

In the decade after his first books were published, Burroughs' work and lifestyle began to seduce musical artists like Bob Dylan, who met Burroughs in 1965 as he set about reshaping the language of rock 'n' roll, investing it with new narrative potency while retaining its raw, unkempt attitude. Soon, what was once a teenybopper phenomenon heard at American sock hops became a religion of rebellion practiced by people the world over. If this chapel has an altar, Burroughs' portrait hangs above it. But before he was the patron saint of outlaw artists, Burroughs was a young man in pursuit of his wildest desires, dodging both responsibility and accountability in a white-knuckled game of chicken with his personal demons.

Steering clear of North America in the aftermath of his wife's death, in 1953 Burroughs went on a second walkabout, once again searching for the powerful psychedelic plant initially encountered in his anthropological research. "*Yage* may be the ultimate fix," Burroughs wrote in the conclusion of *Junkie*, his debut novel published the previous year. He made his second excursion with the same amount of planning as the first—which is to say, close to none. Burroughs' philosophy of "do easy"—that is, expend only the minimum amount of effort toward achieving a goal—improbably led to his getting his hands on the substance after a chance encounter with a friendly, English-speaking botanist specializing in rare and mind-altering flora. A local shaman prepared the *yage* for ingestion and served as a guide for Burroughs' inner voyage.

Burroughs' correspondence with Allen Ginsberg during this period—first published in 1963 as *The Yage Letters*—predates the so-called acid tests masterminded by Beat disciple Ken Kesey, where tripped-out hippies grooved to a live soundtrack by the Grateful Dead, led by Burroughs enthusiast Jerry Garcia. The music of that era is forever associated with the young men sent to Vietnam, with bands like Iron Butterfly and Vanilla Fudge providing aural bombast to weary soldiers fighting an unpopular and brutal war in the jungles of Southeast Asia. Burroughs' own tour of the tropics was less threatening, though hardly a cakewalk. "Do easy" had its limits, and the tendency for Burroughs' most basic plans to fall apart put him in a sour mood within the first few weeks. Having been delayed in Panama and stuck on a cramped swift boat with bickering Europeans, Burroughs was already fed up with South America by the time he made it to Ecuador. At least this time he managed to locate his quarry.

In his letters to Ginsberg, Burroughs calls *yage* "the most powerful drug I have ever experienced. . . . It produces the most complete derangement of the senses." Ingestion was marked by serious nausea, which Burroughs attributed to *yage*'s all-encompassing perceptual distortions. "There is a definite sense of space-time travel that seems to shake the room," he wrote. In his mind, the vomiting wasn't due to foreign toxins, but rather "time-space motion sickness." Whatever the discomfort, it was a minor price to pay for achieving a legendary high. Burroughs was now, in the parlance of psychedelic rocker Jimi Hendrix, "experienced."

Upon his return, Burroughs checked in with his parents in Palm Beach, where Mote and Laura operated a knickknack shop and looked after his son, Billy, now a precocious six-year-old who had begun to wonder about his absent father. Burroughs then spent a few weeks at the end of 1953 kicking around in Rome with writer and playwright Alan Ansen. The city wasn't at all to his liking, but it did offer an opportunity to burn through the monthly allowance his parents still sent. Soon, boredom and the work of writer Paul Bowles drew him to Tangier, Morocco—an international port city then under the joint administration of France, Spain, and Britain. There Burroughs spent long days and torpid nights getting high, looking for sex, and channeling the radioactive prose that formed the basis of his best-known work, *Naked Lunch*.

For the other Beats, the times were a-changin'. In the period leading up to Joan Vollmer's death and *Naked Lunch*'s publication in 1959, two members of the original trinity—Allen Ginsberg and Jack Kerouac—were overtaken by sudden notoriety. This opened the door for other members of the tribe, including Burroughs. Soon he would emerge as an important voice whose twisted vignettes pushed the limits of what was considered acceptable in literature. But not until Ginsberg's long-form poem "Howl" blew minds from coast to coast, heralding the arrival of a new literary movement that in turn inspired many a rock 'n' roller. "For other would-be movers and shakers, the poet had sparked intense dreams of transformation beyond the literary sphere," Simon Warner writes in *Text and Drugs and Rock 'n' Roll: The Beats and Rock Culture*.[1]

Ginsberg's turbulent verse originally appeared in 1956, creating a firestorm of interest and no small amount of controversy. It is difficult in our current times to imagine a poem having such intense social impact, but "Howl," with its unflinching take on generational and interpersonal transitions, was the Beat shot heard 'round the world. The next salvo came with Kerouac's *On the Road*—something like a proto-GPS for restless bohemians. Based on the author's real-life adventures with Neal Cassady, *On the Road* crisscrosses the country, its thrill-seeking protagonists making a pit stop in Louisiana to visit a certain Old Bull Lee. This erudite and drug-addled character was, of course, based on Burroughs:

It would take me all night to tell about Old Bull Lee; let's just say now, he was a teacher, and it may be said that he had every right to teach because he spent all his time learning; and the things he learned were what he considered to be and called "the facts of life," which he learned, not only out of necessity but because he wanted to. He dragged his long, thin body around the entire United States and most of Europe and North Africa in his time, only to see what was going on.... There are pictures of him with the international cocaine set of the thirties—gangs with wild hair, leaning on one another, there are other pictures of him in a Panama hat, surveying the streets of Algiers.... He was an exterminator in Chicago, a bartender in New York, a summons-server in Newark. In Paris he sat at cafe tables, watching the sullen French faces go by. In Athens he looked up from his ouzo at what he called the ugliest people in the world. In Istanbul he threaded his way through crowds of opium addicts and rug-sellers, looking for the facts. In Chicago he planned to hold up a Turkish bath, hesitated just for two minutes too long for a drink, and wound up with two dollars and had to make a run for it. He did all these things merely for the experience.

Kerouac and Ginsberg weathered the highs and lows of postwar celebrity, which included both media hype and outrage. It was a lot like being a rock star. Ginsberg handled the attention well enough, but Kerouac bristled. By 1957, he had moved with his enabling French Canadian mother into a Florida cottage where he could drink himself to death without interruption. Ginsberg made the best of his growing role as cultural influencer and intellectual matchmaker, helping to bridge the Beat movement with the emerging psychedelic '60s and its anything-goes values. (Burroughs had little love for hippies, though they did buy his books and attend his readings, which finally helped him achieve financial independence at age fifty.)

As the Beats' reputation and influence grew, so did Burroughs' personal fixation on Ginsberg. Though the two men deeply loved one another, their closeness never resulted in a long-term romantic partnership. Ginsberg resisted Burroughs' cloying attempts to achieve a "soul bond" between them; the rail-thin and pale Burroughs was simply not his physical type, and Ginsberg was put off by his emotional carrying on. Still, Ginsberg's deep respect for Burroughs' talent compelled him to serve as his earliest assistant and literary agent. Over the years, Ginsberg would aid in the preparation of several manuscripts, including the sprawling and deeply experimental *Naked Lunch*—a work that would influence artists from Bob Dylan to U2, even if only some of them read it cover to cover.

Born Under a Bad Sign

Apocryphally, Burroughs' career began only after his bullet penetrated Joan Vollmer's forehead. In actuality, he had been writing in fits and starts since his boyhood in Saint Louis. An imaginative, somewhat peculiar child, "Billy" Burroughs longed to be an author, imagining writers as exotic, globe-trotting types with dangerous habits and acquaintances. Burroughs' earliest published work bears little resemblance to the lacerating prose for which he would later become known. "Personal Magnetism" was his 1929 entry in the literary journal of the John Burroughs School (no relation). The writing is as tortured as one might expect from a brighter-than-average fifteen-year-old struggling to fit in. But its topic—the use of secret techniques to manipulate minds—is William S. Burroughs all the way:

> "Are you bashful? Shy? Nervous? Embarrassed? If so, send me two dollars and I will show you how to control others at a glance; how to make your face appear twenty years younger; how to use certain Oriental secrets and dozens of other vital topics."

> I am none of these things, but I would like to know how to control others at a glance (especially my Latin teacher). So I clipped the coupon, beginning to feel more magnetic every minute.

> In a week, I received an impressive red volume with magnetic rays all over the cover. I opened the book and hopefully began to read. Alas! The book was a mass of scientific drivel cunningly designed to befuddle the reader, and keep him from realizing what a fake it was....

. . . Did I find out how to control others at a glance? I certainly did, but never had the nerve to try it. Here is how it is done: I must look my victim squarely in the eye, say in a low, severe voice, "I am talking and you must listen," then, intensify my gaze and say, "You cannot escape me." My victim completely subdued, I was to say, "I am stronger than my enemies." Get thee behind me Satan. Imagine me trying that on Mr. Baker!

I think the book was right in saying that by following its instructions I could make myself the center of interest at every party. Interest is putting it mildly!

The desire to control others stemmed from an inability to fit in. Burroughs' childhood was defined by a persistent sense of otherness that made him act in ways he knew would only deepen his estrangement from family and peers. It was as if he had been invaded by an indescribable presence that made him isolated and disaffected. Such feelings of alienation are hardly unique to Burroughs. Many people—creative and otherwise—struggle with a sense of apartness that can result in a lifetime of difficulties with parents, siblings, classmates, teachers, employers, colleagues, friends, and lovers. As Burroughs himself noted, something always seemed to drive him to self-sabotage, even when things were going well enough. Later he would attribute this phenomenon to an entity within him he called "the Ugly Spirit," but as a kid, it just felt like a curse.

Curses also had a practical purpose in Burroughs' life: they were protection against a threatening cosmos. The family's Irish cook was a practitioner of Old World witchcraft, which fascinated and terrified the boy in equal measure. It was she who opened his eyes to the concept of a magical universe, where the manipulation of words, sounds, and objects could make something a person imagined happen in real life. The cook taught him the curse of the blinding worm—a dose of Celtic folk magic whereby moldy bread is threaded through with a needle, after which it is buried under a fence in a pigsty. Then came the incantation, which Burroughs recited to biographer Ted Morgan: "Needle in thread, needle in bread, eye in needle, needle in eye, bury the bread deep in a sty."

In addition to the Irish cook, Burroughs learned a curse or two from his nanny, Mary Evans—a woman he claimed could start a fire by simply commanding it to light. He was deeply attached to Evans up until the age of four, when an incident involving her and her boyfriend so traumatized the young boy that he blocked out the specific memory of what happened. He was confident that it was sexual in nature, and he was able to recall a few details from before and after the episode. It all started with an excursion with Evans on a day when she wasn't on the clock. There was a drive somewhere remote with the boyfriend. Walking into the woods, the nanny urging him on. Big brother Mort wondering if they should tell Mother. . . . But still so much missing . . . like a story with sections cut out by a razor. Did the incident actually happen? Burroughs needed to believe. "He kind of reified it, ultimately," Grauerholz said. "In the way you will when you take drugs and undergo hypnosis and everything else trying to get to something. Because you have to get to *something*."[2]

Whether or not the event took place, Burroughs used it as a predicate to self-understanding. He turned to psychoanalysis and, briefly, Scientology in an attempt to find an unconscious rationale for his impulses. "It's a matter of him feeling very, very vulnerable," Grauerholz said. "He was the younger child. His older brother was tight with his dad and played with the tools in his dad's workshop, whereas William's hands were rapped if he touched a tool. When with his mother, she would tell stories, and they would have seances. He was very much a mama's boy."[3]

Burroughs' notoriously harsh views on women are explained to an extent by an upbringing in which he was alternately coddled and ostracized. "It's not misogyny as such," Grauerholz said. "And it's not exactly internalized gay self-hatred. His mother had simply doted on him so intently. Of course, he wouldn't have attributed it to Laura. He'd attribute it to the upper-class women of the central West End, like Doctor Senseny's wife, who said, 'That child is unwholesome. He looks like a walking corpse.'"[4] These formative experiences drove Burroughs' attempts to both understand and escape himself. The same can be said for the musicians he influenced—all of whom pursued transformation by any means necessary, whether that meant creative innovation, drug experimentation, occult exploration, body modification, or some combination of the above.

Metamorphosis is a key theme in Burroughs' life and work. Often his efforts were directed at himself, though he also sought to transform the outside world by cutting up, rearranging, and playing back its artifacts—namely, text, image, and sound. Burroughs' ideas and techniques can be applied in many different contexts, music among them. Of course, one must have the proper tools. For Burroughs, these were his typewriter, tape recorders, camera, scissors, and voice. We can think of them as Burroughs' divine weapons, which he used to assert his visions upon reality. This is a fundamentally occult conceit. Drawing inspiration and energy from symbols, sigils, recitation, and charged objects, practitioners enter non-normative states during which their will—or desire—is projected into the day-to-day world where it is meant to have an impact. The effectiveness of a creative or magical act is a matter of sticking the mark. A curse needs an objective, just as a work of art needs an audience. A bullet requires a target. The circuit finds its path to completion.

Burroughs' experiments in reality-hacking took some interesting turns. In the early 1970s he allegedly made a London restaurant that treated him poorly go out of business (a feat accomplished by playing prerecorded tapes of a car accident cut up with everyday sounds captured on the cafe's sidewalk). Curses became an essential part of his creative and emotional armory, allowing him to launch broadsides against Control while protecting himself from psychic or even physical injury (or so he believed). It also helped maintain a connection to the child he once was—the scrawny kid with a thing for influence schemes and exotic adventure stories. Through radical acts of expression, Burroughs sought to reshape his own reality, changing the world in the process. In his case, the spell worked; not only did he send thunderbolts through the literary community, his influence permeates the broader culture thanks to the artists who carried forth his ideas and methods. According to Patti Smith, "William seemed to have a connection with anything and everything. You see a movie like *Blade Runner*, then you find out the phrase 'blade runner' came from him. The term 'heavy metal' is attributed to him. . . . There's so many phrases and names of groups that come from William's work. He's like another kind of Bible."[5]

Appetite for Destruction

Is Burroughs a good influence or a bad influence? The answer probably depends on the observer. Nevertheless, it is telling that so many other artists found something relatable in his work, lifestyle, attitude, and intellect. Musicians are often outsiders who struggle to fit in, much as Burroughs did. Their expression can evoke great yearning and powerful disaffection of the romantic, social, and spiritual kind. To some extent, these sensitivities are universal. After all, even those with lots of friends and admirers may sometimes feel lonely or oppressed. In young people, such emotions can build up until the predominant urge is to scream at the top of one's lungs. This is the very impulse that gave life to rock 'n' roll: the desire to push back, to reject, to overcome. The eccentrics and ne'er-do-wells who make this music are outlaws by design. But even antiheroes have heroes, and for a certain breed of artist—including Bob Dylan, Patti Smith, Lou Reed, and Thurston Moore—William S. Burroughs is the paladin.

Artists often lead lifestyles enabled by charity or desperation: survival by any means necessary. Sometimes it's record label advances. Sometimes it's drug-dealing and pimping. Sometimes it's a crisp white envelope accompanied by a letter from one's long-suffering parents. Artists also tend to be driven by compulsion, which can be an aid to productivity. The flip side of creative realization is self-destruction; for proof, one has to look no further than the long list of musicians who died before their time, victims of one or another ill-advised choice or behavior. These impulses have likely been a part of the creative experience since art first became a popular pursuit. "The Imp of the Perverse" is an Edgar Allan Poe story from 1845 that describes in great detail the author's irrepressible desire to do the exact wrong thing merely because the option to do wrong exists. The narrator's awareness of this dynamic is its own special torture, as it is for any artist who self-sabotages even as they produce works of undeniable brilliance.

The dual impulse to create and destroy enjoins any number of musicians. Billie Holiday, Jerry Lee Lewis, Johnny Cash, Keith Richards, Lou Reed, Iggy Pop, Mark E. Smith, Shane McGowan, Amy Winehouse—all walked the razor's edge between rapture and ruination. "Every time I thought I'd got it made, it seems the taste was not so sweet," David Bowie sings in "Changes," from 1971's *Hunky Dory*. Then there is Burroughs, the patron saint of doing the wrong thing at precisely the right time. But where does this impulse come from in the first place? Burroughs believed it is hardwired in our neurology via word commands that we respond to like Pavlov's dogs to the strike of a bell. As he describes in *The Job*:

> Consider another pair of commands that contradict each other: "to make a good impression or to make a bad impression." Everyone wants to make a good impression. His self-regard, livelihood, sexual satisfaction depend on making a good impression. Why does the subject when he is trying most desperately to make a good impression make the worst impression possible? Because he also has the goal to make a bad impression, which operates on an involuntary automatic level. This self-destructive goal is such a threat to his being that he reacts against it. He may be conscious or partly conscious of the negative goal but he cannot confront it directly. The negative goal forces him to react.

The destructive impulse is more than bad behavior or a lack of self-discipline. The Imp of the Perverse is one of Control's most effective agents. It feeds on anxiety and aversion to failure. "Negative goals are implanted by fear," Burroughs wrote.[6] And fear is cemented by words and symbols presented in a repetitive—though not necessarily predictable—fashion. Burroughs points to ancient elites who used the calendar as a device to create the impression of godlike omniscience. Maya priests could seemingly foresee any astrological or agricultural event, which created an impression of omniscience among the people. Burroughs imagined that contemporary society can be similarly controlled through electronic media, cut up and juxtaposed by computers for maximum psychic impact, much like today's memes. "I advance the idea that in the electronic revolution, a virus is a very small unit of word and image," Burroughs said.[7] In an age of instant communication, fear becomes weaponized and ever more contagious. In his view, the job of the artist is to subvert this malignant apparatus with the tools at one's disposal.

It is tempting to dismiss all of this as the fantasies of a drug-addled mind. But Burroughs was a serious student of Mesoamerican anthropology with a focus on linguistics, and his studies took up much of his productive time in Mexico. Such investigations form a natural extension to Burroughs' lifelong fascination with the mechanics of power and mass influence—from the Maya to Scientology to mind-blasting hard rock acts like Led Zeppelin. He ultimately came to see his mission as a fight against the forces of Control. No wonder, then, that so many creative outlaws have been drawn to him.

Throughout his life, Burroughs was distracted by addiction, run-ins with the law, family drama, and later, a seemingly endless parade of hangers-on. Yet he maintained remarkable focus, spending long hours writing and revising, dreaming and experimenting. It is here that he found true freedom. Creative absorption, much like an orgasm or junk rush, temporarily eliminates worldly concerns. There is no longer anything to attain; the work is the center and circumference of one's comprehension. In a trancelike state, artists become a conduit for energies bigger than themselves. Burroughs admirer Jerry Garcia put it well in 1991: "I was thinking about the Dead and our success. And I think the idea of a transforming principle has something to do with it. Because when we get onstage, what we really want to happen is, we want to be transformed from ordinary players into extraordinary ones, like forces of a larger consciousness."[8]

Burroughs' work is both a play at transformation and a bid for immortality. He believed that words on a page or sounds on tape take on a life beyond the person who put them there. To Burroughs, creative expression is a ticket to the eternal, which he called "the Western Lands":

> Personal immortality in a physical body is impossible, since a physical body exists in time and time is that which ends. A step toward rational immortality is to break down the concept of a separate personal, and therefore inexorably mortal, ego. This opens many doors. Your spirit could reside in a number of bodies, not as some hideous parasite draining the host, but as a helpful little visitor.[9]

Burroughs' books, recordings, essays, and interviews are those "little bodies" in which the author lives on. All one has to do to conjure Burroughs in the here and now is to read or listen to his words. When the day comes that we lose Bob Dylan (hopefully not anytime soon), we will still be able to experience his gifts by playing any one of his nearly 400 original compositions. It may sound like hokum, but the essence of the idea is that great art lasts because great artists dare. This certainly applies to both Burroughs and Dylan, whose timelessness was earned through the persistence of effort.

There is a photograph of a young Burroughs standing before a sign reading D-A-N-G-E-R that somehow exemplifies the perilous allure of creativity. The quest for artistic immortality is not for the weak of heart. Perhaps that's why we champion its pursuit in literature and music alike. Burroughs' lifestyle alone was probably destined to make him a beacon to musicians, who are known to push boundaries even at the expense of their health and psychological well-being. How many rock stars took drugs in order to "break on through"? How many have an abiding interest in the occult? How many were involved in violence or wantonness? More than there are days in the Mayan calendar.

Fallout Boy

The road to artistic immortality can be long and torturous, with the first steps often taken in rebellious youth. As a teen, Burroughs raged against the machine as a student at the Los Alamos Ranch School in New Mexico, where he experienced an outdoorsy "education" that bordered on child abuse. His class-conscious mother— who was once featured in a homemaker spread in *Life Magazine*— believed his persistent sinus issues would be improved by spending his last two years of high school in a drier clime among other affluent lads of the American Midwest. At fifteen, Burroughs was, like many boys of that age, gangly and awkward. Yet his flint-blue eyes evinced a fierce intelligence and also a hint of aloofness.

Burroughs arrived at the Boys School in 1929, where he was weighed and inspected like a piece of livestock. Grauerholz believes that Los Alamos is key to understanding the man behind the mythos. "It's not 'I am the Great and Mighty Oz,'" he said. "Patti Smith worshipped the Great Oz, and everybody worshipped the Great Oz, when actually, the little man behind the curtain is this young kid at Los Alamos Boys School."[10] There was no yellow brick road leading to the hardscrabble spread of Los Alamos; US Highway 501 wouldn't be built until the 1970s. Burroughs was not impressed by the campus, with its plain cabins and boredom-inducing remoteness. He might have been had he known that the US government would later purchase the school to serve as home base for its top-secret Manhattan Project. Nearly twenty years after Burroughs arrived at Los Alamos, a mysterious explosion rocked the desolate New Mexico terrain, frightening and confusing area residents in the early morning hours of July 16, 1945. Army officials attempted to calm nerves by blaming it on an ammunition explosion, a tough explanation to swallow, what with the ash raining from the sky. The blast was, of course, a nuclear detonation at the nearby Trinity test site, marking the moment when America split the atom and ushered in an entirely new reality for humankind. The scientists at Los Alamos had cleared a dangerous path for the planet from which there would be no going back. "No atomic physicist has to worry, people will always want to kill other people on a mass scale," Burroughs remarked.[11]

Slice the atom or slice the page and see what happens. "When you cut into the present, the future leaks out," Burroughs would say of the cut-up method. As an adult, his work would alarm the literary establishment much like the Trinity detonation shocked the residents of Los Alamos. As it turns out, "the Bomb" is also a decent metaphor for the self-annihilation of a junk fix. The Velvet Underground's "White Light/White Heat" captures the intensity, even if it skips the fallout:

White light, white light goin' messin' up my mind.
White light, and don't you know it's gonna make me go blind.
White heat, aww white heat, it tickle me down to my toes.
White light, oh have mercy, white light have it goodness knows.

Like drugs, music can make the world around us disappear. Whether it's a powerful live performance or a captivating record album, we are reduced to dumbstruck awe, as those observing the Trinity nuclear tests must have been. Mushroom clouds blossom over a black-and-white horizon. Jimi Hendrix bends a note beyond the stratosphere in napalm bursts of kaleidoscopic sound. The air shudders; we are consumed by the blast. The bombs keep falling, and the hits keep coming: *Naked Lunch* in 1959, the Beatles on *Ed Sullivan* in 1964, Bob Dylan at the '65 Newport Folk Festival, Patti Smith at St. Mark's Church in '71—each incident produced tremendous cultural shockwaves. These chain reactions continue to ripple into the future, yet we can return to the past at any time simply by rewinding the tape.

This was Burroughs' basic idea of time travel: media, pregnant with associations from the time of its genesis, can be used to hop-scotch across past, present, and future. Events can be rearranged or even excised, provided one has the right tools and mindset. Songs, with their recurring leitmotifs and memory triggers, are an especially efficient vehicle: "We are continually moved backward and forward on the time track by repetition and rearrangements of musical themes," Burroughs wrote.[12] Bob Dylan certainly understood music as a time-travel device; his early songs were informed by much older traditions, from populist folk anthems to the grimly evocative ballads of Appalachia. By the time the two met in person in 1965, Dylan was ready to jettison the past and embrace the future. He was inspired to no small extent by Burroughs' own visionary techniques and creative nerve.

Gotta Serve Somebody

The most intrepid creators and thinkers—people like Burroughs and Dylan—continually seek new vistas, different ways of being that can be expressed to others in the form of possibility. At first, this impulse can be nothing more than a desire to escape—a means of probing beyond the drudgery of daily existence, a way to imagine something greater, to dream of a more meaningful future. Back in Los Alamos, young Burroughs craved nothing more than to break free of his stultifying surroundings, though his options at the time were limited.

Burroughs' days at the camp were highly regimented, beginning with a 6:30 a.m. "all rise" bell, at which point boys gulped down two tall glasses of ice-cold water and headed outdoors for a day of strenuous activity meant to harden them into junior Captains of Industry. Tutelage at Los Alamos was rooted in survival fetishism with a dash of laissez-faire economics—the kind of cosplay Darwinism favored by men who never had to worry about where their next meal was coming from. Tuition was expensive, and Burroughs' peers were scions of wealthy American families who could afford to send their sons. Although Burroughs was upper middle class—his family's fortune came from selling the last of their company stock for $200,000 just before the market crash—he felt like a peasant next to these kids. Still, he shared with them a healthy distaste for government regulation, which he viewed as an affront to the natural order. Politicians had no business messing in people's labors. Not that he was one for strenuous activity. Burroughs bristled at the calisthenics and mandated community work at Los Alamos. There was a rule that the boys had to remain outdoors between 2:30 and 4:30 every afternoon, regardless of the weather. Burroughs biographer Ted Morgan spoke with a classmate who recalled Burroughs standing in the doorway of a campus cabin, soaked to the bone from buckets of rain, waiting for the signal that he could come inside.

Burroughs kicked off a life of drug experimentation in New Mexico. At age sixteen, he snuck away to a pharmacy while on a trip to nearby Santa Fe with his visiting mother and schoolmate Roger Scudder. Burroughs asked the man at the counter for chloral hydrate—then known as knockout drops. Why would a kid want something like that? "To commit suicide," he croaked facetiously.[13] This apparently did not trouble the druggist, because a few days later, Scudder saw Burroughs being steadied by the school nurse who accompanied him across the calisthenics field where he had just collapsed.

Burroughs got in trouble again when he attempted to get back at one of his teachers, Henry Bosworth, who had been giving him a particularly hard time. After breakfast one morning, Bosworth was appalled to see above the fireplace a plaster-of-Paris figure dressed up like a Boy Scout hanging by a mini-noose with a sign pinned on the uniform reading, "Bozzy-bitch, goddamn him." Was it a prank or a hex? With Burroughs, one can never be entirely certain. He might have been more harshly disciplined but for the fact that Bosworth was under suspicion of improper contact with a student. Undeterred by reprimands, Burroughs continued to act out, even managing to get himself incarcerated while on a field trip to Santa Fe.

He was picked up for vagrancy after sneaking away from the group in the hunt for some local hooch (this was during Prohibition). He spent the night in a jail cell and was subsequently put on probation by the increasingly irate headmaster. An outlaw was born.

By the time he was shipped off to New Mexico, Burroughs' sexual preferences were cemented. Still, he would struggle to form healthy romantic relationships throughout his life. It wasn't that he didn't desire to be loved or enjoy intimate companionship; in fact, he desperately longed for both. It was that he was somehow convinced that he was unlovable, which drove him to be attracted to men who were not in a position to reciprocate. Either they were straight, or mostly straight, or not interested for other reasons. He had made peace with his attraction to men, yet he was stymied by a tendency to become completely subservient to the objects of his attraction. At Los Alamos, it was another boy who first consented to, then rejected, sexual play with Burroughs, who only became more obsessed the more his desires were denied.

"That's why he flees after a year-and-a-half," said Grauerholz.

He was fooling around with another boy who outed him and told everyone that "William Burroughs is a fairy." He had kept a diary, and it was filled with these loving thoughts about Russ Faucett, who was the scion of Faucett Publishing.... Faucett said, "I couldn't stop him! He's mad for that sort of thing!" And so William fled. Then he's waiting for his stuff to be shipped home, and the minute the trunk arrives, he digs through it, throwing things over his shoulder until he gets to the diary. And without even looking at the offending pages, he destroys them.[14]

Burroughs' embarrassment was so profound it would put him off writing for almost a decade.

This incident and other humiliations meant that the Los Alamos Ranch School would be no haven for William S. Burroughs. Neither was Saint Louis—not anymore. By the time he was accepted to Harvard in 1932, Burroughs was hungry for autonomy and a change of scenery. Perhaps the elbow-patched airs of Cambridge, Massachusetts—later a major hub of the emerging folk music revival—would finally provide him with a sense of belonging.

Most Likely You Go Your Way (and I'll Go Mine)

At Harvard, where he would graduate with honors in 1936, Burroughs became enamored of Coleridge, who composed "Rime of the Ancient Mariner" while in an opium haze. (Dylan, too, was fond of the epic poet; his yearning ballad "If Not For You" owes much to Coleridge's delicately lyrical "Frost at Midnight.")[15] Burroughs' literary horizons continued to expand at Harvard. There were courses on Chaucer and Shakespeare, and T. S. Eliot gave a lecture that Burroughs attended his freshman year. He was a member of the exclusive Adams House dormitory but joined no clubs and was treated as an outsider by his peers. By then he was used to not fitting in and simply went about his business. "If Harvard doesn't bother me, I won't bother Harvard," was Burroughs' mantra.[16]

Crucially, there were no arrests or written reprimands mailed back to Saint Louis. In lieu of pharmaceuticals, he made bathtub gin. Mostly, he just read in his room, playing with his pet ferret and trusty .38 pistol. The revolver was at the center of an incident that serves as alarming foreshadowing of the shooting of Joan Vollmer. While goofing off one day in his dorm with friend Richard Stern, Burroughs pointed the gun—which he thought was unloaded—at the young man's stomach. Stern, a fencer, deftly twisted his body as Burroughs pulled the trigger, leaving a hole just behind where Stern had stood a moment before. There is no record of any discipline resulting from the incident. He later remembered putting a bullet in the chamber while home in Saint Louis—and vowed that he'd never again point a gun at someone without being certain it was completely empty unless he intended to use it.

Burroughs' lack of sexual experience led to no small amount of awkwardness. While hanging out with his Harvard classmates, he let slip that he thought babies were born from women's navels. His peers were kind enough to explain things. Eventually, his urges drove Burroughs to a whorehouse in Saint Louis where he had perfunctory sex with a motherly woman. As a senior, he managed to have a sexual experience conforming to his orientation. Unfortunately, the street hustler gave Burroughs a case of syphilis that took two years to show up and almost as long to get rid of. By then he had graduated, skipping commencement due to those ever-present feelings of alienation. As a gift, his parents sent him to Europe with a friend. The pair made their way through Paris and Vienna and passed through Salzburg, where they encountered Nazi brownshirts striking authoritarian poses. Burroughs and his companion eventually found themselves in Croatia (then Yugoslavia), where they were introduced to a hip Jewish woman named Ilse Klapper who knew everyone worth knowing in Dubrovnik. Burroughs found her refreshingly unpretentious and funny. Klapper showed him around the city, and he had such a good time that when his vacation was up, he decided to enroll in medical school in Vienna, even though he had none of the traditional prerequisites.

By 1937, fascism was ascendant, with rampant anti-Semitism and discrimination against homosexuals. (Ironically, Burroughs' uncle Ivy Lee—an innovator in "crisis communications" whose main client was the Rockefeller family—did publicity work in the United States on behalf of one Adolf Hitler.) Klapper's Yugoslavian visa was about to expire, and the two decided it would be best for her to ditch Europe permanently. So Burroughs dropped out of medical school (where he was doing terribly) and married the older woman as a means of securing her passage to America. But immediately after the wedding, Klapper returned to Yugoslavia, and Burroughs went back to Cambridge, where he shared a rented house with his old friend Kells Elvins.

In 1939, Burroughs set about getting Klapper out of Yugoslavia permanently. Putting on his WASP charm, Burroughs convinced immigration authorities that his marriage was one of true love, not convenience, and thus she arrived in the city a few weeks later. The two lived apart but remained friendly, seeing each other socially until Burroughs' new boyfriend, Jack Anderson, began taking up more and more of his time. True to pattern, Anderson was beautiful and anti-intellectual, which meant he was no good for Burroughs. Also, Anderson would bring men and women to their cramped quarters at the Taft Hotel on Seventh Avenue near Times Square and have loud sex with them. This drove Burroughs to buy a pair of poultry shears and cut off the tip of his left pinky finger in a fit of romantic pique. The two eventually split for good, throwing Burroughs into a deep depression until Allen Ginsberg came into his life.

Burroughs' altruistic marriage to Klapper—the two officially divorced in 1946—and his self-mutilation for Anderson indicate a confused but compassionate individual who defies the stereotype of bitter misanthrope. No doubt he struggled personally, especially in those early years. Even as a young man, Burroughs questioned whether anyone really had any control over their own life. He came to advance the idea that the universe itself was a recording, and everything we see, feel, think, do, or touch is pretaped. But by whom? "Control" was what he called it. Still, there was a silver lining: if everything was recorded, that meant it could be edited. One could regain agency by disrupting the Control program. This was Burroughs' entire raison d'être. He took his mission seriously, and he also took care to arm himself properly for it. Besides his .38, Burroughs' trustiest weapons were the typewriter and the tape recorder. Always an intrepid agent, Burroughs deployed globally, with stints in Mexico City, Tangier, Paris, London, and New York. Of course, his mission required a cover story, lest he become compromised. International man of letters would do just fine.

Secret Agent Man

In the wake of the surprise success of *Naked Lunch*, Burroughs began employing cut-ups in his writing. The technique informed his Nova trilogy of the early 1960s, which included *The Soft Machine*, *The Ticket That Exploded*, and *Nova Express*. Cut-ups gave him the perfect weapon to fight against the tyranny of the Word, and he could even create his own viruses. Being a published author also provided a terrific cover identity. Now he could really get down to business. He felt like the gangster Dutch Schultz working under-cover as a G-man. Or maybe it was the other way around. Either way, there was a job to do. Control wasn't going to smash itself.

A little known fact about Burroughs is that he nearly made it into the CIA, or at least its precursor. The Office of Strategic Services, or OSS, was a wartime agency that collected dirt on Hitler and his cabal, plotting ever more outrageous adventures to defeat the Axis powers. Incredibly, before Ginsberg helped convince Burroughs to write *Junkie*, before the obscenity trial for *Naked Lunch* cleared a path for many of the record albums referred to in this book, before the cut-ups and their digital offspring, memes—there was William S. Burroughs, would-be secret agent.

Way back in 1939, Burroughs attempted to join the navy but was denied on account of his poor eyesight and flat feet. Desperate, he turned to the American Field Service, but the wartime ambulance corps rejected him due to the enlisting officer being a Harvard man who was unimpressed with Burroughs' lack of extracurriculars. Then his father told him about a new kind of spy regiment being put together by one Colonel William "Wild Bill" Donovan. With his status as a recent Ivy League graduate, Burroughs managed to win an audience with Donovan in Washington, DC. They got along well enough, and for a brief moment it seemed that Burroughs was on track to become a bona fide intelligence operative. Ready to close the deal, Donovan introduced him to his director of research and analysis, another Harvard man. Burroughs' stomach dropped, and for good reason: it turned out the officer was none other than his former housemaster, James Phinney Baxter, who was fond of nei-ther Burroughs nor his pet ferret. When Baxter nixed the arrange-ment, Burroughs' dreams of becoming a spy for the United States were dashed. The rest of us are left to imagine how the world might have been different if "Lee . . . Bill Lee" had somehow replaced James Bond, the famous creation of fellow writer and former spy Ian Fleming.

Burroughs wrote himself into the role of mutating secret agent in *The Soft Machine*. The book's central plot, if it can be said to have one, concerns Inspector J. Lee, who possesses the ability to shape-shift at will and who travels through fluid realities with the aid of a homemade time machine. *The Soft Machine* boasts the first use of the word "heavy metal" and blew the minds of such rockers as Iggy Pop, who name-drops the character Johnny Yen in his spazzy street anthem "Lust for Life." It also inspired a group of longhaired progressive rockers from Great Britain to take their name from the book's title. That band's leader, Daevid Allen, first met the author in Paris in 1963. "Burroughs hired my jazz trio to participate in a dramatized excerpt from his book, *The Ticket That Exploded*," Allen said.[17] "He was dressed in a nun's costume and jumped from a gigantic syringe to begin the show." Burroughs gave Allen permission to use the title for his band, and also offered what the musician claimed was the best advice he ever received: "Keep your bags packed and ready to go at all times."

Bringing It All Back Home

Crushed at his rejection from covert service, Burroughs went back to New York City, where his father managed to get him a job at a struggling advertising agency where he would work as a copywriter. This wasn't exactly what he wanted to be doing with his life, but it did give him an opportunity to play around with words for the purpose of influencing mass behavior. Burroughs never went back to the ad game after the firm went under, but it's fair to call the experience formative. Like the cartoonist Robert R. Crumb, whose earliest gig was as a greeting card illustrator and whose later psychedelic comics still bore what he called "the cuteness curse," Burroughs retained something of Madison Avenue's unvarnished vernacular. Ad copy was also familiar to Dylan, who grew up around sales slogans in his father's electric appliance shop. Experiences like this tend to rub off in subtle and not-so-subtle ways. Take the lyrics to "It's All Right, Ma," from *Bringing It All Back Home*:

Disillusioned words like bullets bark
As human gods aim for their mark
Made everything from toy guns that spark
To flesh-colored Christs that glow in the dark
It's easy to see without looking too far
That not much is really sacred

It is perhaps ironic that Bob Dylan and many of his contemporaries criticized materialism while making a very good living selling records and performing in cities around the world. As Burroughs might say, traveling salesman makes for a great cover.

If it is challenging to get a clear read on Burroughs, it is equally difficult with Dylan. Another son of the Midwest, Robert Zimmerman was born in Duluth, Minnesota, on May 24, 1941, six months before the United States entered World War II. He enjoyed a quiet and uneventful childhood, or so the official story has it. Anyone even passingly familiar with Bob Dylan knows his reputation as chameleon and enigma. Whether the "real Dylan" even exists, or who that person might be, is beyond the purview of this book. And yet Dylan, like most classical heroes, has an origin story, and his connects directly to Burroughs. "I met Bob Dylan when he was just starting in New York," Burroughs said in a BBC interview in 1982. "He said he was going to become a star.... He seemed to be very definitely planning his career, and it has worked out."[18]

Dylan and Burroughs have more in common than midwestern proximity (such as it is). Much like Burroughs wanted to be a writer from an early age, the young Dylan—then known as Robert Zimmerman—nurtured his creative ambitions over other pursuits. "I always wanted to be a guitar player and a singer," he told Cameron Crowe in 1985. "Since I was ten, eleven or twelve, it was all that interested me.... That was the only thing that I did that meant anything really."[19] According to Minnesotan musician Tony Glover, Dylan first discovered Burroughs in late 1959, after Glover lent him a copy of *Naked Lunch*.[20] Though it would be several years before the influence began showing up in his work, it seems likely that the book's hallucinatory prose made an impression on the young songwriter.

After graduating from high school in 1959, Dylan set out for Minneapolis, where he attended classes at the University of Minnesota while playing coffee shop gigs in Dinkytown—then an enclave for artists and musicians, many of whom no doubt modeled themselves after the Beats. It was during this time that Dylan became drawn to recordings by Big Bill Broonzy, Roscoe Holcomb, and Leadbelly—the latter of whom Kurt Cobain claimed to have discovered via Burroughs. According to Dylan, America of the early 1960s was "still very straight, post-war and sort of into a gray-flannel suit thing, McCarthy, commies, puritanical, very claustrophobic."[21] Finding alternatives took both dedication and diligence. "Whatever was happening of any real value was happening away from that and sort of hidden from view," Dylan noted.[22] He became obsessed with the new artistic underground, of which Burroughs' work was a cornerstone. "It had just as big an impact on me as Elvis Presley, Pound, Camus, T. S. Eliot, e. e. cummings," he said, expressing fondness for "expatriate Americans who were off in Paris and Tangiers . . . Burroughs, *Nova Express* . . . it all left the rest of everything in the dust. . . . I knew I had to get to New York though, I'd been dreaming about that for a long time."[23]

Like Burroughs, Dylan is a mirror: we see what we want to see in his work, and sometimes what we don't. Dylan operates under multiple identities and seems to invent a new one with each record release or interview. One thing is for certain: the eager mimic with a thing for trains who first came to New York in 1961 is not the artist who emerged from his encounter with Burroughs in 1965. At least not judging by the difference between his self-titled 1962 debut—a charming but hesitant acoustic folk record—and *Highway 61 Revisited* and *Bringing It All Back Home*, both of which arrived the year he met Burroughs.

Greenwich Village in the early 1960s was a hotbed of creativity, especially in music, where the sounds emanating from the Lower East Side—including jazz, blues, and folk—helped usher America into a new era, one in which the repression, prejudices, and injustices of earlier decades were rejected by a broad and intersectional movement united in pursuit of progress. These trends continued throughout the decade and beyond, with multiple cultural, social, and civic sectors undergoing rapid transformation. This revolution naturally required a soundtrack. Before psychedelia and free love, there was the sound of fingerpicked guitars and harmony vocalists singing cardinal narratives of American hardship and perseverance.

The rebellious youth of the early 1960s were hip to marijuana and also turned on to traditional American music—from bluegrass and Appalachian ballads to gospel spirituals and Delta blues to protest songs and workers' anthems. The kids went gaga for what they perceived as a more authentic sound than the saccharine pop they heard on the AM dial, with its focus on boy-girl relationships. Soon these same radios would broadcast folk heroes like Peter, Paul and Mary and Shirley Collins. This didn't always go over well with participants in the American folk revival, who saw themselves as part of a commerce-rejecting vanguard. Theirs was a revolution of the human spirit, one that sought freedom for all peoples, regardless of race or class. And their brightest hope was a reedy-throated kid named Bob Dylan.

Dylan arrived on the scene with a beat-up acoustic guitar and a voice that David Bowie later compared to "sand and glue" in his "Song For Bob Dylan" from *Hunky Dory* (1971). That track is both an echo and parody of an early Dylan number written for Woody Guthrie that appeared on his self-titled debut. Within a few short years, Dylan found himself at a creative crossroads. He was infuriated by those who wanted to place limits on him or force him into a mold. Burroughs' lifestyle and intellectual product, all slashing wordplay and Billy the Kid attitude, looked like freedom. Dylan's talent and ambition bred resentment within the scene that gave him his initial boost. More than a few of his fellow artists viewed Dylan with a combination of jealousy and skepticism. Traditionalists thought he was hopelessly self-absorbed; even his supporters fretted over his growing recognition beyond the cloister. Dylan was desperate for a new identity. Inspired by Burroughs, the young folkie set about cutting up and rearranging the character of "Bob Dylan" into exciting, confounding, and ever-changing forms.

Burroughs' quicksilver abstractions opened up new creative possibilities for Dylan, who had only recently taken a more impressionistic approach to songwriting. "Hey, you dig something like cut-ups? I mean, like William Burroughs?" Dylan asked interviewer Paul J. Robbins in a conversation published in the *Los Angeles Free Press* in 1965. Burroughs had left Tangier that spring and returned to New York, where he hoped to get clean and benefit from what Ginsberg assured him was his emerging status in the counterculture. Ginsberg was already on friendly terms with Dylan, but not yet the groupie he'd become. "Tell him I've been reading him and that I believe every word he says," Dylan told Ginsberg about Burroughs.[24] But what wisdom could an aging, junkie author impart to a twenty-four-year-old on the verge of superstardom? Maybe he could teach Dylan how to disappear in plain sight. Help a wet-behind-the-ears agent learn what makes a good cover story. Give him tips on keeping it straight in his head. Burroughs not only knew the score, he knew how to score it. It was time to make introductions.

Burroughs and Dylan took their meeting at a small café in Manhattan's East Village, the precise location of which has been lost to time and memory. "He struck me as someone who was obviously competent," Burroughs later told Victor Bockris. "If his subject had been something that I knew absolutely nothing about, such as mathematics, I would have still received the same impression of competence. Dylan said he had a knack for writing lyrics and expected to make a lot of money." Personally, Burroughs had little use for money beyond its utility in purchasing narcotics and avoiding hard labor. But he could easily spot élan, which Dylan had in spades. "He had a likable direct approach in conversation, at the same time cool, reserved," Burroughs later recalled to Bockris. "He was very young, quite handsome in a sharp-featured way. He had on a black turtleneck sweater." Although they only met once in person, Burroughs left a mark on the younger artist. According to critic R. B. Morris,

"There's no doubt that he was greatly influenced by Burroughs' wild juxtaposing of images and scenes, as well as subject matter."[25] After encountering Burroughs, Dylan's work became even more abstract, caustic, and surreal.

The indestructible Iggy Pop, himself a Burroughs acolyte, notes the Dylan connection in a BBC Radio profile of the author. "He's even in Dylan's 'Tombstone Blues'!" Pop exclaims, before firing up the track, which includes a verse believed to reference Burroughs: "I wish I could give Brother Bill his great thrill / I would set him in chains at the top of the hill / Then send out for some pillars and Cecil B. DeMille / He could die happily ever after." To Dylan, Burroughs was impossibly hip—James Joyce with nasty habits, T. S. Elliot with a cane sword. Dylan's evolution from shy folkie to idiosyncratic icon was greatly accelerated by his immersion in the rhythm and meter of Burroughs' writing. As scholar James Adams notes, "Without Burroughs and his experiments, Dylan might not have been pushed to compose lines that resemble cut-ups but still emerge from some more personal, purposeful, honest, and human place like those Dylan wrote in 1965."[26] Take, for example, the lyrics from "Gates of Eden," which evoke the illumination made possible by cut-ups:

With a time rusted compass blade
Aladdin and his lamp
Sits with utopian hermit monks
Side saddle on the Golden Calf
And on their promises of paradise
You will not hear a laugh
All except inside the Gates of Eden

Burroughs also inspired bravery. In July 1965, Dylan drove a stake through the heart of acoustic purism with an electrified set at the Newport Folk Festival. This was an unforgivable offense in the eyes (and ears) of the folk cognoscenti, but for Dylan, it was all about following his instincts. At twenty-five, he was a creative sponge, and the East Village offered plenty in the way of sop. It is likely that Dylan attended a pair of readings Burroughs gave at the East End Theater in the same YMCA building that Burroughs would call home a decade hence. The author recited sections of *Naked Lunch* and *Nova Express*—works that Dylan claimed as an influence.[27] In 2016, Dylan would win a Nobel Prize, which included recognition for his 1965 novel, *Tarantula*. The book owes much to Burroughs, including, perhaps, its title, which may have originated in a bit of stagecraft described in a *New York Times* review of one of Burroughs' readings:

> Mr. Burroughs, a lean, formal man who sounds something like the late Will Rogers as he reels off dry jokes, read a story that conveyed the idea that various bizarre characters were in a port seeded with atomic mines. The people wanted to leave, but Mr. Burroughs' audience did not. Warmed by such interest, he livened up his one-syllable-at-a-time reading with sudden bursts of dramatic activity, eventually ripping down a white-sheet backdrop and uncovering a painting of horrifying tarantulas.

Dylan was also a self-admitted practitioner of cut-ups, though it is unclear how often he employed the technique. He claims not to have used them in his songs due to the need to rhyme. On the other hand, there is evidence that some of his compositions featured cut-ups, such as the line "The ghost of electricity howls in the bones of her face" from "Visions of Johanna," released the year after his meeting with Burroughs.[28] Dylan denies that *Tarantula* was a cut-up work, which seems dubious to anyone familiar with the technique or the book itself. Nevertheless, recently released bonus footage in D. A. Pennebaker's quintessential early Dylan biopic, *Don't Look Back*, shows Dylan giving a how-to on cut-ups, complete with the four-panel arrangement. This shows that Dylan was familiar with Burroughs' then-new creative approach. In some ways, Dylan's shadowing of Burroughs is like a junior operative on a training mission with an older spy. As Dylan wrote in "Desolation Row," from *Highway 61 Revisited*:

Now at midnight all the agents
And the super human crew
Come out and round up everyone
That knows more than they do

As a creature of the Village, Dylan was also exposed to the underground literature of the day, known as "mimeo magazines"—a kind of precursor to the "zines" of the 1990s. These homemade publications contained the works of avant-garde writers and artists from all corners of the underground. More well-known contributors like Burroughs and Dylan used mimeos as a venue for new ideas or works-in-progress. Dylan was a fan and occasional stringer for rags like *Broadside*, offering early songs and poems. He also enjoyed mimeos from around the world, including *Gnaoua*, which originated in Tangier and featured several pieces by Burroughs: "Notes on Page One," "Pry Yourself Loose and Listen," "Just So Long and Long Enough," and "Ancient Face Gone Out." The same copy of *Gnaoua* graces the cover of Dylan's *Bringing It All Back Home* LP, laid out among other objects dear to the songwriter.

Like Cobain, Dylan's Burroughs obsession may have inspired him to try hard drugs. As he said in a 1966 interview, "I had a heroin habit in New York City. I got very, very strung out for a while. I mean really, very strung out. And I kicked the habit."[29] Did Dylan make this up to seem more like an outlaw, someone with a dangerous backstory, like Burroughs? Maybe, but he maintained the story for at least a decade. "I had taken the cure and had just gotten through / staying up for days in the Chelsea Hotel / Writing 'Sad Eyed Lady of the Lowlands' for you," he sings in the song "Sara" from his 1976 album *Desire*.

That same year, Burroughs turned down an offer to join Dylan on his Rolling Thunder Revue tour, which also featured Ginsberg.

There were plans for Burroughs to appear in the film of the tour, giving a how-to on cut-ups using Dylan lyrics and the writings of Edgar Allan Poe as source text.[30] Burroughs claimed that he didn't want to be another one of Dylan's hangers-on, but the real reason he skipped out was because Dylan didn't offer him a per diem. And so their meeting in the spring of 1966 was, as far as anyone can confirm, the only time Dylan and Burroughs met. Their lone appointment nevertheless galvanized the songwriter, who, like his onetime hero, did not look back. An exceptional agent, Dylan would adopt many cover stories over a long career: vagabond, fortune teller, hedonist, actor, evangelical, radio host, lingerie pitchman, and Nobel Prize winner among them.

Like a junkie Mary Poppins, Burroughs floated back to England, where he would soon enter the stories of a pair of game-changing acts, the Beatles and the Rolling Stones. His uncanny ability to show up at crucial times in other artists' careers is *Zelig*-like. But Burroughs never told his young charges how they should live their lives. As Poppins herself says in the P. L. Travers classic, "Don't you know that everyone has a fairyland of their own?"

Here, There, and Everywhere

Rock and Roll adolescent hoodlums storm the streets of all nations. They rush into the Louvre and throw acid in the Mona Lisa's face.

WILLIAM S. BURROUGHS, *Naked Lunch*

The Future Leaks Out

In 1966, Burroughs was fifty-two and living in Great Britain, where he had come to reside six years prior. Moving like a thin, gray mist through the fog of Swinging London, he made no attempt to mingle with the spiritual seekers and acid eaters on every High Street corner. And yet, without so much as trying, Burroughs left his mark on a number of young artists and intellectuals bristling at the drab postwar world of their parents. It's hard to picture this taciturn relic of the Jazz Age serving as inspiration to the psychedelic minstrels of the mid-sixties. And yet the fabbest of the fab, the Beatles, put Burroughs on the cover of their seminal album, *Sgt. Pepper's Lonely Hearts Club Band*. His wan visage appears alongside several dozen luminaries, including Mae West, Aleister Crowley, Lenny Bruce, Aldous Huxley, and Carl Jung. Hardcore Beatles fans know that songs like "Being for the Benefit of Mr. Kite," "Good Morning, Good Morning," and "A Day in the Life" are informed by avant-garde composer Karlheinz Stockhausen. Fewer are aware of how Burroughs' tape experiments encouraged Paul McCartney to try new approaches in the studio. In fact, even before the Beatles entered Abbey Road to produce their masterpiece, Burroughs was making recordings in Ringo Starr's flat using equipment provided by McCartney.

The success of *Sgt. Pepper* helped take Burroughs-style cut-ups out of the underground and on to the hi-fi, completely changing how we relate to recorded sound. First there was audio tape, then digital samplers, and finally, the Internet, where distinctions between high and low art are obliterated in a relentless stream of memes and mash-ups. In today's online world, source material only matters inasmuch as it reveals something in juxtaposition. Pink Floyd's *Dark Side of the Moon* betrays strange synchronicities when played as the soundtrack to *The Wizard of Oz*. Donald Trump's sniffles are spliced together to form dope beats. DJ Girl Talk subverts pop music by mixing together songs by Elton John with Notorious B.I.G. Today's time-warp culture jammers may not realize it, but they are the direct descendants of Burroughs, who played doula to the future through his work with cut-ups.

The painter Brion Gysin stumbled onto cut-ups in 1958. One day he was trimming canvases and discovered that he'd also sliced a newspaper into sections, rearranging them in the process. He began playing with different combinations, achieving a broad range of permutations with just a few text sources. Gysin correctly intuited that cut-ups had the potential to transform his friend Burroughs' approach to writing. The pair would spend the next two decades advancing cut-ups as a populist revolution. The literary world, with its fixation on authorship, remained resistant. "Writing is 50 years behind painting," Gysin frequently countered.[1] To Burroughs, anything or anyone that served as a filter for self-expression was just another form of Control. Gysin's and Burroughs' dreams of a future liberated from gatekeepers eventually came to fruition with the Internet, where the de-authoring of text, sound, and image is commonplace. Of course, the network and its billions of users also present a tremendous opportunity for Control. What would Burroughs have thought about mass digital surveillance, corporate data mining, and algorithm-powered propaganda?

The original cut-up method still works like a charm. The beauty is in its simplicity. Anyone can perform a cut-up. You can do it right now, with this book, provided you have a physical copy. Exhibit A, performed with the text from this very page:

Interspersing sounds from a range of users also presents tremendous television broadcasts, for example. A thought about mass digital surveillance effects could be achieved with two tape recorders. The original cut-up method still works.

Simply take a page and slice it into four quadrants, then reassemble the sections. Do it with a magazine or newspaper, a brochure or Scientology tract. Cut 'em up and stick 'em back together. See how the random combinations reveal new narratives. You may even catch a glimpse beyond the here and now. As mentioned earlier, Burroughs was fond of saying, "When you cut into the present, the future leaks out."[2] Well, that leak is now a deluge.

Urged on by Gysin, Burroughs soon took cut-ups beyond the printed page. This involved interspersing sounds from a range of sources: spoken word, street noise, and radio broadcasts, for example. A simple audio cut-up involved Burroughs reciting text into a microphone and playing back the recording out of sequence. More complex effects could be achieved with two tape recorders: one to play back the original recording, the other to cut in audio from a totally different source. These days one can achieve the same results using a smartphone. Back then, however, the process required a degree of technical know-how and no small amount of attention. Burroughs would spend hours recording, rewinding, slicing, and manipulating tape in order to produce his audio cut-ups. He can be heard explaining the method on "Origin and Theory of the Tape Cut-Ups," a track from the LP *Break Through in Grey Room* (Sub Rosa, 1986):

> The first tape recorder cut-ups were simply extensions of cut-ups on paper. There are many ways of doing these, but here's one way: you record, say, ten minutes on the recorder. Then you spin the reel backwards or forwards without recording, stop at random, and cut in a phrase. Now, of course when you've cut in that phrase, you've wiped out whatever's there, and you have a new juxtaposition. Now, how random is random? We know so much that we don't consciously know that we know, that perhaps the cut-up was not random. The operator, on some level, knew just where he was cutting in.

Further results can be heard on *Nothing Here Now but the Recordings*—a 1981 Burroughs LP originally released on Industrial Records, the label of UK noise pioneers Throbbing Gristle, and recently reissued under the Dais imprint. Here Burroughs' sandpaper incantations are interlaced with disembodied broadcasts and so-called "electronic voice phenomenon," or EVP. The overall product is disorienting and can hardly be described as musical. Still, one can see why Patti Smith referred to Burroughs as "a shaman . . . someone in touch with other levels of reality."[3]

Checking In, Checking Out

Before Burroughs haunted Old Blighty, he spent several crucial years in France, where his breakthrough work, *Naked Lunch*, was first published. Disenchanted with the encroachment of tourists in Tangier, in January 1958 Burroughs boarded a plane to Paris, where Ginsberg and his lover Peter Orlovsky were staying. Sometime after, Burroughs' friend Harold Norse recommended an English-language bookshop on Rue de la Bucherie, which faced the cathedral of Notre Dame. It was here that Burroughs met young electronics whiz and future Beatles engineer Ian Sommerville, who was working as a clerk. Their initial introduction was like a romantic comedy meet-cute, with Sommerville accidentally dropping a book on Burroughs' head while standing on a shelf ladder. A tall, pale lad with red hair and a flair for mathematics, Sommerville had recently arrived in Paris in an attempt to learn French by immersion. He would become instrumental in Burroughs' life, serving as both a companion and assistant in the creation of audio cut-ups. Within a few short weeks, the two were in a romantic relationship. The next thing Sommerville knew, he was helping Burroughs kick a nasty codeine habit with a reduction cure in room 15 at 9 Rue Gît-le-Coeur—forever known as the Beat Hotel.

The Beat Hotel was hardly a hotel at all—more like a flophouse for artists, junkies, and social outcasts. Situated near the Left Bank, the building still stands, a small plaque marking it as the onetime residence of several important figures of the Beat movement and their associates: Brion Gysin, Harold Norse, Gregory Corso, Allen Ginsberg, Peter Orlovsky, Ian Sommerville, and Burroughs. The rooms in the Beat Hotel were drab and dingy, but they were at least cheap, starting at ten francs per night (about fifty cents in US currency). All were equipped with a single straw-stuffed bed and an army blanket, along with a small table and chair, a faucet that ran only cold water, and a couple of hooks to hang one's outerwear. The pricier quarters came with a telephone and gas stove. Burroughs paid something like twenty-five dollars a month for his accommodations, which boasted a bare lightbulb and a window that looked into the dim hallway. A lone bathtub on the first floor served the residents of all forty-two rooms, and there was a small bistro on the first floor that offered drinks and food.

Overseeing the building and its residents was Madame Rachou, who purchased the property with her husband in 1933 and ran it as a class 13 residential hotel. This was the lowest ranking for public lodgings in France, and the place was barely fit for habitation. Still, Madame Rachou loved her tenants and took great pride in renting to artists, homosexuals, and mixed-race couples. She also provided safe haven to members of the movement against the French occupation of Algeria. The narrow hallways of the Beat Hotel reeked of hashish, of which Burroughs and his guests regularly partook. Here, in a small gray room, Burroughs and his associates would assemble the array of vignettes composed in Tangier into the first edition of *Naked Lunch*.

Burroughs also spent time at the Beat Hotel engaged in what we would today call "personal work." Drawing from an introduction to Tibetan Buddhism at Harvard, he developed a mindfulness practice that involved sitting and allowing his thoughts to come and go without judgment. In this way he began to come to grips with the disturbing fantasies and obsessions that had previously held sway over his interior. Some darkness could not be so easily dispelled, however. No matter how long he sat in contemplation, he was unable to pinpoint the trauma stemming from the childhood incident with his nurse. Over the years, Burroughs would spend considerable energy attempting to relieve this distress with drugs, psychotherapy, a brief flirtation with Scientology, and his writing.

Burroughs felt at home at the Beat Hotel in part due to the number of companions who also lived in the building. Allen Ginsberg and Peter Orlovsky stayed for a time, and Gregory Corso was a fixture. The Dutch painter Guy Harloff laid his head next door, and novelist and critic Herb Gold regularly stopped by. Burroughs frequented cafés and bars where folk singers like Alex Campbell and Derroll Adams—a compatriot of Ramblin' Jack Elliot—would entertain and fraternize. Another fixture was the American writer Baird Bryant, who had recently taken to composing pornography for Paris-based publisher Olympia Press, which brought out the first edition of *Naked Lunch* in 1959. Despite his overall grounding, Burroughs nonetheless got hooked on paregoric, an opium tincture readily available at local pharmacies. Soon after, he made the acquaintance of Jacques Stern, the son of a countess and an affluent banker. Stern's privilege afforded him a steady stream of heroin, of which Burroughs was a willing beneficiary.

Ginsberg went back to the States in July 1958, but before he left, he and Burroughs made their trek to visit the irascible Louis-Ferdinand Céline. This was one of several bonding experiences in Paris between Burroughs and Ginsberg that helped dispel the negative energy that was the result of Burroughs' petulance over his unreturned affections. It was also during this period that he and Brion Gysin would cement a highly collaborative friendship. Although they both had lived in Tangier at the same time, the two were not close. In fact, Burroughs thought Gysin was a snob; Gysin didn't think of Burroughs at all. It's perhaps fitting that chance led to their becoming fast friends after a random encounter on Place Saint-Michel led to a conversation that carried on for days, weeks, months, and years.

Life of Brion

Brion Gysin is probably as important to Burroughs' work as Burroughs himself. One of the twentieth century's most undersung media artists, Gysin is far from a household name. Burroughs' notoriety far eclipsed that of his friend and collaborator, yet he took pains to attribute the cut-up method to Gysin and promote him as a visionary at every turn. Burroughs' occult ideas were further honed by Gysin, and the two would spend much of their time at the Beat Hotel conducting paranormal experiments.

Born in Canada in 1916, Gysin was the son of a British expat and his Canadian wife. He never knew his father, who returned to England to fight in World War I and was killed in the Battle of the Somme. A precocious child with a tendency for self-mythologizing, Brion developed his artistic instincts at an early age. He attended the prestigious Catholic institution Downside College in Somerset, UK, where his appreciation of art and history took deeper root. In 1934 he moved to Paris, where he fell in with the surrealists. At the tender age of nineteen, his paintings were part of a group show at the Galerie des Quatre Chemins alongside works by Picasso, Duchamp, Dalí, Magritte, and Man Ray. Unfortunately, he managed to draw the ire of André Breton, who demanded that Brion's paintings be removed. It turns out that Gysin's poster for the show featured a cow bearing no small resemblance to Breton, to which the older surrealist took offense. The pain of excommunication meant that Gysin would never again seek comfort from cliques, even when it might have furthered his career.

During World War II, Gysin served in both the US and Canadian armies. Upon armistice, he obtained American citizenship. In 1946 he published a book about slavery in the States and Canada and kept on painting through his relocation to Morocco in 1950. There he became enamored of the country's musical and magical traditions. Gysin experienced the power of local magic when the restaurant he owned and operated, 1001 Nights, was cursed by shamans known as *shawafa*. Apparently, these conjurors were peeved about notes and sketches Gysin had made about Moroccan magical practices. He claimed the *shawafa* first attempted to poison him. When that didn't work, they cast a spell in the restaurant's kitchen ventilator using seven shards of a broken mirror and seven seeds in their pods placed around a paper packet sealed with menstrual blood, pubic hair, and the eyes of a newt. The text within called upon a *djin* to drive Gysin from the establishment. One week later, his business partners—a pair of Scientologists from the States—foreclosed on his loan, and he lost the restaurant to them.

In Paris, Gysin would spend long days making paintings with Burroughs observing closely. Transfixed by his creativity and methods, Burroughs wrote to Ginsberg, "I see in his painting the psychic landscape of my own work. . . . He regards his painting as a hole in the texture of so-called 'reality' through which he is exploring an actual place in outer space. That is, he moves into the painting and through it, his life and sanity at stake when he paints."[4] Burroughs was struck by the interdimensional aspects of his friend's art, seeing "a sort of toy world, and one that is somehow alarming, populated with mechanical insects attacking each other, and men in armor from other planets."[5]

The uncanny visions extended beyond the canvas edge. In November 1958, Burroughs visited a Parisian magic shop where he picked up a keychain with a small stainless steel ball on the end. When Gysin saw it, he hipped Burroughs to the occult practice of scrying, whereby the seer gazes into a reflective surface to perceive images of future or past events. Scrying works best when one relaxes the eyes and mind while remaining focused on the object. Having already clocked numerous hours staring at his shoes while in a narcotic stupor, Burroughs was a natural. In one experiment using a mirror, he saw himself transformed into an alien creature complete with pale tendrils, like something out of an H. P. Lovecraft yarn. He wasn't the only one to behold the vision: a nice straight kid from Kansas named Jerry Wallace recoiled with terror while bearing witness to the mutation from across the room. Baird Bryant had a paranormal experience when peering into a coconut shell filled with cold tap water. A saxophone player and author from Texas named Sheldon Thomas saw a coffin in a library, a vision shared by Burroughs, Gysin, and Jacques Stern. Never one to be outdone, Gysin spent thirty-six hours in a single scrying session, during which he saw many a strange sight.

For Burroughs, it was all a blast. "The thing about it for me, about magic and that whole area of the occult is that it is FUN!" he told biographer Ted Morgan. "Fun things happen. It's great. And none of it ever bothers me, you can't get too extreme." His psychic experiments and work with cut-ups helped him get a grasp on Joan Vollmer's death. One of Gysin's cut-ups shone additional light on the tragedy: "Raw peeled winds of hate and mischance blew the shot." Under his friend's guidance, Burroughs came to see the Ugly Spirit as a real and inescapable component of his identity, "a hateful parasitic occupation," as he referred to it in his introduction to *Queer*.

Gysin also helped Burroughs recognize that art and the occult work according to the same principles. A desire or ideal is codified in symbol, charged in absorption, and transmitted through opportunity. The latter often takes the form of random chance, which is why cut-ups became so important: they are the means through which chance is introduced in art, prophetic or otherwise. Burroughs would slice into his back pages and set his own words against material that could come from anywhere—Rimbaud, the Koran, or even the grocer's circular. The resulting text would be combined with visual elements in scrapbooks that served as a kind of mixed-media grimoire. Audio cut-ups were another potent weapon in his arsenal. Burroughs would continue to use these and other methods in his lifelong quest to subvert everyday reality.

Getting Naked

As important as the cut-ups were to Burroughs' work, his best-known book was written before he and Gysin discovered and developed the technique. Although sometimes mistaken as a cut-up novel, *Naked Lunch* was composed conventionally at a typewriter during epic writing sessions in Tangier. In a preview of coming abstractions, its chapters were sequenced at random by a small group of collaborators, including Gysin, Ginsberg, and Kerouac. The book's vignettes were so bizarre and intense that Kerouac had trouble sleeping while assisting with the manuscript:

> When I undertook to start typing it neatly double-space for his publishers . . . I had horrible nightmares . . . like of pulling out endless bolognas from my mouth, from my very entrails, feet of it, pulling and pulling out all the horror of what Bull saw, and wrote. . . . [6]

Naked Lunch reads like the work of a sexually obsessed beat reporter trapped in a Hieronymus Bosch painting. Or perhaps a scathing satire in the mode of Jonathan Swift, had Swift been an unrepentant junkie on the run from authorities. "In writing, I am acting as a mapmaker, an explorer of psychic areas," Burroughs said. "And I see no point in exploring areas that have already been thoroughly surveyed."[7]

As exploratory as rock music would get in the coming decades, it still pales in comparison to the headfuck that is *Naked Lunch*. Any number of musicians have attempted to capture the novel's essence, either in spirit or through direct reference. Arch jazz-rockers Steely Dan took their name from a dildo mentioned in the book ("Mary is strapping on a rubber penis: 'Steely Dan III from Yokohama,' she says, caressing the shaft.") Post-punks Joy Division recorded "Interzone," named after the book's most outlandish location, for their debut. Electro act Klaxxons have a tune called "Atlantis to Interzone." The alt-country band Clem Snide took their name from a recurring Burroughs character who first appeared in *Naked Lunch*. The Mugwumps, a 1960s folk act, also borrowed from the book, as did psychedelic improv act the Insect Trust. The list goes on.

Naked Lunch moves through exotic locales like a dance DJ's tour itinerary. Established characters morph into entirely new entities, like a mash-up of classic songs from wildly different genres. Is there a point to the insanity? That depends on the reader and what they're willing or able to relate to. Addiction, sexual obsession, and the dangers of authority are among the book's chief obsessions. Perhaps that's why it still holds up. "Control, regimentation, these are merely symptoms of a deeper sickness that no political or economic program can touch," Burroughs wrote. He repeatedly invoked sinister forces who attempt to eliminate individuality and personal freedom. In Burroughs' epic dystopia—and it is epic in the classic meaning of the word—man becomes "an automaton, an interchangeable quantity in the political and economic equation."[8]

Naked Lunch is well calibrated for an age where every paranoid half-thought can be amplified through digital media, whether the speaker is the president or simply off their meds. Though not a work of science fiction, the book is attuned to humankind's evolving relationship with technology: "The study of thinking machines teaches us more about the brain than we can learn by introspective methods. Western man is externalizing himself in the form of gadgets," states one foresighted passage. *Naked Lunch* is like a musical earworm; it sticks with you whether you like it or not. "I know this one pusher walks around humming a tune and everybody he passes takes it up," Burroughs wrote. "He is so grey and spectral and anonymous they don't see him and think it is their own mind humming the tune."[9]

Doctor, Doctor

The bulk of what would become *Naked Lunch* was written in Tangier between 1954 and 1957. During those years, Burroughs was strung out and unhappy, living off of his parents' allowance and getting deeper and deeper into addiction. He had friends but rarely saw them, preferring to spend days at a time staring at his shoes while ensorcelled in a narcotic haze. Were it not for his trip to Great Britain in the spring of 1956 to take an experimental cure administered by Dr. John Yerbury Dent, Burroughs may have wasted away in Tangier having produced only one novel, *Junky*, that few even read. According to Burroughs, *"Naked Lunch* would never have been written without Dr. Dent's treatment."[10]

The doctor maintained a small practice at 34 Addison Road in London, where he administered a substance known as apomorphine, created by boiling morphine in hydrochloric acid. Although it produced no high and resulted in violent nausea, Dent believed that apomorphine recalibrated the junkie metabolism in such a way that the craving for opioids was eliminated. To Burroughs, the cure was a miracle. Of course, his recovery was greatly aided by the personal attention he received from Dent, who would stay up with him all night when he had trouble sleeping. The two would discuss Burroughs' experiences with *yage*, as well as their shared enthusiasm for archaeology. Burroughs would evangelize the apomorhine cure well after the doctor died in 1962.

Following his rehabilitation in England, Burroughs spent a couple of weeks with Alan Ansen in Venice, a city for which he felt little affinity. Then it was back to Tangier, where his newfound focus allowed him to log the various scenes and routines that became *Naked Lunch*. At the time, it was impossible to predict the impact the book would have on the broader culture. With its depictions of drug addiction, erotic debasement, and nightmarish creatures, *Naked Lunch* serves as a random-access invitation to deviance. No wonder so many rock, punk, and experimental musicians dig it. It doesn't hurt that the book is often laugh-out-loud funny. Take the character of Dr. Benway, another important MD in the Burroughs story. Whenever the bad doctor appears, readers are assured of two things: a disturbing medical procedure and at least one solid belly laugh. Benway's lunatic schtick is both gory and amusing, not unlike the stage antics of shock rocker Alice Cooper. Here's an example:

The lavatory has been locked for three hours solid. . . . I think they are using it for an operating room. . . .

NURSE: "I can't find her pulse, doctor."
DR. BENWAY: "Maybe she got it up her snatch in a finger stall."

NURSE: "Adrenalin, doctor?"

DR. BENWAY: "The night porter shot it all up for kicks." He looks around and picks up one of those rubber vacuum cups at the end of a stick they use to unstop toilets.... He advances on the patient.... "Make an incision, Doctor Limpf," he says to his appalled assistant.... "I'm going to massage the heart."

Dr. Limpf shrugs and begins the incision. Dr. Benway washes the suction cup by swishing it around in the toilet-bowl....

NURSE: "Shouldn't it be sterilized, doctor?"

DR. BENWAY: "Very likely but there's no time." He sits on the suction cup like a cane seat watching his assistant make the incision.... "You young squirts couldn't lance a pimple without an electric vibrating scalpel with automatic drain and suture.... Soon we'll be operating by remote control on patients we never see.... We'll be nothing but button pushers. All the skill is going out of surgery.... All the know-how and make-do.... Did I ever tell you about the time I performed an appendectomy with a rusty sardine can? And once I was caught short without instrument one and removed a uterine tumor with my teeth. That was in the Upper Effendi, and besides ... "

DR. LIMPF: "The incision is ready, doctor."

Dr. Benway forces the cup into the incision and works it up and down. Blood spurts all over the doctors, the nurse and the wall.... The cup makes a horrible sucking sound.

NURSE: "I think she's gone, doctor."

DR. BENWAY: "Well, it's all in the day's work."

Dr. Benway made his first appearance in "Twilight's Last Gleaming," a collaboration with Kells Elvins rejected by *Esquire* as "too screwy, and not effectively so for us."[11] In the essay "Remembering Jack Kerouac," from *The Adding Machine*, Burroughs recalled how he and Elvins developed the character. "We acted out the parts, sitting on a side porch of the white frame house we rented together, and this was the birthplace of Dr. Benway," he wrote.

Dr. Benway is one of Burroughs' most memorable characters. That's probably why references to the mad MD litter pop culture like so many bent syringes. Noise-rockers Sonic Youth would reference the doc on "Dr. Benway's House," a song recorded for the 1990 Burroughs collaboration *Dead City Radio*. A layered slab of micro-pandemonium, the track comes on like a kiss from a Mugwump and doesn't let up for a whole minute and seventeen seconds. "It's basically a 16-track loop," guitarist Lee Renaldo explained. "We started recording on one track, and we had a tape stretching across the room." Drummer Steve Shelley added, "We did a couple passes mixing all the sounds that were piled on, and that became the track."[12] Burroughs, too, experimented with layering on his tape recordings, which he achieved through the recording and playback mechanisms of two tape machines.[13]

Though often played for laughs, Doctor Benway is a potent metaphor for authority gone berserk. Benway is both entitled and inept, conducting ill-advised operations without a second thought as to the patient's well-being. He is the loutish summation of everything Burroughs found repellent in those whose influence is derived from exploiting the public's naïve faith in authority figures. One would not be shocked to see Dr. Benway leering psychopathically among the candidates in an upcoming general election. Actually, there is something of Donald Trump in Dr. Benway's asinine egomania. "The man is not to be trusted," Burroughs wrote. "Might do almost anything. . . . Turn a massacre into a sex orgy. . . . Or a joke."[14]

I Fought the Law

Naked Lunch is inseparable from its author, which tends to happen with certain major works. The book may be the only Burroughs title many literature buffs can name. It would make a great early round *Jeopardy* prompt: "After shooting his wife, William S. Burroughs wrote this book in a narcotic haze in Tangier and Paris." In terms of name recognition, *Naked Lunch* is a bit like Miles Davis' *Kind of Blue*, which also arrived in 1959. Radical for its time, *Kind of Blue* now sounds quaint, though it is undeniably a masterwork. *Naked Lunch*, on the other hand, can still produce feelings of confusion and unease among readers. This is likely why publishers didn't exactly fall over one another to bring it to market more than half a century ago. Lawrence Ferlinghetti of the legendary San Francisco imprint City Lights told Allen Ginsberg that no one would risk printing this "flow of junk and jizzom,"[15] and he was nearly correct.

Olympia Press took a chance on *Naked Lunch* in 1959, but it would be three years before Grove Press published the US edition. Both imprints invited reprisal in making the material available to the public; each did so based on the understanding that this was a work of major significance, destined to be a landmark in the evolution of the novel. Perhaps expectedly, certain members of the Establishment saw *Naked Lunch* as coarse, vulgar, and lacking in literary merit. The US edition faced a highly publicized obscenity trial, the outcome of which ultimately paved the way for numerous other works—including record albums—to find audiences. But first came the Olympia Press edition, published in Paris as *The Naked Lunch* in an initial run of five thousand copies. And thus Maurice Girodias of Olympia Press gets a good deal of the credit for helping establish William S. Burroughs as an international literary phenomenon.

Girodias was born Maurice Kahane to a Jewish father and Catholic heiress mother in 1919. When money got tight during the Depression, his father made ends meet by publishing erotic literature in Paris, aimed at English tourists who were unable to get their hands on such material at home due to UK obscenity laws. (France had a similar prohibition, but it did not apply to works published in English.) At the onset of World War II, he adopted his mother's maiden name to avoid Nazi persecution. By age fifteen, Girodias was working in his father's business, which in addition to tawdry pornographic tracts published provocative literary fare by Henry Miller and Anaïs Nin. He assumed full publishing duties at age twenty, bringing forth *Zorba the Greek*, by Nikos Kazantzakis, and *Sexus*, by Henry Miller. Girodias launched the Olympia Press imprint in 1953 and published Vladimir Nabokov's *Lolita* just two years later. His love of literature resulted in angry letters from pornographic consumers who were upset that the book wasn't sufficiently titillating. (Imagine a similar reaction to *Naked Lunch:* "It's not so much the orgasmic executions and centipedes, it's that there's not *enough* orgasmic executions and centipedes.")

Girodias rejected *Naked Lunch* when Allen Ginsberg first presented it to him in 1957. The manuscript Ginsberg delivered was a pile of dog-eared pages with loose bits of text haphazardly pasted over half-legible words underneath. Content aside, Girodias had trouble seeing the unwieldy palimpsest as a printable book. He told Ginsberg that if the mess of text could be fashioned into something readable, he'd be happy to give it another look. Burroughs was in no great rush. He had a new companion in Ian Sommerville, a burgeoning collaboration with Brion Gysin, his meditation and occult practices, and a nasty paregoric habit to keep him busy.

Portions of *Naked Lunch* were already finding their way to readers by the time Girodias saw a second draft. In 1957, the final edition of the *Black Mountain Review* ran an excerpt credited to William Lee, Burroughs' go-to nom de plume. Another section landed in the *Chicago Reader* in the spring of 1958. Publisher Irving Rosenthal was particularly impressed with Burroughs' unflinching depictions of homosexuality, which defied the effete stereotypes of the day. When the *Chicago Reader* ceased production, Ginsberg and Burroughs took a tip from Jack Kerouac and hit up the new literary journal *Big Table*, which published ten *Naked Lunch* vignettes. A few hundred copies were almost immediately seized by the Chicago post office. This only served to bring national attention that helped the issue sell out at newsstands. The ACLU sued the post office, and in 1960, federal justice Julius J. Hoffman ruled that the use of offensive language in a work does not necessarily make the work obscene.

This was the first green light for *Naked Lunch* as a novel, and an opening for challenging expression yet to come. It's safe to say that a great many rock records would have never seen release had *Naked Lunch* not beat its obscenity rap.

The incident bestowed upon Burroughs a modicum of notoriety. When Maurice Girodias caught wind of the controversy, he wrote a letter to Burroughs asking to have a another look at *Naked Lunch*. In July 1959, Burroughs was informed that he had ten days to get the manuscript prepared for printing. Enlisting his friends at the Beat Hotel, piles of text were assembled into publication-ready chapters. That November, Burroughs was among those profiled in a *Life* magazine piece on the Beats. It was harsh. "The bulk of the Beat writers," wrote Paul O'Neill, "are undisciplined and slovenly amateurs who have deluded themselves into believing their lugubrious absurdities are art simply because they have rejected the form, style and attitudes of previous generations and have seized upon obscenity as an expression of 'total personality.'" (These criticisms are a lot like those levied two decades later at punk, a movement whose artists tended to worship Burroughs.)

Burroughs' mother, Laura, a consummate conservative homemaker, was highly displeased. It was bad enough that she and her husband frequently had to bail out their son. That at least was a private matter. Seeing him described as a junkie writer of filth in a national magazine was a true affront to the family's dignity. She went so far as to suggest that Burroughs never return to America on pain of losing his monthly allowance. He responded in an amusingly terse letter that included a reference to the occultist Aleister Crowley:

> In order to earn my reputation, I may have to start drinking my tea from a skull, since this is the only vice remaining to me.... I hope that I am not ludicrously miscast as the wickedest man alive, a title vacated by the late Aleister Crowley—who by the way could have had his pick of Palm Beach invitations in a much more

straitlaced era despite publicity a great deal more extreme. . . . And remember the others who have held the title before . . . Byron, Baudelaire, people are very glad to claim kinship now.[16]

Burroughs was emboldened to dismiss his mother's criticisms because of the $800 advance he received from Girodias, who claimed a third of the English-language rights. It wasn't a lot of dough, but the money gave him a shot of confidence. Problem was, Girodias had a reputation for not paying author royalties, having repeatedly stiffed Nabokov on his cut of the sales for *Lolita*. Girodias also struggled to find a publisher for the American edition of *Naked Lunch*. Even so, Burroughs felt that his luck had finally changed. Not only was he was getting attention as an author, he'd just gotten off the hook from yet another drug bust.

In October, Burroughs had been tried in Paris for a mostly bogus trafficking offense stemming from a brief trip back to Tangier in 1959. Authorities mistakenly thought Burroughs was at the center of an international heroin-smuggling operation; in actuality, he had a half-baked idea to bring a small amount of Moroccan marijuana to France. At trial, one of the judges read portions of Burroughs' preface to *Naked Lunch* to demonstrate his standing as a man of letters, which may have served to mitigate his punishment. (It's a good thing they didn't read the "Talking Asshole" routine.) Burroughs received a suspended sentence and a fine of eighty dollars. This was very different from how the case would have been prosecuted in America, Burroughs thought. He maintained a sour outlook on his home country, and not just because of his history of legal trouble. "America is not a young land: it is old and dirty and evil before the settlers, before the Indians," he wrote in *Naked Lunch*. "The evil is there waiting."

When Grove Press finally brought *Naked Lunch* to the United States, it provoked almost immediate censure. Barney Rosset, who owned the imprint, was willing to stand up for the work. Like Girodias, Rosset had a reputation for publishing provocative novels, including *Lady Chatterley's Lover*, by D. H. Lawrence. But nothing was like *Naked Lunch*, with its scary monsters and super-creeps. Burroughs describes once such beast, the Mugwump: "Thin, purple-blue lips cover a razor-sharp beak of black bone with which they frequently tear each other to shreds in fights over clients. These creatures secrete an addicting fluid from their erect penises, which prolongs life by slowing metabolism."[17] Taken alongside the semen-doused deaths by erotic asphyxiation and the grim accounts of heroin dependency, the book was designed to provoke the uptight, including civil authorities.

"Censorship, of course, is the presumed right of governmental agencies to decide what words and images the citizen is permitted to see,"[18] Burroughs said at the International Writers Conference in Scotland in 1962, his first appearance at a major literary event. Burroughs appeared on a panel that also included Henry Miller, Norman Mailer, and Mary McCarthy, all of whom had established profiles. Burroughs impressed with his sagacity. "What is considered harmful would of course depend on the government exercising the censorship," he said. "In the Middle Ages, when the Church controlled censoring agencies, the emphasis was on heretical doctrine. . . . In English-speaking countries the weight of censorship falls on sexual words and images as dangerous."[19] The conference helped put Burroughs on the literary map, even though *Naked Lunch* still hadn't been published in the United States at the time of his appearance.

In November, *Naked Lunch* finally hit US shelves, enjoying brisk sales out of the gate. And then, expectedly, the hammer came down. Boston detectives arrested bookseller Theodore Mavrikos for carrying the title after area residents complained. Rosset sprang into action, hiring First Amendment attorney Edward de Grazia to take the case. Interestingly, de Grazia had read *Naked Lunch* and recognized it as an important work. He worked with the Massachusetts attorney general to make the trial about the book itself rather than the bookseller. It was a big gamble, but if they prevailed, it could protect other challenging yet important works of art. The case went before Superior Court Judge Eugene A. Hudson on January 12, 1965. Witnesses for Burroughs testified that he was a moral writer who dealt in unsavory subject matter in order to illuminate certain truths for readers. Norman Mailer suggested that the work and its author were too brilliant to suppress. "The man has extraordinary talent," he said. "Perhaps he is the most talented writer in America, and as a professional writer, I don't like to go about bestowing credit on any other writers."[20]

Mailer's glowing testimonial failed to affect the verdict. On March 23, 1965, Judge Hudson issued his opinion: *Naked Lunch* was indeed obscene, based on his own standards rather than precedent, which by then included a ruling in favor of *Tropic of Cancer*. It was a blow, but de Grazia appealed to the Massachusetts Supreme Court, which delayed a decision until the US Supreme Court got around to spelling out what constitutes obscenity for several cases under review. On March 22, 1965, nine justices laid out a three-pronged obscenity test that lower courts could employ in cases like *Naked Lunch*:

1. The dominant theme of the material taken as a whole appeals to a prurient interest in sex.
2. The material is patently offensive because it affronts contemporary community standards relating to the depiction or representation of sexual matters.
3. The material is utterly without redeeming social value.

With guidelines in place, the Massachusetts Supreme Court had little difficulty rendering its decision. It was obvious that *Naked Lunch* had value as literature, and its themes weren't solely reflective of a "prurient interest in sex." Offense to community was debatable, but certainly not every community would take offense. Since all three elements were required to be true for a work to be judged obscene, the court ruled in favor of *Naked Lunch* on July 7, 1966.

Two decades later, *Naked Lunch* fan Frank Zappa would testify at a US Senate committee hearing put together by the Parents Music Resource Center—a coterie of politicians' wives upset about rock music content they deemed to be harmful to children. Zappa, who gamely recited the *Naked Lunch* routine "The Talking Ass-hole" at a 1978 tribute to Burroughs in New York City, did not mince words. If Burroughs was watching, he surely felt pride at his friend's performance:

> While the wife of the Secretary of the Treasury recites "Gonna drive my love inside you" and Senator Gore's wife talks about "Bondage!" and "oral sex at gunpoint" on the CBS Evening News, people in high places work on a tax bill that is so ridiculous, the only way to sneak it through is to keep the public's mind on something else: "Porn rock."

> Is the basic issue morality? Is it mental health? Is it an issue at all? The PMRC has created a lot of confusion with improper comparisons between song lyrics, videos, record packaging, radio broadcasting, and live performances. These are all different mediums, and the people who work in them have the right to conduct their business without trade-restraining legislation, whipped up like an instant pudding by The Wives of Big Brother....

> It is unfortunate that the PMRC would rather dispense governmentally sanitized heavy metal music than something more uplifting. Is this an indication of PMRC's personal taste, or just another manifestation of the low priority this administration has placed on education for the arts in America?

Like Maurice Girodias and Barney Rosset, music executives know full well that provocative content sells. In fact, a great deal of resources are devoted to segmenting consumers by lifestyle in order to persuade them to try the companies' wares. This matches Burroughs' assessment of drug dealers: "The junk merchant doesn't sell his product to the consumer, he sells the consumer to his product," he wrote in *Naked Lunch*. "He does not improve and simplify his merchandise. He degrades and simplifies the client."

By the time the *Naked Lunch* manuscript made it out of 9 Rue

Gît-le-Coeur, Burroughs' addiction was in full flower. Ian Sommerville, who shows up in Burroughs' works as the Subliminal Kid (also the nom de plume of Burroughs devotee DJ Spooky, That Subliminal Kid), was there to help him kick it. It was a slog. As Sommerville told a visitor, "I never want to go through this again. Hallucinations, convulsions, freakouts, the edge of insanity. But it's been worth it. He's getting well."[21] Helping the writer kick a habit was a surefire way to earn his trust. And so, when Sommerville returned to Great Britain, Burroughs was not far behind.

London Calling

Burroughs found a room at the Hotel Rushmore in the Earls Court neighborhood of London in 1966. Unfortunately for him, Sommerville already had another boyfriend. Still, the two kept up their audio collaborations, at least for a time. Previous sessions recorded at the English-language bookstore in Paris had recently been made public via Burroughs' 1965 spoken word debut, *Call Me Burroughs*. The LP was a smash with London hipsters and was a personal favorite of Paul McCartney. In 1966, Sommerville lucked into work as an engineer on Beatles recordings and built a recording studio in a flat owned by Ringo Starr at 34 Montagu Street in London. McCartney rented the space from Starr and personally paid for the equipment with which Sommerville was meant to record material for a spoken word label operated by the band.

With its smoked glass mirrors and gray silk wallpaper, Ringo's pad was very different from the sterile recording environments of the day. And unlike EMI Studios, where engineers still wore white lab coats, smoking hashish was perfectly acceptable. Though small, it was comfortable enough for Sommerville to also live there, which meant Burroughs—who still had hopes of rekindling their romantic relationship—was around quite often. Burroughs and McCartney would chat about cut-ups and computers making the music of tomorrow, as the future Knight of the Realm listened to Burroughs' sonic experiments, such as the twenty-minute "K-9 Was in Combat with the Alien Mind-Screens." As McCartney told *Q Magazine* in 1986, "I used to sit in a basement at Montagu Square with William Burroughs and a couple of gay guys he knew from Morocco doing little tapes, crazy stuff with guitar and cello."

No doubt Beatles collectors would love to get their hands on these recordings, which have long since been lost. McCartney's memories are now all that remain of those heady sessions. "We used to sit around talking about all these amazing inventions that people were doing . . . it was all very new and exciting, and so a lot of social time was taken up with just sitting around chatting," he recalled.[22] It was a productive and friendly environment for McCartney and Burroughs. "I thought, let Burroughs do the cut-ups, and I'll just go in and demo things. I'd just written 'Eleanor Rigby' and so I went down there in the basement on my days off on my own. Just took a guitar down and used it as a demo studio."[23] Burroughs later spoke to Victor Bockris about the day McCartney penned one of his most classic compositions. "The three of us talked about the possibilities of the tape recorder. He'd just come in and work on his 'Eleanor Rigby.' Ian recorded his rehearsals so I saw the song taking shape. Once again, not knowing much about music, I could see he knew what he was doing. He was very pleasant and prepossessing. Nice looking young man, fairly hardworking."[24]

Burroughs inspired McCartney to cut in found sounds on Beatles recordings, including alarm clocks, automobile horns, and circus atmospherics. This, in turn, gave Brian Wilson—whose Beach Boys were locked in a kind of cross-continental musical arms race with the Fab Four—the gumption to add barking dogs and bicycle horns to his own masterpiece, *Pet Sounds*. The formal name for such experimental composition is *musique concreté*. Much as Burroughs didn't consider himself knowledgeable about popular music, he would have twitched his lips disapprovingly at the suggestion that he belonged to a Western compositional school. Nonetheless, his direct influence is felt throughout twentieth-century and millennial music culture, more often than not at the level of composition.

Burroughs got to hear an early cut of *Rubber Soul* during a visit with McCartney. In typically inscrutable fashion, he said little and merely nodded occasionally. McCartney thought he didn't like the record. In actuality, Burroughs was stung by Sommerville's new relationship and was having trouble focusing on much of anything. The Beatles' satellite studio had become another way for Sommerville's attention to be diverted. Eventually, it seemed to Burroughs, his former partner even lost interest in their tape experiments.

Their Satanic Majesties Request

In July 1966, Burroughs moved into an apartment on Duke Street near Piccadilly Circus. Not long after, he was pulled into the chaotic universe of the Beatles' erstwhile rivals the Rolling Stones. London in the mid-1960s was a place of creative cross-pollination and the breaking down of social boundaries. Hip art gallery owner Robert Frazier facilitated the connection between Burroughs and the band. "Sometimes Bill ran into the Stones at Frazier's salon, which focused on bringing artists of all professions together," Bockris said.[25] "Both the Beatles and the Stones talked of using Burroughs cut-up techniques to write some of their lyrics." In 1970, Nick Roeg's film *Performance*, starring Mick Jagger, worked Burroughs' name into the script, and the characters quoted from his books on several occasions. "He was not so much having an impact on this generation of musicians as becoming part of that rock rebellion," Bockris said.[26] Jagger was even slated to play the lead in a musical film adaptation of *Naked Lunch* by director Antony Balch, for which Burroughs wrote the screenplay. The project collapsed after Jagger and Balch had a falling out. (Director David Cronenberg's version, starring Peter Weller as William Lee, hit cinemas in 1991.)

Their Satanic Majesties Request—the Stones' uneven response to *Sgt. Pepper*, which also arrived in 1967—is a clunker with a few standout cuts, including the lysergic "2000 Light Years From Home" and the jaunty "She's a Rainbow." More interesting but less commercial is *Brian Jones Presents the Pipes of Pan at Joujouka*, captured by the Stones guitarist in Morocco during the weeklong

Pipes of Pan festival the following year. Released on the Rolling Stones' vanity record label in 1971, the album includes liner notes by Burroughs, who described the music as "the primordial sounds of a 4,000-year-old rock 'n' roll band."

Jones looked to his Moroccan adventure as an escape from the pressures of his reality. It worked for Burroughs after all. Shortly before he made departure, Jones was arrested for possession of marijuana. He had already been pinched the previous year for pot, cocaine, and methamphetamines. Now he was potentially facing a much harsher sentence, which could include incarceration. Jones was also bored with playing guitar in a rock band, preferring instead exotic sounds and instruments from abroad. The Master Musicians of Joujouka—a group of Sufi trance musicians whose lineage can be traced back to 800 AD—would end up becoming an obsession for Jones in his final year on Earth.

Brion Gysin discovered the Master Musicians of Joujouka from a painter friend named Mohamed Hamri in 1950. Fifteen years later, Gysin found himself face-to-face with members of the Rolling Stones, who came to Tangier to experience firsthand the alluring environs described by writers like Paul Bowles and Burroughs. The increasingly drugged out Jones, mere weeks from being sacked by the band, had a secondary motive: to record the Master Musicians. The group, all but unknown to the rest of the world, rarely performed outside the namesake village where their music was an integral part of residents' spiritual and social lives. As Gysin related to Genesis P-Orridge of Throbbing Gristle years later:

Brian was with Anita [Pallenberg] at that time, and they came to Tangier, where they joined Mick and Marianne [Faithfull], who were already there, as I remember. . . . It was decided the next day that Brian and Anita would go to Marrakech. When Brian came back, he discovered [the band] had all left. . . .

He was swallowing fistfuls of pills; god knows what they were. He and Anita were doing things I didn't like very much, like wearing

Nazi uniforms. . . . But when he played the guitar, it was a complete surprise to me—I considered that none of these rock people had really anything behind them at all, it was all PR and very little talent. So I was amazed at his musical talent.

[Brian] was not meant to record in Joujouka at all. No, he pulled a fast one by getting George Chkiantz out to do the recording without telling me that that's what he was going to do. Because there was never an agreement with the musicians, and there was an awful struggle to ever get any money for them. Burroughs was there, too, and he and I talked it over: what should one do about this illicit recording that had been done?[27]

Jones spent considerable time and money experimenting with the tapes in the studio—applying effects, splicing, playing sections in reverse, et cetera. His work would be abruptly cut short. Not long after midnight on July 2, 1969, Jones was found drowned in his own swimming pool. Coroners ruled it a "death by misadventure," pointing to an enlarged heart and liver brought on by persistent drug and alcohol abuse. (Some suggest that he was actually murdered by Frank Thorogood, a construction worker hired by Jones to make some improvements to the property.)

When the Rolling Stones' business management got the bill for Jones' studio work on the Joujouka tapes, they were furious. Eventually, they decided to cut their losses and release the project on the Stones' own label. The broader exposure to the music of Morocco inspired other artists, including free-jazz maestro Ornette Coleman, who accompanied Burroughs to record the Master Musicians in the early 1970s. The music of Morocco was personally appealing to the author, who kept a cassette tape of the Brian Jones recordings. According to Bockris, "Bill played it for the rest of his life."[28]

Joujouka-style rhythms can be heard on the Rolling Stones track "Sympathy for the Devil" from 1968 all the way up to "Continental Drift," which is on the 1989 Stones comeback album, *Steel Wheels*. A more direct Burroughs influence is found in some of the band's lyrics. Speaking about the 1983 single "Undercover of the Night," vocalist Mick Jagger said, "I'm not saying I nicked it, but this song was heavily influenced by William Burroughs' *Cities of the Red Night*, a freewheeling novel about political and sexual repression."[29] Burroughs would return the favor by turning Mick Jagger into a thinly veiled and largely unsavory character in the follow-up, *The Place of Dead Roads*.

A decade prior, the Stones had made use of Burroughs' cut-up method for the lyrics of "Casino Boogie," from the 1972 album *Exile on Main Street*. "That song was done in cut-ups," Jagger explained to *Uncut* in 2010. "It's in the style of William Burroughs. . . . We just wrote phrases on bits of paper and cut them up. This is the conceit. The Burroughs style. And then you throw them into a hat, pick them out and assemble them into verses." Burroughs was allegedly a visitor during recording sessions for *Exile* in 1971, though it hasn't been officially confirmed. Sessions took place in Keith Richards' rented Villa Nellcôte—a sixteen-bedroom former Nazi crash pad on the French Riviera. "It was like trying to make a record in the Führerbunker," Richards told *GQ* in 2010. "Upstairs, it was fantastic, like Versailles. But down there, it was Dante's Inferno." Regular deliveries of heroin ensured that the band and guests got their "rocks off," to borrow the title of *Exile*'s seedy opening cut. "The sunshine bores the daylights out of me," Jagger howls over a cacophony of careening guitar chords. A decade earlier, a smacked-out Burroughs said to Harold Norse at the Beat Hotel: "Hate . . . the sun . . . never . . . go . . . out."

Miles Ahead

Burroughs owes a good amount of his UK notoriety to Barry Miles, who has two excellent Burroughs biographies to his credit: *El Hombre Invisible: A Portrait* and *William S. Burroughs: A Life*. He also happens to be the guy who turned Paul McCartney on to hashish. A rare combination of intellectual and scenester, Miles worked at Better Books at 94 Charing Cross in London, where Allen Ginsberg would give a reading in 1965. This initiated a series of events co-hosted by Miles called the International Poetry Incarnation. Soon he was running his own place in Mason's Yard, called Indica Gallery and Bookshop, supported in part by McCartney. It was here that Yoko Ono first met John Lennon in 1966. The Beatles even rehearsed an early version of "Tomorrow Never Knows" at Indica before recording it for *Revolver* that year. As the scene began to coalesce, Miles helped launch the *International Times*, a series of underground newspapers that featured the work of occultist Kenneth Grant, legendary DJ John Peel, and William S. Burroughs. "The Invisible Generation"—something of a call-to-arms for audio cut-ups—was published in the *International Times* in 1966. It is an assault on Control as well as standard punctuation:

> yes any number can play anyone with a tape recorder controlling the sound track can influence and create events the tape recorder experiments described here will show you how this influence can be extended and correlated into the precise operation this is the invisible generation he looks like an advertising executive a college student an american tourist doesn't matter what your cover story is so long as it covers you and leaves you free to act you need a philips compact cassette recorder handy machine for street recording and playback you can carry it under your coat for recording looks like a transistor radio for playback ...

> ... for example i am playing back some of my dutch schultz last word tapes in the street five alarm fire and a fire truck passes right on cue you will learn to give the cues you will learn to plant events and concepts after analyzing recorded conversations you will learn to steer a conversation where you want it to go the physiological liberation achieved as word lines of controlled association are cut will make you more efficient in reaching your objectives whatever you do you will do it better record your boss and co-workers analyze their associational patterns learn to imitate their voices oh you'll be a popular man around the office ...

It also shows Burroughs' continued obsession with charismatic influence, which goes back to his first published essay in grade school. Remember that for him, writing it down was the way to make it happen. Influencing others with his words was what he wanted, and that is what he got. That doesn't mean he was keen on babysitting a bunch of musician dilettantes, however. But he had no problem capitalizing on rock as a movement, provided it paid the bills and advanced the fight against Control.

Victor Bockris claims that Burroughs did have a fondness for rock—or at least its ambassadors. "Anybody who read Burroughs' *Crawdaddy* columns in *The Adding Machine* can see how much he appreciated and supported the rock bands who were so obviously strong players in spreading the counterculture's messages around the world," he said.[30] "For example, when the Sex Pistols released their summer 1977 single 'God Save The Queen,' he wrote them a letter of support. It was the fame game, the loose association of his name with theirs that sometimes made him uncomfortable. He did not like the worship of heroism."

Watch That Man

Man is an artifact designed for space travel.
He is not designed to remain in his present
biologic state any more than a tadpole is
designed to remain a tadpole.

WILLIAM S. BURROUGHS

In September 1974, a gaunt David Bowie crouched over a table covered with scraps of paper and lines of cocaine backstage at the Universal Amphitheater in Los Angeles. He struggled with a pair of scissors, audibly sighing as the blades sliced through various words and phrases. "What I've used this for more than anything else is igniting anything that might be in my imagination," he said of the cut-up method evangelized by Burroughs.[1] Framed by a flaming red pompadour, Bowie's pale, angular face was made more striking by the lack of brows above his eyes, themselves a mesmerizing mismatch of crystal blue and aquamarine. "I've tried doing it with diaries and things, and I was finding out lots of amazing things about me and what I've done and where I was going.... It seems that it would predict things about the future, or tell me a lot about the past.... I suppose it's a kind of Western tarot."[2]

That same year, Burroughs returned to New York City from London; shortly before his departure, he found himself face-to-face with Bowie for an article published in a 1975 issue of *Rolling Stone*. But which Bowie and which Burroughs met on that gray London afternoon? Both men played fast and loose with identity to the extent that it isn't easy to separate fact from fiction, concept from reality, mask from wearer. And each understood that immortality—the artistic kind, anyway—depends on the masks we leave behind, and how these masks are perceived, rearranged, and repurposed by those who remain in this world.

Bowie and Burroughs used their art to make sense of personal traumas, affect reality, and transform themselves through a creative alchemy that involved character play and the calculated or chance juxtaposition of media artifacts, symbols, and archetypes. This idiosyncratic approach to self-understanding bears much in common with psychoanalyst Carl Jung's radical framework for "individuation." In response to his own nervous breakdown in 1914, Jung pioneered techniques meant to synthesize the disparate elements of personality into a more holistic, integrated self.[3] Through the exploration of dreams, active imagination, role-playing, and free association, individuation brings into harmony the subjective facets of self-identity with the archetypes of the collective unconscious. According to Jung and his followers, these psychological substrates—or masks, if you will—shape our apprehension of reality regardless of our conscious awareness of their influence.

Burroughs was well aware of Jung and his pioneering methods; Bowie, too, was familiar. In fact, the singer had already begun to pursue his own creative approach to individuation by the time he met Burroughs in late 1974. That didn't mean he couldn't learn something from the master. By age sixty, Burroughs was a mask-wearer nonpareil: he'd been a privileged son, a petty criminal, a pharmacological adventurer, a committer of accidental homicide, an erotic tourist, an occult experimenter, and a literary provocateur. Throughout it all, he did battle with any and all conditioning forces, all part of Control—the primary enemy of spiritual and psychic liberation. Burroughs believed humanity is imprisoned by this hostile power, which perpetuates itself through the virus of language and establishes a foothold through what he called "the algebra of need."[4] Anything that can be used to condition behavior is an asset of Control. And yet the same tools can be used to fight back. Employing words, sounds, and images—reordered and weaponized—Burroughs sought to demolish pernicious systems of repression and degradation, including social, civic, and religious dogmas. In turn, he inspired countless other artists—Bowie among them—to use similar methods to rattle the status quo in ways that even Burroughs could not anticipate.

Bowie was particularly fascinated by Burroughs' lifestyle. A drug user and homosexual at a time when society treated both activities with outright enmity, Burroughs spent much of his life dodging authorities and rankling the Establishment on multiple continents. Bowie took as much to the author's overall mien as he did any specific work. He did, however, draw heavily from Burroughsian techniques, including experiments with cut-ups and altered states of consciousness. Like Burroughs, Bowie used his notoriety to inspire others to pursue individualism, even as he recognized identity itself as a series of manufactured illusions. Music brought Bowie's many masks to vivid, sensational life, attracting attention and adulation beyond his wildest dreams. His sound and vision will surely be obsessed over well past his time as a flesh-and-blood being, just as Burroughs' prose continues to inspire and offend decades after he made his departure for the Western Lands.

In the early 1970s, English music fans were hooked on the day-glow decadence of glam rock. As the crown prince of this movement, Bowie already had a well-established reputation in the UK by the time he sat down with Burroughs. He was riding high with his most celebrated of avatars, Ziggy Stardust—an extraterrestrial being packaged and sold to Great Britain's youth as a vaguely messianic figure of licentious fantasy. Teenage wildlife scoured second-hand shops and costume merchants for outrageous attire, painting lightning bolts on their foreheads in homage to their far-out Fagin. As Neil McCormick, pop and rock music critic for *The Telegraph*, wrote, "For me, Ziggy Stardust is the Seventies' most iconic star, personifying the marriage of grit and glamour, a space-age hero rising from decay, depression and existential crisis with mud on his silver platform boots."[5] Under Bowie's guidance, fans embraced gender-bending and the open mocking of institutions—a harbinger of the anti-Establishment attitudes of the punk movement still on the horizon.

Bowie was pro-mutant, which is to say that transformation formed the basis of his creative campaigns. His identikit approach takes certain cues from Burroughs' most celebrated work, *Naked Lunch*, which boasts a coterie of characters who morph and evolve with little adherence to narrative logic. Then there is *Nova Express*, whose antagonists are literal viruses programmed to infect reality with the Control agenda. Burroughs' anti-Establishment broadside *The Wild Boys* was especially influential for Bowie. Artist and designer John Coulthart called it "a homoerotic utopia/dystopia where gangs of teenage boys hide out in depopulated regions, waging war against the rest of humanity with sex, magic and a mastery of weapons, including biological and viral varieties."[6] On roller skates, no less. Bowie used *The Wild Boys* as inspiration for his Ziggy Stardust character—right down to his outrageous look, which also borrows from Anthony Burgess' *A Clockwork Orange*. "They were both powerful pieces of work, especially the marauding boy gangs of Burroughs' Wild Boys with their Bowie knives," the singer said.[7]

Burroughs was the shot Bowie needed to engineer a new rock 'n' roll contagion. "I'm definitely under his spell," he claimed. "That guy messed me up when I first started reading him in the late '60s, and I've never gotten over it. That kind of writing and performance I can really throw myself into."[8] By the time of their first meeting in 1974, Bowie had already gone from cheeky crooner to glam innovator. And he still had light-years to go.

Future Legend

Born David Jones in Brixton, UK, in January 1947, Bowie always knew he wanted to be an artist. Early years were spent playing the recorder and listening to American rhythm and blues like Little Richard and his all-time favorite, Elvis Presley. He formally studied design at the all-boys Bromley Technical High School and, like Burroughs, took a job as a junior advertising executive. Bowie's older stepbrother Terry Burns—who suffered from mental illness his entire life, eventually committing suicide in 1985 by lying on a train track—had an outsized role in his creative development. For one thing, it was Terry who turned David on to jazz and literature, including the Beats.

Exposed to the mania and malaise of mental illness, Bowie reflected his stepbrother's struggles—albeit abstractly—in songs like "After All," "The Man Who Sold the World," "The Bewlay Brothers," and "All the Madmen." In the latter, Bowie sings of "mansions cold and grey," despairing of an era "when a nation hides its organic minds in a cellar." The title of *Aladdin Sane* from 1972 is a pun on the phrase "a lad insane." In tribute to his stepbrother, Bowie penned "Jump They Say" for *Black Tie White Noise* (1993), an album that reignited his career following a mid-1980s nadir. Just as Burroughs spent a lifetime "writing his way out" from under his Ugly Spirit, Bowie used his music and image to come to terms with what he saw as the precariousness of identity, perhaps staving off his own breakdown by adopting and discarding personas at will.

On September 16, 1965, David Jones made a clumsy play at transformation. "I seriously wanted a name change," he said. "The first attempt at several. One I adopted for about three weeks; I even did a photo session for it, apparently."[9] Turns out the name Bowie picked, Tom Jones, was already taken. He briefly considered sallying forth as himself, but Davy Jones of the Monkees was by that point a household name. Eventually, he borrowed "Bowie" from the American knife manufacturer, a fact that tickled Burroughs when they met in late 1974. "The weapon of the Wild Boys is a Bowie knife, an 18-inch Bowie knife, did you know that?" Burroughs inquired. "You don't do things by halves, do you?"[10] the singer replied. Bowie would refer to his adopted moniker as "the medium for a conglomerate of statements and illusions"—a perfectly Burroughsian conceit.[11] With these two, even the masks wear masks.

In July 1969, Bowie scored a transatlantic smash with "Space Oddity." The song features one of his most indelible characters, Major Tom, an astronaut spinning into the void following a mishap with his rocket ship. Major Tom would return a decade later as a junkie "strung out in heaven's high" on "Ashes to Ashes" from *Scary Monsters (And Super Creeps)*; he is also visually referenced in the video for "Lazarus," from Bowie's 2016 farewell, *Blackstar*. Bowie's extraterrestrial fascinations persisted throughout his career and mirror Burroughs' own interest in alien intelligences and time-space travel, which he believed heralded the final stage in humanity's evolution. "This is the space age, and we are here to go!" the author often exclaimed at readings.

"Space Oddity" briefly sent Bowie's career into the stratosphere, but it plunged quickly back to Earth when the thrill of the 1969 moon landing waned. Bowie reinvented himself as a hard-rock ruffian for *The Man Who Sold the World* (1970) and a hippie mystic for *Hunky Dory* (1971), but it was *Ziggy Stardust and the Spiders from Mars* (1972) that delivered the most riveting Bowie yet: alien messiah. The album and supporting performances excited British kids at a level not seen since the Beatles, and Bowie's interstellar Ziggy had everything to do with it. *Aladdin Sane* hit shelves the following year, after which he tired of the spaceman schtick. Even for the attention-seeking Bowie, the fan worship was getting to be too much. The Burroughs doctrine would help him break out of his glitter prison and become a decorated agent of change. "I have always been drawn to the Bill Burroughs of this world, who produce a vocabulary that is not necessarily a personal one, but something that is made up of ciphers and signifiers which are regurgitated, reformed and re-accumulated," Bowie said.[12]

He used cut-ups on *Diamond Dogs*, a transitional record from 1974 originally intended as a musical theater interpretation of George Orwell's *1984*. When he was unable to secure rights, Bowie borrowed themes from *The Wild Boys* and started slicing up and re-assembling the songs he had already written for the project. As Burroughs said, "You cannot will spontaneity. But you can introduce the unpredictable spontaneous factor with a pair of scissors."[13] Bowie prized the element of chance in his work, which is one reason he continued to use cut-ups through his final two albums, *The Next Day* and *Blackstar*, released in 2013 and 2016, respectively.

The cut-up technique finds its origins in the early twentieth-century Dada movement. Avant-garde poet Tristan Tzara suggested at a 1920s surrealist rally that a poem be created on the spot using words drawn from a hat, introducing random chance to text-based composition.[14] This may not seem all that groundbreaking to anyone who has ever owned refrigerator magnet poetry. But it was radical at the time, and still was when Burroughs and Gysin evangelized their version.

Bowie described the "how" of cut-ups to the *Daily Mail* in 2008:

> You write down a paragraph or two describing several different subjects, creating a kind of "story ingredients" list, I suppose, and then cut the sentences into four or five-word sections; mix 'em up and reconnect them. You can get some pretty interesting idea combinations like this. You can use them as is or, if you have a craven need to not lose control, bounce off these ideas and write whole new sections.[15]

In other words, not every cut-up is left as is. Once rearranged, sentences can subsequently be edited to convey more or less of the author's intent. Cut-ups can also be used to evoke narrative points of view that go beyond common focal perspectives. As David Buckley says in *Strange Fascination: David Bowie, The Definitive Story*: "The sense of randomness appealed greatly to Bowie. He would write a song both in the first and third person and then randomize these two perspectives to create a 'new' subjectivity."[16]

Later in his career, Bowie worked with software developer Ty Roberts on a program that would make cut-ups easier to produce. "If you put three or four disassociated ideas together, the unconscious intelligence that comes from those pairings is really quite startling, quite provocative," Bowie said in the mid-1990s. "I'll take articles out of newspapers, poems I've written, pieces of other people's books, and put them all into this little warehouse of information and hit the button, and it will randomize everything."[17]

The choice resided with Bowie about how much control to apply in the final mix. "I'll either take sentences verbatim as it spews them out, or there might be something within a sentence that triggers off an idea," he said.[18] Bowie's machine-assisted cut-ups were a natural extension of the experiments undertaken by Burroughs and Sommerville in 1960s London. An early computer programmer, Sommerville would feed a sentence into a machine that would render every possible combination of individual words and spit them out in new formulations.[19] This process was a primitive version of Bowie's program, which, in a rare creative misfire, he called "the Verbasizer."

Bowie's cut-up app was used on the 1995 album *Outside*—a stormy affair that its creator described as "a non-linear Gothic Drama Hyper-cycle." The technique would continue to be applied right up to Bowie's final album, *Blackstar*. Director Michael Apted featured Bowie waxing psychedelic about cut-ups in his 1997 documentary about creativity, *Inspirations*; Burroughs might have appreciated the singer's remarks. "It's almost like a technological dream in its own way," Bowie said. "It creates the images from a dream state, without having to go through the boredom of having to go to sleep all night. Or get stoned out of your head."[20]

Cracked Actor

Getting stoned was a major focus for Bowie during the rollercoaster 1970s. Like Burroughs, Bowie sought visionary experiences by whatever means necessary, including narcotics. Though Bowie and Burroughs did not advocate drug use, both experienced the agonies of addiction, including withdrawal and paranoia. Still, Bowie had few regrets. "The more mediocre, vacuous personalities in that period ended far worse than the ones who really put themselves through the mill," he said in a 1990s career retrospective.[21]

And people like Bill Burroughs—you can't meet an ostensibly healthier, fitter older guy. Bill Burroughs probably had more needles in him than a pincushion. It's just interesting that people who make those explorations, if they go through the cusp of those explorations, they do tend to come out the other side—in a way, better people for it. That's a dangerous thing to say, but it's true in my case.[22]

Unlike Burroughs, Bowie preferred uppers to opiates. By the mid-seventies, his diet consisted solely of whole milk, red peppers, and cocaine.[23] The latter allowed him to skimp on sleep as he masterminded a new identity. Tired of glam and losing money due to increasingly expensive stage sets, Bowie "killed" Ziggy live on stage on June 3, 1973. "Of all the shows on the tour this particular show will remain with us the longest, because not only is it the last show of the tour, it's the last show we'll ever do," he said to an aghast audience decked out in platform shoes and rainbow eyeshadow.[24]

As it turns out, Bowie was only retiring his latest persona, not giving up music entirely. He dismissed the Spiders from Mars in favor of a soul-r&b crew assembled from Philadelphia's heaviest musical hitters. When he ducked into Sigma Sound studio on break from the *Diamond Dogs* tour, he emerged with a new sound he called "plastic soul." This would form the basis for his next LP, *Young Americans*, which featured a young Luther Vandross on backing vocals. Gone were the costumes inspired by the rampant hooligans of Burroughs' *The Wild Boys*. Now Bowie donned crisp suits that looked like spendier versions of Burroughs' seersuckers. (Both men admired Marlene Dietrich, who could definitely rock a suit.)

Like Burroughs' characters, whose identities and agendas are elastic, Bowie's changes tended to happen suddenly and with no advance warning. And, like Burroughs, he would not hesitate to drop anything that he felt held him back in his quest for individual fulfillment. Sometimes this meant discarding costumes, stage sets, and entire genres. Other times it meant discarding people, like Mick

Ronson, his glam-era axman. Or Angie Bowie (née Barnett), his saucy American wife. Or Carlos Alomar, his longtime rhythm guitarist and arranger. Still, it is hard to argue with the results. Bowie's Machiavellian streak made him one of the most successful rock stars across generations, much as Burroughs' dangerous and peculiar habits only served to cement his indelible notoriety.

Other popular '70s acts like Jackson Browne and the Eagles fell into softness, but Bowie's edges only got sharper. His debonair charm masked a killer's instinct, like a handsome cane that hides an icy blade. With cocaine abuse and sleep deprivation pushing him further into the red, Bowie channeled that instinct into making music for a new century—one where political, economic, and social violence was an everyday reality. Like an advance scout, Burroughs had already surveyed this apocalyptic terrain in his Nova trilogy, which invoked impending chaos of cosmic magnitude.

Such a perilous future demanded new techniques to fight Control. One of them was sound. Here a more obscure connection between Burroughs and Bowie comes to the fore. Burroughs believed sound could affect people at the molecular level, like junk rearranges the cellular makeup of biological organisms. He also recognized the power of rock bands like Led Zeppelin, whose sonic Sturm und Drang unleashed powerful energies, leaving audiences dazed and confused. He even pondered whether certain "bad vibrations" in the lower sonic frequencies could result in total system collapse among those targeted.

Bowie was interested in weaponized sound, but he was far too polite to use it on paying customers. Still, he talked about the idea often and even came up with a pet name for it: "black noise." As he explained to television host Dick Cavett in a rambling interview from 1974: "Black noise is something that Burroughs got very interested in. It's one facet of black noise is that . . . um . . . like a glass if an opera singer hits a particular note, the vibrations of that hit the metabolism of the glass and cracks it, yeah? So a black noise is the register within which you can crack a city or people. . . . It's a new Control bomb."[25] Somebody's been freebasing Burroughs.

The technical term for such weapons is "infrasound," or sound that is below 20 Hz in frequency. Infrasound is often outside the normal range of human hearing, yet it can produce intense, even dangerous effects. Certain frequencies are known to cause feelings of fear and deep unease among those exposed; some have even reported odd sensations of the supernatural. At its most extreme, infrasound can cause disruption to bodily functions, including dizziness, headaches, loss of vision, paralysis, and uncontrollable bowels—the infamous "brown note."[26] All of this appealed to Burroughs greatly, and one suspects it interests electronic acts like Skrillex, who deploys gut-rumbling "bass drops" in his EDM compositions.

The military's enthusiasm for sonic weapons isn't just theoretical: it has been put to test in the field. In 1989, US troops blasted Panamanian strongman Manuel Noriega with music from Van Halen and Guns N' Roses to drive him out of the Vatican compound where he was holed up.[27] Intelligence personnel used Metallica and Slipknot tracks as "enhanced interrogation" tools against suspected members of Al Qaeda.[28] Powerful sound cannons were turned on Dakota Access Pipeline protesters[29] and those taking to the streets in Ferguson, Missouri[30]—not far from Burroughs' own Saint Louis. More recently, there have been reports of brain injuries and hearing loss among US diplomats stationed in Cuba—the alleged result of a sonic attack.[31] There is little doubt that such weapons will continue to be deployed as civil unrest becomes status quo.

The idea of using music to kill is apparently an old one. A 2016 article from *FACT Magazine* describes an instrument that would have been of particular interest to Burroughs:

> One of the most frightening recently discovered weapons of sound is the Aztec Death Whistle, a pottery vessel, often shaped like a skull, that was used by Mexico's pre-Columbian tribes. Blowing into it makes a sound that has been described as "1,000 corpses screaming." Used en masse, an army marching with death whistles would surely have been terrifying.[32]

Some music fans willingly subject themselves to annihilating noise. Consider the popularity of black metal, with its windstorm guitars and guttural shrieks. The epitome of caustic, the genre is beloved by metalheads in all corners of the globe. Certain extreme music is basically already infrasound. Doom overlords Sunn O))) cause audiences to lose control of basic motor functions with their earth-rumbling drones. Dark ambient artist Lustmord hypnotizes with low-frequency hums. Noise pioneer Merzbow sounds like microphone feedback from Mars. Laptop trickster Tim Hecker serves up symphonies of static. And these are just a few examples. Black noise is coming to a concert hall or street riot near you—just as Burroughs and Bowie predicted.

Watch That Man

Like Burroughs, Bowie faced blowback from the Establishment for his supposed amorality and negative influence on youth. Critics, too, were distrustful, often dismissing him as a dilettante or poseur compared to artists like Bob Dylan and Joni Mitchell. Burroughs seemed sensitive to this when he met with Bowie for a 1974 *Rolling Stone* profile. "They try to categorize you," he said by way of commiseration. "I think the most important thing in the world is that the artists should take over this planet because they're the only ones who can make anything happen. Why should we let these fucking newspaper politicians take over from us?"[33]

The meeting had been arranged by the magazine's main man in London, A. Craig Copetas, and was published as "Beat Godfather Meets Glitter Mainman" in the February 28 edition. The pair met at Bowie's London home in November, shortly before Burroughs accepted Allen Ginsberg's invitation to come back to New York and take a teaching gig at City College. Copetas set the scene:

> Bowie's house is decorated in a science-fiction mode: A gigantic painting, by an artist whose style fell midway between Salvador Dali and Norman Rockwell, hung over a plastic sofa. Quite a con-

trast to Burroughs' humble two-room Piccadilly flat, decorated with photos of Brion Gysin—modest quarters for such a successful writer, more like the Beat Hotel in Paris than anything else.

Soon Bowie entered, wearing three-tone NASA jodhpurs. He jumped right into a detailed description of the painting and its surrealistic qualities. Burroughs nodded, and the interview/conversation began. The three of us sat in the room for two hours, talking and taking lunch: a Jamaican fish dish, prepared by a Jamaican in the Bowie entourage, with avocados stuffed with shrimp and a beaujolais nouveau, served by two interstellar Bowieites.

Bowie, like Dylan a decade prior, was at a creative crossroads when he sat down with Burroughs. He craved the kind of credibility rarely extended to teen idols at the top of the pops; chatting up a notorious Beat writer for a major American publication was a great way to establish his bona fides as a visionary thinker. For his part, Burroughs understood that paying the rent meant staying in the public eye to some extent. At least this new generation was more interesting than the hippies, who Burroughs thought were milquetoast. "The only way I like to see cops given flowers is in a flower pot from a high window," he once remarked.[34]

Burroughs and Bowie hit it off, sharing their views on a range of topics, from the media to love to yogic techniques. But if Bowie's aim was to appear as a sophisticated student of letters, he mostly fell short:

BURROUGHS: What is your inspiration for writing, is it literary?
BOWIE: I don't think so.
BURROUGHS: Well, I read this eight-line poem of yours and it is
     very reminiscent of T. S. Eliot.
BOWIE: Never read him.

Bowie had taken a deeper dive into the Burroughs oeuvre before their meeting and could barely hang on to himself. The author's prose was gloriously hideous in a way that was almost tactile. "That's the way I get off on writing, especially William's," he said. "I can't say that I analyze it all and that's exactly what you're saying, but from a feeling way I got what you meant. It's there, a whole wonderhouse of strange shapes and colors, tastes, feelings."[35]

Bowie explained his vision of a stage show incorporating Burroughs-style concepts. "*Nova Express* really reminded me of *Ziggy Stardust*, which I am going to be putting into a theatrical performance," he promised. "Forty scenes are in it and it would be nice if the characters and actors learned the scenes and we all shuffled them around in a hat the afternoon of the performance and just performed it as the scenes come out. I got this all from you, Bill." Burroughs was intrigued. "That's a very good idea, visual cut-up in a different sequence," he said. The production never came to pass.

In 1979, Jeffrey Morgan of *CREEM* got Burroughs to revisit his conversation with Bowie:

MORGAN: What did you think of [Bowie] when you met him? Did he seem to be the kind of guy who was bullshitting his way through life or did he seem to be walking the straight and narrow?

BURROUGHS: Well, neither one. He's not bullshitting, he's very, very clever and I think very calculating. I think he knows exactly what he's doing and where he's going and how to get there.[36]

As the 1970s drew to a close, the challenge for Bowie wasn't getting there; it was finding his way back.

The Supermen

Like Burroughs, Bowie was very much interested in the occult. He believed, as Burroughs did, that art was a gateway to the realm of magic, where word, symbol, and sound can be harnessed to produce real-world results. To everyday practitioners, "the occult" is any system or technique that brings about change through processes unexplained or unexamined by classical physics. Or, even more simply, anything beyond our everyday apprehension that informs or impacts reality. Becoming an occult adept does not require an admission exam at Hogwarts; all one needs is an open mind. Or perhaps no mind at all. "Exterminate rational thought," the William Lee character says in the film adaptation of *Naked Lunch*. David Bowie definitely got the memo: he spent the back half of the '70s in a drug-fueled fugue state.

Bowie covered his rented Los Angeles home in arcane symbols, much as Burroughs' fictional double Kim Carsons "drew magic circles in the basement and tried to conjure demons" in *The Place of Dead Roads*. Bowie's occult preoccupations turned up in his music with increasing frequency. "Don't look at the carpet / I drew something awful on it," he sings in a tremulous baritone on "Breaking Glass" from the 1977 album *Low*. His skeletal frame and sallow complexion looked something awful indeed. To watch Bowie perform "Young Americans" on live television that year, cadaverous limbs angled painfully around a guitar that likely weighed more than him, is to see a man who would be lucky to survive the decade. That he did is a testament to a fierce desire to realize his ambitions. "Do what thou wilt shall be the whole of the law," states the Aleister Crowley maxim. And what Bowie "wilt," besides piles of drugs, was to achieve lasting impact through his art by whatever means necessary—including a little light sorcery.

Like Burroughs, Bowie's approach to the occult was intuitive rather than academic, though he was fairly well informed on a wide array of esoteric subjects, from Crowley to Wicca to Eastern philosophy. "Bowie has constructed his public persona from the various parts of the puzzle that are at the roots of modern occultism," Peter R. Koenig said in his epic online essay *The Laughing Gnostic: David Bowie and the Occult*. "This is the recurring motif of his quest for the authentic self."[37] That quest is the purpose and directive of Gnosticism.

But what is Gnosticism? A really old word virus, for starters. In ancient Greek, *gnosis* means knowledge. The aphorism *gnothi seauton*, or "know thyself," has echoed through mystical schools across the ages and was etched upon the entrance to the internal temple at Luxor in ancient Egypt. In a modern occult context, Gnosis is both the path to self-knowledge and the destination itself. A 1986 essay archived at the Chaos Matrix website describes Gnosis as:

> The key to magical abilities—the achievement of an intense state of consciousness known in various traditions as No-Mind, One-Pointedness, or Sartori. Awareness is emptied of all information except the object/subject of concentration. Various methods of achieving gnosis can be resorted to, from frenzied dancing to the rapt contemplation of an idea. Whatever method is chosen, the practitioner continues it until s/he is taken into Ecstasy.[38]

If that is indeed the case, there is little doubt that music can be a potent instrument of illumination.

In the nineteenth and early twentieth centuries, organizations such as the Hermetic Order of the Golden Dawn and the Ordo Templi Orientis synthesized Gnostic concepts into something called "Western Hermetics."[39] This spiritual system incorporated the wisdom of older cultures, including those supposedly originating with the Knights Templar. It also made extensive use of Jewish esoteric teachings rooted in the Kabbalah—a set of divine emanations that correspond to one another within a metaphysical hierarchy called the Sepher Sephiroth, or Tree of Life. These and other esoteric practices would eventually fall under the umbrella of "magick," a term coined by Aleister Crowley to distinguish occult practice from tricks performed by illusionists. (And that's what we'll be calling it from here on out.) Crowley also promoted "sex magick," a more intimate discipline that makes use of the energies, and sacred bodily fluids, brought forward through acts of unbridled lust, wasting none of their vitality. Perhaps that's why magick so appealed to Bowie and other horny rock stars. It also provides some context for the seemingly nonstop flow of ejaculate in Burroughs' novels.

One of Bowie's most occult compositions is "Station to Station" from the 1977 album of the same name. Over a jagged guitar riff and a cyclical beat, he references the Stations of the Cross, magical circles, astral projection, the poetry of Aleister Crowley, and the Kabbalistic Tree of Life:

Here are we, one magical moment, such is the stuff
From where dreams are woven
Bending sound, dredging the ocean, lost in my circle
Here am I, flashing no color
Tall in this room overlooking the ocean
Here are we, one magical movement from Kether to Malkuth
There are you, you drive like a demon from station to station

Like Burroughs' paranormal activities at the Beat Hotel, Bowie's occult forays led to some pretty weird situations. Then again, it might have been "the side effects of the cocaine," to borrow another quote from "Station to Station." At one point, the superstar believed a satanic coven was attempting to steal his bodily fluids to conceive the Antichrist; to prevent this, he began storing his urine in the refrigerator. Bowie claims to have witnessed a demonic presence in his backyard pool; this at least was corroborated by his then-wife Angie.[40] He even suspected Led Zeppelin guitarist Jimmy Page— who was interviewed by Burroughs for *Crawdaddy* in 1975—of placing a curse on him.[41] By decade's end, Bowie's strange fascinations had him completely unspooled.

That was all a far cry from the wide-eyed eagerness of "Quicksand," from Bowie's pre-glam masterpiece *Hunky Dory*. Over soft hollows of acoustic guitar, the singer reveals intimate spiritual yearnings. "I'm closer to the Golden Dawn / Immersed in Crowley's uniform of imagery," he croons. Bewildered by forces bigger than himself, Bowie seeks to balance the extremes of his awareness. "I'm torn between the light and dark / Where others see their targets, divine symmetry." His esoteric paean also makes mention of

"Himmler's dream reality," which is a likely reference to the Nazi regime's supposed interest in the occult and its artifacts. This would not be the last time Bowie would wink at fascism in his music or commentary.

Boys Keep Swinging

One wonders what Bowie and Burroughs would make of the young crypto-fascists waging online war in support of the most retrogressive politics the world has seen in nearly a century. These self-styled "edgelords" congregate at sites like 4Chan and Reddit and claim to have gotten Donald Trump elected through "meme magick." Like the army of nihilist delinquents in *The Wild Boys*, they aim for total overthrow but will settle for LOLs.

As a young man, Bowie was drawn to the Mod gangs of '60s Great Britain and later became fixated on the fictional hoodlums in Burroughs' books—as did songwriter Robyn Hitchcock, who got the name for his band Soft Boys by combining the above with *The Soft Machine*, which had already been claimed by Daevid Allen. In any case, the fictional gang in *The Wild Boys* care nothing for functional political or social systems; they're here to tear down institutions. Compare them to today's alt-right movement—a global virus carried almost exclusively by disaffected young men for whom tolerance and inclusion are signs of weakness that must be eradicated with extreme prejudice. (Apparently, homosexuality gets a pass; the openly gay Milo Yiannopoulos is one of the movement's biggest stars.)

Decades earlier, Burroughs anticipated a contagion that would benefit from distributed communications networks. Recall his claim that in "the electronic revolution a virus is a very small unit of word and image." It's all fun and games until an actual fascist comes to power. Social media users are no doubt familiar with the cartoon frog that appeared all across the Internet during the American presidential election of 2016. His name is Pepe, and he originated in a comic by Matt Furie called *Boy's Club*. Pepe has since been appropriated—against his creator's wishes—by alt-righters who believe he is an avatar of a frog-headed Egyptian god named Kek. You read that right: some portion of voters went into the 2016 elections believing the Internet resurrected an ancient amphibian to challenge the globalist system. But is that the whole story? Not according to Tara Isabella Burton, who explored the post-ironic sensibilities of the alt-right in an article for *Real Life*:

> Most of the people posting about Kek don't actually *believe* that Pepe the Frog is an avatar of an ancient Egyptian chaos god, or that the numerology of 4chan *"gets"*—when posts are assigned a fortuitous ID number—somehow predicted Donald Trump's presidential victory. . . . It's a joke, of course—but also not a joke. As one self-identified active member of the alt-right told me, "I don't believe in God. But I say *'Praise Kek'* more than I've ever said anything about God."[42]

Belief creates reality; masks coalesce identity; writing makes it real. A cursory scroll through Twitter confirms that Kek Corps is still on the march. And instead of Bowie knives, they've got memes.

It's probably coincidence that Bowie dressed up as an Egyptian pharaoh for a 1971 photo shoot. Less ambiguous is a *Playboy* interview from 1976 where he called Adolf Hitler "one of the first rock stars." This, too, was probably playacting, but in today's political climate, Bowie's words are chilling: "Look at some of the films and see how [Hitler] moved," he enthused.[43] "I think he was quite as good as Jagger . . . he used politics and theatrics and created this thing that governed and controlled the show for those twelve years. The world will never see his like again. He staged a country." That same year, Bowie was roundly criticized for giving what some believe was a stiff-armed Nazi salute while greeting fans at London's Victoria Station from the back of a Mercedes convertible. In a separate interview with the *New Musical Express* in 1975, Bowie predicted and endorsed the rise of a demagogue who will remake the political landscape: "There will be a political figure in the not too distant future who'll sweep through this part of the world like early rock 'n' roll did. You probably hope I'm not right but I am.... You've got to have an extreme right front come up and sweep everything off its feet and tidy everything up."[44]

Most Burroughs aficionados are well aware that he shot his wife and made many misogynistic statements. Far fewer Bowie fans know that he flirted with fascist ideology. Perhaps this is because he worked so closely with black musicians, who often made up more than half of his band. Bowie married a Somali fashion model, Iman, in 1992 and stayed with her for the remainder of his life, all the while supporting antiracist causes and publicly chastising MTV for its initial refusal to air videos by black performers. Could a bigot make *Young Americans*? Fans can sleep easy: the preponderance of evidence suggests that Bowie was not a Nazi. His earlier remarks may have been more playacting, like Burroughs' routines—delivered for shock value. Though they may not have reflected personal beliefs, as prophecy they're chilling.

Burroughs, for his part, "didn't have any fundamental bigotry," according to James Grauerholz. "If no other proof were produced, look who he let screw him in Morocco."[45] In fact, Burroughs' father came from a family of northern abolitionists who took civil rights very seriously. "William's great-grandfather named his grandfather after abolitionist William Henry Seward," Grauerholz said. "Now, his mother's family, the Lees, were southerners from Georgia. But they were part of the New South, the enlightened South.... There are stories about William's grandfather laying down his cape over a mud puddle so that a black couple going to church could walk over."

Though there are plenty of artists with racial prejudices, exposure to different cultures is of demonstrable benefit to creativity. It's hard to imagine what Burroughs' books would look like had he not lived in Tangier, where he encountered music and mysticism practiced by inhabitants over centuries. And everyone knows rock 'n' roll would not exist but for jazz and blues, whose practitioners are by overwhelming majority black. Bowie's temperament and travels invited much cross-pollination in terms of creative ideas. To soothe his stinging psyche, he also turned to the wisdom traditions of other cultures.

Seven Years in Tibet

Bowie first encountered Tibetan Buddhism at age thirteen, when he read "The Rampa Story," by T. Lobsang Rampa, and began visiting the Tibet House in London several times a week. "I was within a month of having my head shaved, taking my vows, and becoming a monk," he later recalled.[46] In 1966, a young monk named Chögyam Trungpa fled Tibet for Scotland's Samye Ling Monastery, which soon attracted several of England's creative cognoscenti, including Tony Visconti, Bowie's bandmate, producer, and lifelong friend who had made an earlier pilgrimage and encouraged the singer to check it out. Bowie spent a good deal of time in the Highlands, sitting on a cushion and focusing on his breathing.

Burroughs knew Trungpa from the talks he gave in the 1970s at the guru's Naropa Institute in Boulder, Colorado. Before that, Burroughs wanted to run his own metaphysical training camp in Scotland, with curricula to include meditation techniques like those he practiced at the Beat Hotel. Burroughs shared his vision for his "Final Academy" with Bowie: "Its aim will be to extend awareness and alter consciousness in the direction of greater range, flexibility and effectiveness at a time when traditional disciplines have failed to come up with viable solutions," he said. "We will be considering only non-chemical methods with the emphasis placed on combination, synthesis, interaction and rotation of methods now being used in the East and West." This appealed to Bowie, for whom Eastern philosophy would hold fascination for the rest of his life. Following his death in 2016, Sonic Youth guitarist Thurston Moore wrote a tribute that described Bowie's early Buddhist practice: "Legend has it that David had considered a life as a monk but his teachers saw his light was needed beyond the monastery and advised him to follow it."[47]

A more sinister strain of Eastern thought likely reached Bowie through Burroughs. The latter's oft-repeated dictum "Nothing is true; everything is permitted" originated with eleventh-century Persian mystic Hassan i-Sabbah, the leader of a radical sect of dagger-wielding ascetics who were the Shiite equivalent of Japanese ninja. These mercenaries meted out assassinations while high on hashish; the Arabic term *hashashin*, used to describe i-Sabbah's order, is the source of the words "hashish" and "assassin." The historical Assassins possessed the ability to adapt to different circumstances and environments by simply assuming a new identity; Bowie might have fit in well. Followers of i-Sabbah were instructed that action, rather than belief, gives shape to the world. Blind faith—including unquestioning adherence to the Koran—is a form of Control. If nothing is true, and everything permitted, corrupting distortions like morals and dogmas are torn away, and true reality is revealed.

Taken out of context, such a philosophy seems to reject any and all restraints on individual behavior—which dovetails nicely with the rock star lifestyle. Given Bowie's ongoing interest in Burroughs, he was no doubt aware of Hassan i-Sabbah. The album *Lodger* features a cut called "Yassassin," and his look at the time was very *Lawrence of Arabia*. There is also a link to Crowley; the British magus espoused a radical freedom agenda that has a lot in common with i-Sabbah's. Burroughs certainly grasped the connection. "If you see everything as illusion, everything is permitted," he said. "The last words of Hassan i Sabbah, the Old Man of the Mountain, the Master of the Assassins. This was given a slightly different twist, but is the same statement as Aleister Crowley's 'Do What Thou Wilt Is the Whole of the Law.'"[48]

Bowie would continue to reinvent himself in the years to follow, but he never abandoned what he learned from Burroughs. In the late 1970s, the singer delivered a trio of groundbreaking albums—*Low*, *Heroes*, and *Lodger*—which applied cut-up techniques not only to the lyrics, but also the music. Recorded in the shadow of the Berlin Wall with producer and musician Brian Eno, the albums made use of Eno's Oblique Strategies—a deck of cards featuring random prompts that can be applied to any situation, and which helped Bowie break through studio logjams. "Do something sudden, destructive and unpredictable," one card states. "Remove specifics and convert to ambiguities," reads another. *Heroes*, in particular, makes extensive use of cut-ups. The album "takes the form of a scattershot collection of displaced phrases pieced together using the cut-up technique," writes Thomas Jerome Seabrook in *Bowie in Berlin: A New Career in a New Town*.[49] Between sessions, Bowie would go clubbing with fellow Burroughs fan Iggy Pop.

Leaning heavily on the random, Bowie and Eno helped lay the groundwork for the post-punk and New Romantic movements that included such acts as ABC, Culture Club, and Spandau Ballet. In 1984, Bowie disciples Duran Duran tipped their hat to Burroughs in their big-budget video "Wild Boys," which was intended to serve as proof-of-concept for a full-length feature film based on the novel. Like Bowie's planned cut-up musical, the project never got off the ground.

Before donning a Colgate grin and peroxide 'do for the Reagan era, Bowie helped another Burroughs fan with his faltering solo career. Lou Reed was an obsession of Bowie's from the moment he first heard the Velvet Underground in the late 1960s. He made sure to drop Reed's name in his meeting with Burroughs. "Lou Reed is the most important definitive writer in modern rock," Bowie gushed. "Not because of the stuff that he does, but the direction that he will take it. Half the new bands would not be around if it were not for Lou. The movement that Lou's stuff has created is amazing. New York City is Lou Reed."[50]

Under Pressure

Did Bowie plant a seed in Burroughs' mind about moving back to New York? It's possible. Allen Ginsberg was certainly on his case about it. It wasn't a hard sell: Burroughs was already fed up with Great Britain, with its high taxes and snobby shopkeeps. The days of smoking hashish with Paul McCartney and making tapes with Ian Sommerville were over. There were some bright spots, like his collaboration with avant-garde filmmaker Antony Balch, whose work ran the gamut from B-horror to soft-core pornography. Balch's collaborations with Burroughs included *The Cut Ups* (1967) and *Bill and Tony and Others* (1972), along with other experimental films of varying length and interest. Burroughs provided the voiceover narration to Balch's 1968 re-release of the 1921 Swedish film *Häxan: Witchcraft through the Ages*, a curious slice of silent cinema boasting fantastical scenes of satanic worship and harsh medieval judgement. One wonders how many Scandinavian metal bands watch this flick on frigid, starless nights. Plenty of them borrow scenes from *Häxan* for their YouTube videos.

The Balch-Burroughs collaborations are now recognized as cornerstones of Beat cinema, which forms its own distinct canon. At the time, however, audiences fled showings of *The Cut Ups* at the Cinephone on Oxford Street in such a rush they left behind their coats, hats, and umbrellas. Looking at the film now, it's hard to see what viewers found so offensive. The random visual-audio juxtapositions are more awkward than jarring; besides, this style of film-making has long since been absorbed by the mainstream, informing everything from the films of David Lynch to Beyoncé videos. One direct homage was a clip in heavy rotation on MTV in 1992—"Just One Fix," by industrial metal stalwarts Ministry. The video features a cohort of junkies (including band members) on the prowl for heroin. These scenes are cut in with performance footage and shots of Burroughs making ominous hand gestures in front of a billowing cloud of black-gray smoke. Later he is seen firing a double-barreled shotgun at a target emblazoned with the word "Control." The video definitely glamorizes drug use, but it also demonstrates the breadth of Burroughs' influence across the media arts.

Without Sommerville around to assist, Burroughs' tape experiments became more singular in purpose: to curse those who threatened, harmed, or offended him. One such hex was targeted at Somerville's new boyfriend, Alan Watson. Always the doormat, Burroughs caved when Sommerville asked if he and Watson could move into his flat at Dalmeny Court on Duke Street. Now he was being driven mad by Watson's effeminate manner and endlessly hovering presence. Burroughs recorded a tape hex mocking Watson's swishy speech and making stern commands for him to vacate the premises. Watson accidentally discovered the recording while relaxing on a city bench and listening to a cassette he thought contained music. When Burroughs' venomous incantations filled his ears instead, Watson got spooked and chucked the tape into a nearby canal.

Subsequent tape hexes would grow more elaborate. In a 1972 operation, Burroughs claims to have made London's first espresso shop, the Moka coffee bar at 29 Frith Street, pull up stakes. This was accomplished by making recordings of an earlier argument in the establishment, cut up with "trouble noise," including police sirens recorded from the sidewalk in front of the premises. Burroughs' aim was to dislodge the Moka bar from its position in space-time by assaulting it with destabilizing sounds from another position on the so-called time track. Every day he would stand in front of the shop and make recordings, which he would then take home and edit—after which he would return to the scene and play back the recordings at a very low volume, barely perceptible over the existing ambience. This apparently caused deep unease among patrons and proprietors. "They are seething in there," Burroughs wrote. "I have them and they know it." The Moka bar closed its doors on October 30, 1972. Burroughs went to all of this trouble on account of rude service and a bad piece of cheesecake. "The single most important thing about Burroughs was his belief in the magical universe," wrote biographer Ted Morgan. "The same impulse that led him to put out curses was, as he saw it, the source of his writing."[51] Burroughs' growing irritation with English life gave him plenty of fodder.

The same year as his magical attack on the coffee shop, Burroughs hexed the Church of Scientology headquarters at 37 Fitzroy Street. Once again he claimed success when they moved to Tottenham Court Road, a nearby location that remains open to this day. Burroughs didn't start off as a Scientology antagonist; he was for a time an eager student. His interest was initially stoked by Gysin during their stay at the Beat Hotel. As Burroughs wrote in a letter to

Allen Ginsberg: "They do the job without hypnosis or drugs, simply run the tape back and forth until the trauma is wiped off. It works. I have used the method—partially responsible for recent changes."[52]

Founded by science-fiction writer L. Ron Hubbard, Scientology is considered a cult by most outsiders, even as it counts celebrities such as Tom Cruise, John Travolta, and Kirstie Alley among its members. There are famous musician Scientologists, too, such as Beck, Chick Corea, Edgar Winter, the late Isaac Hayes, and briefly, members of the Grateful Dead. But why would Burroughs, with his profound allergy to Control, want anything to do with an organization whose leader, Hubbard, demanded absolute fealty? It was the techniques that interested him foremost. If Scientology helped him locate the Ugly Spirit, it didn't matter if the Easter Bunny was at the helm. Too, Burroughs liked the emphasis on the reactive mind, which acts as a vault of negative experiences that limit personal advancement. In Scientology, one's demons are vanquished through a technique called "auditing" that makes use of something called an E-meter. A cross between cans on a string and a lie detector, the device is employed in interview sessions during which a specially trained interlocutor offers a series of prompts meant to uncover hidden hang-ups. Over time, and with considerable financial commitment, "engrams"—the troublesome emotions and experiences implanted in this and previous lives—are eliminated, or at least that's the idea.

Burroughs had already spent years in analysis, and he'd done plenty of contemplation on his own. Drugs and booze had failed to dissolve his traumas—and at points exacerbated them. Burroughs believed that Scientology might help him achieve relief in a much shorter period of time. (He clearly did not understand the organization's business model.) Burroughs was all about Scientology's methods, but he bristled at leader Hubbard, whose followers treated him like some kind of god. Burroughs demonstrated his non-allegiance by using photos of Hubbard for air pistol target practice. Neverthe-. less, he submitted to a two-month intensive retreat at the organization's East Grinstead estate in 1968, dutifully consuming the literature and submitting to audits. Sommerville, tired of all the prattling on about operating thetans and engrams, moved out before Burroughs even finished his course. Now Burroughs was truly left to his own devices: his typewriter, tape decks, and E-meter.

Burroughs' anti-Establishment views found outlet in articles and interviews for men's magazines like *Rat* and *Mayfair*, no doubt raising his profile among a new generation of thrill-seekers and cultural renegades. In 1970 he issued a series of cassette tapes called the *Revised Boy Scout Manual*. Topics included "assassination by list," "random assassination," "chemical and biological weapons," "biological warfare proper," "deadly orgone radiation," and "infrasound." He took a morbid interest in the then-recent murders committed by the Manson family, noting members' connection to Scientology.[53] Manson, of course, was a failed musician. He might have even crossed Burroughs' path one day had he been as effective at impressing record executives as he was at brainwashing young people to commit murder.

In his final days in London, Burroughs hit both the bottle and the Piccadilly Circus rent-boy scene. But he was running out of money— and quickly. His hopes for a film adaptation of *Naked Lunch* were dashed in 1971 when the producer Chuck Barris—creator of *The Dating Game*, host of *The Gong Show*, and self-confessed CIA assassin—lost interest in the project. In January 1973, Burroughs once again found himself in Morocco, reporting on jazz icon Ornette Coleman's date with the Master Musicians of Joujouka for the men's magazine *Oui*:

Musicians are magicians in Morocco and they all bear the mark of the conjurer the magic man. They are evokers of the djenoun forces, spirits of the hills and the flocks and above all the spirits of music. . . . [Ornette Coleman] is clearly an expert in this musical splicing—"musical surgery" he calls it—and the music that emerged as the session developed was a palpable force felt by everyone present. Magnetic spirals spun through the room like clusters of electronic bees that meet and explode in the air releasing the divine perfume, a musty purple smell of ozone and spice and raw goatskins, a perfume you can hear, smell, and see.

Burroughs was not a music writer, yet his imagistic copy for *Oui* is competitive with rock scribes such as Lester Bangs and Richard Meltzer. Magazine writing padded Burroughs' income, but London's high cost of living continued to strain his finances—and he didn't even have a habit. In 1973, Barry Miles and Brion Gysin helped Burroughs catalog his archives, which were delivered to a financier in Lichtenstein in exchange for a briefcase of cash. Meanwhile, people close to Burroughs had died. His father passed in 1965, Neal Cassidy in 1968, and Jack Kerouac in 1969. His mother spent her final years losing her mind in a nursing home; Billy Jr. paid his grandmother visits, but his dad hadn't seen her in ages. The older Burroughs received a telegram in October 1970 informing of his mother's death. He felt regret for not having been more present in her later life. He was not, however, inspired to pay more attention to Billy, who was now in his early twenties.

Burroughs continued to be welcomed among London's movers and shakers. He attended the Stones' tax exile going-away party and was name-dropped by Anita Pallenberg in the 1970 film *Performance*. "Maybe we ought to call Dr. Burroughs, give him a shot," she coos. But the hipster scene was wearying, and these were not his people. Burroughs had at last given up on Scientology, taking the church to task in a *Mayfair* article called "I, William Burroughs, Challenge You, L. Ron Hubbard":

Some of the techniques [of Scientology] are highly valuable and warrant further study and experimentation. The E Meter is a useful device . . . (many variations of this instrument are possible). On the other hand I am in flat disagreement with the organizational policy. No body of knowledge needs an organizational policy. Organizational policy can only impede the advancement of knowledge. There is a basic incompatibility between any organization and freedom of thought.

He was harsher still in a 1972 issue of *Rolling Stone*, where he called Scientology "a model control system, a state in fact with its own courts, police, rewards and penalties."

With no real love in his life, Burroughs gave his affections to male prostitutes such as John Brady, a sweet and simple lad with a violent temper who moved in with the author in 1972. Visitors could plainly see that this was not a healthy relationship. When Ginsberg visited England in 1973, he offered Burroughs a lifeline. Come back to New York, he cajoled. Burroughs could take a teaching gig at City College and bask in the adoration of his many admirers. So, just before Christmas of 1974, Burroughs returned to the city that birthed the Beats.

New York in the mid-1970s was a metropolis on the edge of a total breakdown. With a major fiscal crisis, high unemployment, blackouts, and surging crime rates, the denizens of the city faced daily uncertainty. Gritty doesn't begin to describe the pothole-ridden streets and trash bags piled past first-story windows due to sanitation strikes. It wasn't all bad though. Cheap rent in the Bowery— soon to be ground zero for punk—enabled poets, painters, and musicians to establish a colony in one of Manhattan's most blighted neighborhoods. In 1970s New York, the art world elite freely mingled with the underground. Ginsberg was part of the scene, but it didn't revolve around the Beats. There was a whole new energy— tougher, sassier, and more cynical—embodied by the likes of Lou Reed, the man who David Bowie said *was* New York.

Men of Good Fortune

Burroughs was an essential part of Lou Reed's creative makeup. His later-life partner, the experimental performer Laurie Anderson, was one of Burroughs' collaborators before she and Reed got together in 1992. Anderson's recorded music debut was one side of an LP called *You're the Guy I Want to Share My Money With*, released in 1981 by Burroughs' friend and onetime assistant, the performance poet John Giorno. Anderson describes how she became a

Burroughs fan: "I heard him speak before I read his books, so it was that voice that grabbed me first, that high-pitched sound made of sharp gravel . . . he was like an odd splice of voodoo doctor and car salesman. There was something about him that was oddly familiar, and yet completely alien."[54] The latter part of her description might as well apply to Reed, who died in 2013 from liver disease following a Coney Island roller coaster of a career. A study in contradictions, Reed's creative gifts seemed poorly paired with his choleric attitude, like a baby angel who lives in a dumpster and chews cigarette butts while hurling invectives at passersby. Thankfully, his talents outshone his personality faults, as evidenced by his influence on modern rock music, starting with the Velvet Underground and continuing through twenty-two solo albums.

A shrewdly insightful writer, Reed rendered potent truths about the human condition in terse, often trenchant prose. His wit was equal parts charming and insufferable, and it blossomed in music that, at its best, reconciled his romantic and cynical sides. Exploding with confidence yet scarred by self-loathing, Reed staked broad musical and lyrical territory in songs both homely and transcendent. Like Burroughs, Reed chronicled desperate characters and squalid situations while refraining from moral imposition. The Velvet Underground's "I'm Waiting for the Man" captures the anxiety of the addict and is a direct descendant of *Junkie*. Even more obvious is "Heroin," a micro-symphony of self-destruction: "I have made the big decision / I'm gonna try to nullify my life / 'Cause when the blood begins to flow / When it shoots up the dropper's neck / When I'm closing in on death / You can't help me now," Reed mumble-sings as drummer Maureen Tucker mimics an accelerating heartbeat. Compare that to Burroughs' description of an opiate high: "Morphine hits the backs of the legs first, then the back of the neck, a spreading wave of relaxation slackening the muscles away from the bones so that you seem to float without outlines, like lying in warm salt water. . . . The physical impact of the fear of death; the shutting off of breath; the stopping of blood."[55]

Reed said Burroughs was "the person who broke the door down ... he alone had the energy to explore the interior psyche without a filter."[56] It wasn't just the inner stuff that caught Reed's eye. He also appreciated Burroughs' ability to describe the harsh realities of drug culture—including its many disreputable yet compelling characters—without a hint of moral imposition. Reed claimed Burroughs "changed my vision of what you could write about, how you could write," which makes perfect sense to anyone who has read *Junkie* and heard the Velvet Underground. Born a generation apart, Reed and Burroughs nonetheless had a few things in common, starting with childhood trauma.

Lewis Allan Reed was born in Brooklyn on March 2, 1942, to a tax accountant father and a former beauty queen mother. His upwardly mobile parents—both native New Yorkers—soon relocated the family to Freeport, Long Island, where Reed enjoyed a comfortable upbringing marked by no small amount of maternal smothering, something he had in common with Burroughs. Younger sister Elizabeth arrived when Reed was five, and although he was very much the devoted older brother, her birth meant his mother's attention was divided. Reed also felt burdened by his parents' standards; his mom and dad wanted him to grow up and become a doctor or lawyer. In a few years' time, he would confound their expectations mightily.

In his seventeenth year, Reed rebelled hard. Already obsessed with rock 'n' roll, he practiced his electric guitar loudly, wore dark clothes, and allegedly exhibited bisexual tendencies, which greatly troubled his conservative parents.[57] In 1959, Sidney and Toby Reed booked their son to see a shrink. The psychiatrist recommended a course of treatment common to the era: electroshock therapy. Reed was schlepped off to Creedmore State Psychiatric Hospital, where his broad brow was strapped with electrodes three times per week for eight weeks, not counting recovery. The effects were heartbreaking. "You can't read a book because you get to page seventeen and you have to go right back to page one again," Reed recalled.[58] He struggled not only cognitively, but emotionally, as he was unable to comprehend the episode as anything but a horrific betrayal. Still, it served to harden his resolve to get out, to fill the newly blank spaces of his psyche with more meaningful stuff than the rot of suburbia.

If not prominence, exactly, Lou Reed came to some notoriety as a member of the Velvet Underground, the perennial favorite of hipsters, musicians, and dope fiends. Originally co-led by Reed and avant-garde cellist and producer John Cale, the Velvets got their start as the house band at the Factory—the famous New York City enclave dreamed into existence by Andy Warhol. Those in Warhol's orbit found themselves positioned like figurines in an avant-garde dollhouse. Forget about the screen-printed soup can labels or stacked Brillo boxes; Warhol's biggest project was people. He loved throwing them together at parties, of which there were many. And, as any good host knows, a party requires music. That is where the Velvet Underground came in. The band regularly performed before Factory audiences teeming with artists, intellectuals, media mavens, street trash, and star-fuckers. Nowadays, people criticize celebrities like Kim Kardashian as being famous for nothing. And yet, for Warhol, this was the idea: anyone can be famous, because fame, like life, is ephemeral.

Warhol also created a space for people whose families had cast them off, or those who never had a family to begin with. That's not to ignore the sleaze at the Factory, which betrayed a near-Roman spirit of indulgence. Reed captures all of this imagistically and succinctly in "Walk On the Wild Side," from the Bowie-produced *Transformer* (1972):

Little Joe never once gave it away
Everybody had to pay and pay
A hustle here and a hustle there
New York City is the place where they said:
Hey babe, take a walk on the wild side
I said hey Joe, take a walk on the wild side

The lyrics owe something to Burroughs, whose just-the-facts report-age in *Junkie* was a cornerstone for Reed. It is street life described by someone who has had to fight every day to maintain a sense of self, to own one sliver of security. Throughout his life, Reed struggled mightily to come to terms with his bisexuality and challenges in communicating. His frequent tantrums, stemming from an inability to connect outside of his work, bear the hallmarks of autism. Was Reed on the spectrum? We will never know for sure. Whatever the root of his difficulties, he spent most of his career self-medicating with smack, booze, and his favorite drug of all, speed. "I take drugs just because in the 20th century in a technological age living in the city there are certain drugs you have to take just to keep yourself normal like a caveman," Reed said.[59] This pharmacological cornucopia made Reed difficult to get along with, but also inspired a lot of amazing music. After all, it was Reed's songs, not his personality, that made David Bowie want to work with him. "There were elements of what Lou was doing that I felt were just unavoidably right," Bowie said. "It's the New York I want to know about.... It was the Beats, it's where we all wanted to escape to. In literature, we have similar likes; we're both Burroughs nuts."[60]

Bowie accelerated Reed's solo career, but it was Warhol who first brought him to market. Sensing bigger opportunities for his doll-house musical act, Warhol paired the Velvet Underground with Teutonic chanteuse Nico, whose flat affect and Germanic palate brought a seductive, alien quality to some of Reed's most beautiful ballads. The band was shoved into the studio and came out with *The Velvet Underground and Nico* in 1967. Warhol designed the album cover, which boasts a bright yellow—and clearly phallic—banana against a shock white background, with the only text being the artist's signature and an invitation to "peel slowly and see." Unfortunately, Warhol's art world celebrity didn't translate to sales in the broader rock scene. That doesn't mean the record didn't make an impact. As Brian Eno told the *Los Angeles Times* in 1982: "I was talking to Lou Reed the other day, and he said that the first Velvet Underground record sold only 30,000 copies in its first five years. Yet, that was an enormously important record for so many people. I think everyone who bought one of those 30,000 copies started a band!"[61]

From there, the Velvets released a string of now-classic albums with music ranging from the densely psychedelic ("Black Angel's Death Song") to the exuberant ("Beginning to See the Light") to the arch ("Sweet Jane") to the itchy ("White Light/White Heat.)" Best among them might be "Pale Blue Eyes," the resplendent centerpiece of *The Velvet Underground* (1969): "Sometimes I feel so happy / Sometimes I feel so sad / Sometimes I feel so happy / But mostly you just make me mad," Reed sweetly intones over a sparse bed of tremulous guitar.

On the Velvet's final album, *Loaded*, the band, now minus John Cale, single-handedly invented what we now call indie rock. Without *Loaded*, there is no Broken Social Scene, no Wilco, no Pavement, no War on Drugs. (Burroughs would surely be okay with that.) However, as celebrated as the Velvets' releases are today, they barely added up to a career for Reed at the time. Burned out and nearly broke, he quit the band three months before *Loaded* hit shelves in November 1970.

Reed's critically panned and commercially ignored 1972 self-titled debut put his career dead on arrival. He must have had angels—or demons—looking out, because as luck would have it, his label, RCA, had just signed David Bowie, a rabid Velvet Underground fan dying to give Reed a makeover. After the suits sorted everything out, Bowie took the helm for *Transformer*, which became Reed's most critically acclaimed and best-selling solo album. After that was *Berlin*, a 1973 rock opera about an imploding relationship, replete with child neglect and drug abuse. Two years later, Reed dropped *Metal Machine Music*, a punishing slab of guitar feedback that confounded audiences and critics while laying the foundations for noise rock. These records make clear the delight Reed took in testing even his most devoted fans, something that was true right up until the end. His final album, *Lulu* (2011), a collaboration with arena bruisers Metallica, was ignored by listeners and savaged by critics. (It had one prominent champion, however: David Bowie called *Lulu* Reed's "masterpiece.")[62]

Throughout it all, Reed battled journalists, romantic partners, managers, record labels, and anyone who happened to cross his path. But the so-called "Phantom of Rock" was more than just a guy with a speed habit and a warehouse of axes to grind. Like Burroughs, his life and work contained complexities that defy ready-made caricatures. They also had childhood trauma in common— Reed's electroshock ordeal and Burroughs' alleged incident with the nanny. These episodes may, in part, be why both men turned to narcotics; the womblike bliss of heroin offered brief respite from their psychological agonies. (For Burroughs, his killing of Joan Vollmer and his neglect of their son were additional torments.) Despite—or perhaps because of—their vulnerabilities, Reed and Burroughs took pains to appear untouchable: Reed with leather and standoffishness, Burroughs with firearms and antipathy. Both men took numerous walks on the wild side and attempted to transcend their distress through creative exploration, offending delicate sensibilities along the way and blazing a trail for other renegades to follow.

Burroughs and Reed were both influenced by the late nineteenth-century Symbolist movement of France, as well as the American author who inspired the Symbolists, Edgar Allan Poe. The Symbolists were a big inspiration for the Beats, who in turn influenced a broad swath of twentieth-century popular culture. The triumvirate of Ginsberg, Kerouac, and Burroughs—along with adjunct provocateur Gysin—echoes the core group of Symbolists: Charles Baudelaire, Paul Verlaine, and Arthur Rimbaud. (The Brion Gysin role belonged to firebrand mystic Joséphin Péledan—an influential but largely forgotten multimedia artist and political raconteur whose Salon de la Rose + Croix included a number of painters, poets, and musicians.) Musicians such as Bob Dylan, Patti Smith, Lou Reed, and Jim Morrison (who as a teenager scored a copy of *Naked Lunch* from a Washington, DC, bookstore)[63] were particularly drawn to Rimbaud and Baudelaire. The latter's *The Flowers of Evil* is a whiff of spiced perfume masking grim decay, while the former's *A Season in*

Hell is a bracing dose of *amor* and ennui. Both are catnip to would-be art stars of any generation, much like Burroughs' own work.

Visions, dreams, and unfettered imagination were the tools Symbolists used to convey deeper truths. They were also obsessed with the occult. Mysticism of many kinds flourished alongside and within the Symbolist movement, and not just in France. In addition to the local occult society Salon de la Rose + Croix, there was the Theosophical Society, the Hermetic Brotherhood of Luxor, and the Hermetic Order of the Golden Dawn—the latter counting literary figures such as William Butler Yeats and Arthur Machen among its members. Symbolists drew from the archetypes and symbols of the occult and used them as both allegory and metaphor. They were also influenced by one of nineteenth-century America's authors, Edgar Allan Poe, whose work laid the groundwork for the hallucinatory prose to come.

Poe's feverish imaginings encouraged Baudelaire, Rimbaud, and Verlaine to let themselves be guided by whatever visions possessed them, however uncanny or abominable. Burroughs, too, adored Poe, whose stories and poems were among his favorites growing up. Toward the end of his life he would recite "The Masque of the Red Death" and "Annabel Lee" on the soundtrack to the 1995 horror video game *The Dark Eye*. Reed was also a Poe devotee. He named a 1979 song and album after one of his poems, "The Bells," and in 2003 he devoted an entire record, *The Raven*, to Poe's stories, poems, and themes.

The Phantom of Rock Meets El Hombre Invisible

Burroughs and Reed had mutual friends, but the two didn't actually meet face-to-face until 1979. By then Burroughs had become a fixture in Manhattan's Lower East Side neighborhood. There, in his windowless, three-room apartment at 222 Bowery, he held court among the musicians, intellectuals, writers, and junkies littering the scene like discarded show posters strewn across the sidewalk of nearby nightclub CBGB. Victor Bockris recorded several conversations between Burroughs and his guests during this period, including a meeting with Reed.

In June 1979, Reed was in town promoting *The Bells* at the nightclub the Bottom Line when Bockris arranged a dinner with Burroughs at the Bunker. Reed's bassist failed to show up for soundcheck, making him forty-five minutes late for the Burroughs meeting—a *major* faux pas with the well-mannered author. When the bandmate finally turned up, Reed tore him a new one, after which he, Bockris, and a bottle of scotch were off to the Bunker.

Bockris recalls that "instead of apologizing for his tardy arrival, Lou cast a withering glance around the room, and abruptly asked if there was a chair, or if he was expected to sit on the floor."[64] Upon being offered a seat, Reed laid in on Burroughs, asking if it was true that he had to sleep with publishers to get his books out, and if he cut off his toe to avoid the draft. (Reed may have misremembered the story of Burroughs slicing his finger in a youthful fit of romantic pique.) Burroughs was not only unruffled, he was amused at Reed's fireplug personality. "Bill really liked Lou Reed because when I took him to the Bunker, Lou was very witty and he asked pointed questions in just the right way," Bockris said, adding that Burroughs made a point to note "how sharp he thought Lou was."[65]

The two discussed how to shoot smack with a safety pin, and the work of John Rechy and Hubert Selby. Reed mellowed somewhat over the course of the conversation, but he still lobbed a few barbs at the man whose writing helped inspire his own career. "There was a quote where someone said about you that you were the only person they ever met who they felt was capable of murder and that you were a very cold person ... is that true?" Reed asked. "I neither confirm nor deny these kinds of rumors," Burroughs replied dryly.[66]

In actuality, Burroughs was quite warmly regarded. "Among those who knew him, Burroughs was well liked, loved and respected," Bockris said.[67] "His original publisher in Paris, Maurice Girodias, told me Burroughs was the kindest and sweetest person he ever met."[68] Bockris said he had a playful side that would reveal itself in the company of friends: "You could always tell when

Bill was really excited because his voice would go up the scale to a high pitched squeak!" On a typical night at the Bunker, "Bill sat at the head of the table. There were always other guests, usually John Giorno and Stewart Meyer would be there when I visited, but there were often others, ranging from Bill's closest friend Allen Ginsberg and his partner Peter Orlovsky to Debbie Harry and Chris Stein of Blondie to Joe Strummer of the Clash to Jean Michel Basquiat." Burroughs took it all in like an "adolescent who delighted in the deepest weirdness of human behavior."[69]

Reed definitely projected deep weirdness, which may be what endeared him to Burroughs. Bockris called their repartee "a hilarious exchange between the Martin and Lewis of the kingdom of junk."[70] Too bad there was no YouTube back then; just imagine a channel about drugs, literature, and music hosted by William S. Burroughs and Lou Reed.

REED: Why did you use the pen name Bill Lee on *Junkie*?
BURROUGHS: William Lee.
REED: Oh, yeah. But why?
BURROUGHS: Because my parents were still alive and I didn't want them to be embarrassed.
REED: But did they read it?
BURROUGHS: Well, they might have.
REED: See, I know you wrote a lot of other books, but I think *Junkie* is the most important because of the way it says something that hadn't been said straightforwardly. . . . Is this boring you?
BURROUGHS: Wha?[71]

Reed could not resist asking an impertinent question about Jack Kerouac: "How could a guy that was so good looking and romantic and writing that myth for generations end up being a fat, dumb asshole—if you don't mind me being crude—sitting in front of television in a t-shirt drinking beer with his mother? What happened to make him change?"[72] Those of lesser manners might have been tempted to point out that Reed himself was presently looking a bit booze-puffed. However, Burroughs took it in stride: "He didn't change that much, Lou. He was always like that. First there was a young guy sitting in front of television in a t-shirt drinking beer with his mother, then there was an older, fatter person sitting in front of television in a t-shirt drinking beer with his mother."[73]

Ever competitive, Reed asked Burroughs what he thought about Patti Smith, with whom the author enjoyed an easy rapport. "Well, yes, I've always liked what Patti does," he replied. "I last saw her I think it was out in New Jersey." Then, quickly pivoting, "Have you ever listened to any Joujouka music?" Reed responded that his only exposure to Joujouka was the Ornette Coleman collaboration, "which I have and play."[74]

After a half hour, Reed said, "Well, those who play can't stay," and it was off to the venue to do the gig. Burroughs stayed behind. As he was getting up to leave, Reed asked, "Would you like to have a quiet dinner so we can talk?"[75] Burroughs said he was game. But they would not see each other again until Burroughs' seventieth birthday party in 1984. "Was Lou too drunk to remember the meeting?" Bockris asked rhetorically. "I don't know, he probably imagined they were big friends. In a way they were. Anyway, I put it on my list of Great First Meetings."[76]

Music and Other Dark Arts

*We must storm the citadels of
enlightenment, the means are at hand.*

WILLIAM S. BURROUGHS

"Rock music can be seen as one attempt to break out of this dead soulless universe and reassert the universe of magic," Burroughs wrote in a 1975 article for *Crawdaddy* profiling Led Zeppelin's Jimmy Page. The British guitarist and bandleader was at the time a devotee of Aleister Crowley, the occultist who had earlier scandalized Victorian society. Crowley's influence was limited during his lifetime, but by the 1960s, his philosophies had begun to attract spiritual seekers like David Bowie. Crowley founded the mystical order Thelema in 1904 upon receiving a psychic download from an extradimensional entity he called Aiwass. In a trance, Crowley dictated to his bride, Rose Kelly, the bulk of *The Book of the Law*, the primary text of an occult philosophy that borrows from Egyptian archetypes and esoteric Judaism. His ideas permeate pop culture, from the "Do What Thou Wilt" sweatshirt worn by rapper Jay-Z to the symbolism in Lady Gaga's "Judas" video. As the primary architect of a world-renowned rock band, Page certainly played a role in the Crowley resurgence. Still, he rarely spoke about his occult interests in interviews, which makes his conversation with Burroughs about the ritual aspects of rock especially interesting.

By 1975, Page had reached the apex of music stardom, cultivating a drug habit and massive audiences along the way. Led Zeppelin's title-free 1971 release, known communally as *IV*, was a transatlantic sensation powered by the enduring "Stairway to Heaven"—a rock 'n' roll canticle with strong pagan overtones. The band's subsequent offerings, *Houses of the Holy* (1973) and the double album *Physical Graffiti* (1975), cemented Page's status as a musical innovator, while world-beating tours earned the group a reputation as one of rock's most dangerous acts. The Starship, Led Zeppelin's private Boeing 720, jetted from city to city like a pillaging craft, leaving trashed hotel rooms and dazed groupies in its wake.

Page had recently acquired Crowley's former estate on Loch Ness and opened an occult bookstore in London called Equinox, which, in addition to Crowleyana, carried tomes on astrology, Rosicrucianism, Kabbalah, alchemy, and Eastern philosophy. He had also begun experimenting with heroin. But Page wasn't just another druggy dilettante with money to burn. His deep appreciation for a range of subjects, from pre-Raphaelite art to Arabic and Indian music, made him a worthy conversation partner for the sixty-one-year-old Burroughs.

Born in West London on January 9, 1944, Page first got his hands on a guitar at age twelve, shortly after his family moved to Surrey. He made fast friends with a couple of other budding axmen named Eric Clapton and Jeff Beck, whose friendly competition over the years brought new and exciting colors to the canvas of rock. Page, Clapton, and Beck would all go on to perform in the progressive blues act the Yardbirds, with Page and Beck briefly sharing lead guitar duties before Beck ditched the band in 1966 while on tour in Texas. Page's tenure as the leader of the Yardbirds was short-lived; by 1968 he had a clear vision for a new act—one that would combine the density of heavy electric blues with enchanting acoustics powered by a precision rhythm section.

Page seemed destined for success even as a young lad, with a twinkle in his eyes that evinced quiet intelligence and determination. He made his first media appearance in 1957 at age thirteen playing skiffle (a kind of upbeat British folk music popular with the day's youth) on the BBC's *On Your Own* show.[1] The earnest boy in pleated pants and casual sweater strummed along with his gawky bandmates on "Mama Don't Allow No Skiffle Playing in Here," after which the host popped over. When asked what he favored in school,

Page answered "biological research" and professed a desire to help find a cure for cancer. It is hard to imagine this buttoned-down young man slinking across world stages, guitar slung almost to his knees, summoning a sonic blitzkrieg.

Before he inherited the lead guitar position in the Yardbirds from Jeff Beck, Page had a comfortable career as a London session musician. Consistently in demand, he played on early cuts by the Who, the Kinks, the Rolling Stones, Donovan, and Joe Cocker, along with more pop-oriented fare from the likes of Petula Clark and Tom Jones. In the studio, Page experimented with then-unorthodox techniques such as placing microphones at a distance to capture depth or playing his guitar with a violin bow and liberal amounts of echo. Such stygian effects can be heard on "Dazed and Confused"— an old Yardbirds number pilfered from folkie Jake Holmes that was given a Luciferian makeover by Led Zeppelin on their 1969 self-titled debut. Page's interest in musical exotica also included experiments with tape loops and non-rock instruments such as mandolin, banjo, and hurdy-gurdy. "Let's put this it way; I had a sitar before George Harrison," Page told an interviewer. "I wouldn't say I played it as well as he did, though."[2]

As the guitarist, chief composer, and producer for Led Zeppelin, Page synthesized acoustic and electric music in bold new ways, delivering trance-inducing heavy rock shot through with Delta blues, British Isles folk, and Eastern drones. "It's really hard for me to say exactly where I got my technique, because it's a combination of a lot of things that were floating around," Page told *Guitar World*. "Sometimes I tell people it's a product of my 'C.I.A. connection'— which is shorthand for Celtic, Indian and Arabic music."[3] In its original forms, this music serves a purpose beyond entertainment; it plays a central role in spiritual and social ceremony. It is the vehicle through which a culture's joys, triumphs, losses, hopes, and dreams are encoded and transmitted across generations.

Attentive listening reveals similarities between seemingly disparate global folk traditions. Celtic, Arabic, and African music—the latter from which American blues is derived—utilize repetition, drone, and cultural narrative in a kind of open-ended conversation with past and present. In blues, the I-IV-V chord progression features a dominant root (the I chord) that repeats as the progression cycles through a fixed number of bars. On guitar, blues is often played in the keys of E, A, and G, which allows for the open vibration of strings that shares something in common with the pedal tones (or drone notes) made by Celtic bagpipes, Indian sitars, Arabian ouds, and Moroccan rhaitas. Rhythmic vernacular varies in so-called world music, but there are similarities in the types of drums used as well as their primary purpose: to heighten or excite emotional and physiological states. The beat provides the foundation, accentuated by cyclical chants or melodies. As Burroughs recognized, this is really not that different from the rhythm section and front line of an electric rock band like Led Zeppelin.

Some of the world's most vital music sprang from non-Christian (or pre-Christian) spiritual practices, even if it later adopted the trappings of Western religiosity. As Peter Bebergal writes in *Season of the Witch: How the Occult Saved Rock and Roll*, these timeworn traditions "endeavor to employ methods of magic—trance, divination, dance—in order to have a direct encounter with the deities." Music is part of humanity's meta-mythical identity, forged in times "when magic and religion were inseparable." It is expression with a purpose, much like Burroughs' routines, cut-ups, audio recordings, photography, painting, and writing—all of which he saw as having the potential to produce real-world impact through occult action.

Burroughs was, by his own account, not much of a music expert. Nevertheless, he came to see how its popular stars in the West could be effective agents against Control. With an attitude of rebellion and the support of millions, certain artists were in a position to use their cultural currency to challenge and provoke, perhaps even usher in an occult revolution against the status quo. He also noted how rock, especially the kind performed by Led Zeppelin, possessed trance-inducing properties not dissimilar to those produced by the Master Musicians of Joujouka, which he called a "4,000-year-old rock and roll band."[4] Burroughs may not have understood what Led

Zeppelin was singing about (duplicitous women and Middle Earth, primarily), but he could appreciate the band's ability to bludgeon their audiences with mind-numbing, gut-rumbling sound.

Fans weren't the only ones affected. Jimmy Page has suggested that when the four individuals in Led Zeppelin—Page, vocalist Robert Plant, bassist John Paul Jones, and drummer John Bonham—performed together, it produced an invisible fifth member that seemed to spontaneously direct them.[5] This kind of alchemy was familiar to Burroughs, who theorized a "third mind" emerging in collaboration with Brion Gysin, revealing synchronicities and arousing ideas that would have been individually inaccessible.[6] When an audience experiences this phenomenon in real time and makes available their own energies in exchange, the intensity becomes exponential. Music seems to open channels for ecstatic communion with the spirit world, which is why it has long been used in ritual in collective settings. The Led Zeppelin fans spontaneously moved to raise their lighters during "Stairway to Heaven" may not have realized this, but the man playing guitar certainly did.

In February 1975, Page's black limousine snaked through the snowy streets of New York City to 77 Franklin Street, where Burroughs made his residence in one of the many vacant industrial lofts being colonized by the city's artists and bohemians. The meeting had been arranged by Burroughs' then-new business manager and assistant, James Grauerholz. A musician himself, Grauerholz understood the importance of being part of the cultural conversation. Burroughs' byline on an article about a well-known artist in a hip rag like *Crawdaddy* would accomplish that, plus it paid. That Jimmy Page shared an interest in trance-based music and the occult was added value.

Up four flights of stairs, the rail-thin rocker found the equally rail-thin author amongst his curios, which included his prized orgone accumulator—the same contraption Kurt Cobain would climb into nearly two decades later. Page politely declined an invitation to try out the device, but he did accept a cup of tea, and later, two fingers of whiskey. Burroughs and Page ended up at the nearby

Mexican Gardens restaurant, where the pair put down margaritas and discussed their shared appreciation for Moroccan music and lists of acquaintances. The latter included Mick Jagger, paranormal investigator John Michell, and experimental filmmaker Kenneth Anger. Page was meant to compose the soundtrack for Anger's movie *Lucifer Rising*, their collaboration rooted in a mutual affinity for Crowley. But when the guitarist turned in just over twenty minutes of tuneless thrum, Anger gave him the boot.[7]

Burroughs had his questions for Page prepared. His angle for the piece came while sitting in the thirteenth row at Led Zeppelin's February 12 performance at Madison Square Garden. The band members were like high priests conducting a ritual whereby hypnotic rhythms and keening wails entrance their subjects. To Burroughs, this was getting it right. "Music, like all the arts, is magical and ceremonial in origin," he wrote. These young Englishmen were tapping the same vein as the Master Musicians of Joujouka, right down to the thunderous beats and piercing high-register notes. Of course, millions more people knew about them than about the Master Musicians, which to Burroughs meant opportunity. "There is at present a wide interest among young people in the occult and all means of expanding consciousness," he wrote. "Can rock music appeal directly to this interest?" Though the focus was Page, Burroughs made sure to advance his own thinking throughout the article:

> Since the word "magic" tends to cause confused thinking, I would like to say exactly what I mean by "magic" and the magical interpretation of so-called reality. The underlying assumption of magic is the assertion of "will" as the primary moving force in this universe—the deep conviction that nothing happens unless somebody or some being wills it to happen. To me this has always seemed self-evident. A chair does not move unless someone moves it. Neither does your physical body, which is composed of much the same materials, move unless you will it to move. Walking across the room is a magical operation. From the viewpoint of magic, no death, no illness, no misfortune, accident, war or riot

is accidental. There are no accidents in the world of magic. And will is another word for animate energy. Rock stars are juggling fissionable material that could blow up at any time ... and as another rock star said to me, "YOU sit on your ass writing—I could be torn to pieces by my fans, like Orpheus."

The pressures of the rock star lifestyle led those who could afford it to acquire private estates—the more remote, the better. Page had recently bought Crowley's Loch Ness ramble, Boleskine House, a property Burroughs once sought for his youth training camp. Nestled in the Scottish Highlands, Boleskine was a perfect retreat for a cultured rock star with a taste for the diabolic. According to legend, the house was erected on the site of an ancient kirk, or church, that burned to the ground with its unfortunate congregants trapped inside. Overlooking a timeworn cemetery, the property is alleged to have a hidden tunnel under the road between the main building and graveyard.[8] Crowley purchased Boleskine in 1899 with the goal of using it as the location for his performance of the Abramelin ritual—a complex ceremony conducted over many months. Through his mystical exertions, Crowley hoped to achieve conversation with his Holy Guardian Angel, a form of higher consciousness that represents the unconditioned self. For Crowley, it was all a part of "the Great Work," his term for unlocking one's true will and purpose. It was nevertheless a perilous affair that involved overcoming various demons from the Goetia, a kind of infernal phonebook found in deeply esoteric Kabbalah teachings. Crowley made considerable progress with the ritual before being summoned to London to settle a disagreement with fellow magus MacGregor Mathers. Gossip among occultists has it that Crowley never performed a proper banishing before he left; some have even blamed him for the appearance of the Loch Ness Monster.[9]

"Jimmy said that Crowley has been maligned as a black magician," Burroughs wrote in the *Crawdaddy* article. "Whereas magic is neither white nor black, good nor bad—it is simply alive with what it is: the real thing, what people really feel and want and are. [Jimmy] told me that Aleister Crowley's house has very good vibes for anyone who is relaxed and receptive. . . . I told Jimmy he was lucky to have that house with a monster in the front yard."[10] Burroughs didn't mention to Page that he had considered buying Boleskine House but ultimately abandoned the idea for lack of funds. On Winter Solstice in 2015, well after Page had sold the property, Boleskine burned nearly to the ground.[11] The cause has never been determined.

Burroughs and Page shared an interest in Crowley and embraced magick as an everyday pursuit. Page struck a more Byronic pose, kindling romantic notions of sages and mystics burning strange oils and incense as they invoke and bind spirits in the pursuit of hidden knowledge, power, or riches. Burroughs viewed the occult more like a tool, not so different from a gun, knife, or sword—implements that could be used in self-defense or targeted attack. Page and Burroughs both believed that art, including music, can be directed for magical purposes—to effect real change in the world. It is here that Page's work with Led Zeppelin connects most to Burroughs.

Burroughs was effusive in describing his experience at a Led Zeppelin performance. "I really, really enjoyed the concert," he said. "I think it has quite a lot, really, in common with Moroccan trance music."[12] Page agreed with this assessment, describing how the song "Kashmir," the epic centerpiece of the about-to-be-released *Physical Graffiti*, made use of an undeviating guitar motif. "Music which involves riffs, anyway, will have a trance-like effect, and it's really like a mantra," Page explained. To Burroughs, this was the whole point. "A rock concert is in fact a rite involving the evocation and transmutation of energy," he wrote in *Crawdaddy*.

Burroughs was hardly a concert reviewer, but he ably recognized the band's fundamental power.

> The Led Zeppelin show depends heavily on volume, repetition and drums. . . . It is to be remembered that the origin of all the arts—music, painting and writing—is magical and evocative; and that magic is always used to obtain some definite result. In the Led Zeppelin concert, the result aimed at what would seem to be

the creation of energy in the performers and in the audience. For such magic to succeed, it must tap the sources of magical energy, and this can be dangerous.[13]

Such hazards can be immediate and physical—like the crush of a crowd—or abstracted in a kind of mob mentality that psychologist Carl Jung called "participation mystique." The energy of audiences can inspire performers to new heights of musicality, just as powerful concert performances can move audiences in ways that even the best home stereos fail to deliver. This feedback loop can also engender aggression, as anyone who has been in the pit at a Slayer show can attest. Even with less extreme music, attendees can sometimes suffer injuries or worse: eleven fans were trampled to death at a concert by the Who in December 1979.

Five years before Page's conversation with Burroughs, the Rolling Stones played a free concert at Altamont Speedway in California that went from debauched to deadly. This was in part because the band had hired the Hell's Angels motorcycle gang to provide security in exchange for $500 worth of beer. As the Stones segued from "Sympathy for the Devil" to "Under My Thumb," an already tense scene turned lethal. Concertgoer Meredith Hunter, high on methamphetamines, attempted to climb on stage and at one point brandished a revolver. He was stabbed five times by a biker and died of his wounds in front of other attendees. The Stones finished their set, got paid, and were whisked away in a helicopter.

Burroughs didn't bring up Altamont when speaking with Page, but he did mention an incident in which a Scandinavian band and their audience were burned alive in a nightclub fire. "It seems to me that rock stars are juggling fissionable material of the mass unconscious that could blow up at any time," Burroughs told Page. "*You* know, Jimmy, the crowd surges forward . . . a heavy piece of equipment falls on the crowd . . . security goes mad, and then . . . a sound like goddamn falling mountains or something." From the thirteenth row, Burroughs pondered the energies invoked by Led Zeppelin, and what they might manifest. "I pointed out that the moment when the stairway to heaven becomes something actually POSSIBLE for the audience, would also be the moment of greatest danger," he said. Page demurred. "The kids come to get as far out with the music as possible," he said. "It's our job to see that they have a good time and no trouble." Page described a recent concert in Philadelphia where overly aggressive security—though thankfully not as hostile as the Hell's Angels—contributed to a vibe that made him "almost physically sick." Page saw himself as a steward of the powerful energies conjured by his band and understood the dangers present. "There is a responsibility to the audience," he said. "We don't want anything bad to happen to these kids—we don't want to release anything we can't handle."

As a musical force, Led Zeppelin was imposing, but rarely subtle. Live, the band indulged in lengthy solos that were varyingly exciting and interminable. They pilfered lines from traditional blues songs and mixed them together with musings on sex, drugs, and *The Lord of the Rings*, with a sprinkling of mystical pomp. Anyone looking for explicit occult instruction in their oeuvre is bound to be disappointed. However, the band did slip in the occasional witchy message between their record sleeves. While readying the release of Led Zeppelin *III* in 1970, Page implored studio engineer Terry Manning to carve "Do What Thou Wilt" into the runoff groove of the first pressing.[14]

He was well aware that mystery was a big part of the band's appeal and took steps to cultivate it. During a particularly sinister performance of "Dazed and Confused" from the 1976 concert film *The Song Remains the Same*, a cutaway scene features Page ascending a moonlit mountain. At its peak stands the Hermit of the Tarot brandishing a staff. Glancing into the figure's gray hood, Page sees his own face, aged many years. The face then grows younger and younger until it morphs into a fetus, only to revert back to a wizened sage. To contemporary viewers, the primitive visual effects may look silly. Still, the scene is eerily Faustian—like the story of Robert Johnson going down to the crossroads to exchange his soul for unearthly six-string skills. As Page and Burroughs both understood, there is a romance in the infernal that can be played up to powerfully subliminal effect. "Black magic operates most effectively in preconscious, marginal areas," Burroughs wrote in *The Western Lands*.[15]

The introduction of occult ideas in music began well before Jimmy Page went plundering with Led Zeppelin. Italian futurist and experimental composer Luigi Russolo applied magical principles to his music in the early 1900s. Russolo used noise as a catalyst for energetic transformation in listeners and was particularly interested in music as an alchemical process. In the late nineteenth and early twentieth centuries, the Hermetic Order of the Golden Dawn and other occult societies initiated composers like Erik Satie and Claude Debussy, who established a new direction for European classical music rich with pagan overtones. Some no doubt became members of occult societies as an excuse to get inebriated and explore group sexuality (not unlike a Led Zeppelin after-show party)—activities evangelized by Crowley as key to the mystical experience.

Even in a modern sense, the occult has had plenty of time to steep. The very first Glastonbury Festival—held near the location where legend has it the body of King Arthur rests—took place in 1914. In the early 1970s, the site was rediscovered by hippies dialed into the mystical frequencies of the location. To this day, Glastonbury plays host to a five-day concert featuring Great Britain's biggest bands. As academic Christopher Partridge of Lancaster University's Centre for the Study of Religion and Popular Culture stated, "occulture is ordinary."[16] And it's big business, too: simply look at all the blockbuster books, films, TV shows, video games, and record albums based on the paranormal.

Though they came from vastly different backgrounds and life experiences, Burroughs and Page had enough mutual interests to make for a genuine connection. Both pursued altered states of consciousness and the harnessing of hidden energies to external effect. Both experimented with audio using portable tape recorders. Both abused intravenous drugs. In addition to Luigi Russolo, Page's aborted soundtrack to *Lucifer Rising* demonstrates an awareness of

Burroughs' tape cut-ups and sound manipulations. The irony is that Led Zeppelin is often lumped in with the preening hair metal acts they inspired, which completely obscures Page's contributions to occult composition. Some of the concepts he explored would serve as the basis for a whole new genre, one that was in theoretical opposition to everything Led Zeppelin represented.

Industrial Strength

Punk was supposed to have slayed so-called dinosaurs like Led Zeppelin. However, ideas are harder to kill than trends. Punk has always lacked a true musical identity, and both its sound and politics find a wide range of expression across a diverse array of subcultures. Minor Threat sounds nothing like the Minutemen; Oi punks don't go to vegan barbecues. At its simplest, punk is an attitude of defiance. This spirit shows up in all kinds of music, from Woody Guthrie to Fela Kuti to Hasil Adkins to Motörhead to Sinéad O'Connor to Erykah Badu. The clothes it wears or slang it adopts matters less than the underlying mindset—which means that as a music genre, punk was always destined to evolve.

One year after Jimmy Page met Burroughs, a new breed of punks took aim at Control using tools and techniques advanced by the author. Formed in 1975, Throbbing Gristle grew out of a performance art troupe called COUM Transmissions. Considered the first industrial band, Throbbing Gristle terrorized British society with an incendiary mix of abrasive sound and provocative theatrics. Members Genesis P-Orridge, Peter "Sleazy" Christopherson, Cosey Fanni Tutti, and Chris Carter invented an entirely new genre—industrial music—and their modus operandi owed everything to Burroughs. The band used tape recorders to play back abrasive noise alongside electric instruments in intensely jarring performances. They filtered the primal DIY energy of punk through the praxis of the occult, borrowing imagery from humanity's history of mass violence and donning paramilitary outfits embossed with a menacing symbol of their own invention. Their confrontational art blew open a door through which a whole host of acts rushed. Bands like Skinny Puppy, Cabaret Voltaire, Joy Division, Ministry, and Nine Inch Nails appropriated Throbbing Gristle's approach, including the use of sampled audio and aggressive mechanized rhythms. P-Orridge explained the group's aesthetic in a 1983 interview that echoes Burroughs' remarks about perceptual reality resembling cut-ups:[17]

> I don't like using the word "real," but in a sense we were trying to make everything more real . . . and to portray, the same way that a cut-up theoretically does: what it's like to be in a house and go along the street and have a car go past or a train and work in a factory or walk past a factory. Just a kind of industrial life, or a suburban-urban-industrial life.

In the 1980s and '90s, P-Orridge would establish an occult order called Thee Temple ov Psychick Youth (TOPY); start another band, Psychick TV (inspired as much by doomed Rolling Stone Brian Jones as industrial noise); and experiment with gender identity in collaboration with his life partner, Lady Jaye Breyer P-Orridge. Along with Lady Jaye, P-Orridge in 1993 embarked on the "Pandrogeny Project," undergoing surgical procedures and adopting shared wardrobes in the pursuit of a blended identity. It wasn't so much that P-Orridge was becoming a woman; she was actively transforming herself in collaboration with her partner, demonstrating that even gender could be cut up. When Breyer died of stomach cancer in 2007, P-Orridge kept her partner's memory alive not only through her art, but also her outward appearance: she now looks like a Mod fairy godmother with a street-punk edge.

Born in Manchester in 1950, P-Orridge was an intelligent and inquisitive child—then identifying as male—whose test scores earned a scholarship to Gatley Primary School from 1961 to 1964. When his father was promoted to manager of a cleaning and maintenance company, he was able to attend a private academy, Solihull School, where he endured "basically four years of being mentally and physically tortured."[18] This abuse no doubt seeded his obsession with altering reality using any means at hand.

In conversation today, P-Orridge (hereafter referred to as "she" except when referencing events before 1993) is completely open but never takes herself—or anything, for that matter—too seriously. She claims Burroughs and Gysin as personal teachers and has spent the better part of the past thirty years advancing their ideas. She confesses that she tended to be more shy around the author than the painter because Burroughs "came across as very learned and serious and we felt we always had to be at our sharpest."[19] (P-Orridge now refers to herself as "we" and uses other idiosyncratic grammar in written communication, such as spelling "the" as "thee.") She is to this day moved by Burroughs' generosity, like the time he wrote a letter of commendation to a British arts council that was considering COUM Transmissions for a grant. "It was incredible that someone of William's stature would do something like that for someone like us," she says.[20] Later, when P-Orridge was facing serious charges for sending postcards that the UK authorities deemed obscene, Burroughs again offered assistance. "He helped us when we got all the legal action against us, with a lot of recommendations and advice, of what to do and what not to do, and to be polite, and not try and turn it into a big battle . . . he's always helped."[21]

In addition to coining the term "occulture," P-Orridge is also responsible for bringing Burroughs' early audio experiments to a wider audience, making a trek with bandmate Peter Christopherson to Lawrence in 1980 to pore through stacks of tapes stored at the author's home. The recordings, some of which were made at the Beat Hotel two decades prior, were released in 1981 as *Nothing Here Now but the Recordings* on Throbbing Gristle's Industrial Records.[22] Burroughs scholars and enthusiasts owe P-Orridge a debt for her efforts in making accessible such important and unique audio documents as "Captain Clark Welcomes You Aboard" and "Last Words of Hassan Sabbah."

P-Orridge wrote at length on Burroughs' and Gysin's importance in *Thee Psychick Bible*, a collection of riffs and rants with the unifying theme of individual and collective evolution. "We are entering a digital future, a holographic universe where, at least theoretically, every sentient being on earth will be interconnected, international and interfaced," P-Orridge said in a 2006 essay.[23] "A future where Burroughs and Gysin and their modern occultural brethren have supplied prophetic, functional skills and nonlocal points of observation which can train us to be fittingly alert and prepared for the unpredictable aesthetic and social spasms to come."[24] An attempt at translation: Through their work with cut-ups, Burroughs and Gysin developed practical techniques to aid human adaptability in an increasingly chaotic world. Whether this is true or not is irrelevant; it is what they practiced and believed. And, as Burroughs and Gysin understood, belief defines reality.

P-Orridge and Burroughs both advocated for freedom: that of self-definition, as well as the right to explore reality without imposed restrictions. Of course, there are powerful forces—religion, school, government, et al.—that do not want people to enjoy such freedoms. For Burroughs and his disciples, this meant war. Psychic war, anyway. According to P-Orridge, the idea was to disrupt "a picture of reality that is designed by those with a vested interest in stasis to maintain our surrender to cultural impotence and all forms of addictive consumption."[25] In her estimation, Burroughs and Gysin were "master magicians" who "grasped the elasticity of reality and our right to control its unfolding as we see fit and prefer."[26]

Burroughs surmised that the universe, or at least what we perceive as reality, is prerecorded, which means it can be edited. But who made the recording? Who fashioned our reality? The Gnostic view holds that a corrupt Demiurge (a kind of deputy deity, if you will) created the world and its dichotomies—light/dark, good/evil, pain/pleasure—in a hostile act against an indivisible super-consciousness. This originating nemesis is akin to Burroughs' concept of Control. Its agenda is simple: assert authority as a means to obtain more of it. In other words, Control is a junkie for control. Burroughs externalized his own struggles with addiction in a metanarrative about the agents and instruments of compulsion and consumption. His work portrays human beings as "soft machines"—fleshy systems imprinted with hidden code that governs everything we do, think, and perceive. Humanity is both defined and enslaved by its appetites, which are the product of crypto-conditioning operating below the threshold of everyday consciousness.

In Burroughs' philosophy, the most important thing an artist can do is fight back by attacking the Control apparatus—that is, the prerecording that constrains us to Control's script. Insurgence is accomplished through "playback," a technique where reality—as represented by its media artifacts—is cut up, cut in, or otherwise disrupted. Playback can also reveal aspects of reality that were previously hidden—like pulling back the curtain on the Wizard of Oz or seeing the hidden code comprising the Matrix. In his article "Playback from Eden to Watergate," Burroughs makes clear the disruptive potential of this technique on politics, in particular: "A Presidential candidate is not a sitting duck like the Moka Bar. He can make any number of recordings of his opponents. So the game is complex and competitive, with recordings made by both sides. This leads to more sophisticated techniques, the details of which have yet to come out."[27]

In Burroughs' view, what most understand of existence is a kind of collective enabled by preprogrammed routines. So what's the reality behind the mirage? Filmmaker, painter, and musician David Lynch posed a similar question in the 2017 series *Twin Peaks: The Return*: "We're like the dreamer who dreams and then lives inside the dream ... but who is the dreamer?" one character asks. Among today's physicists, there are those whose research indicates we exist in a simulation created by more advanced beings. Tech entrepreneur Elon Musk claimed that "there's a billion to one chance we're living in base reality."[28] "Interzone" was Burroughs' base reality for a time—an environment brought to vivid life through acts of imaginative and pharmacological indulgence. As technology progresses, it opens up new possibilities to alter individual and consensus reality through advanced computational processes. Artificial intelligences and neural networks are already fashioning digital worlds beyond humans' ability to wholly fathom, even as we participate en masse. Algorithms increasingly choose what we see and hear, and can even compose music.[29] Feeding on the cut-up data of millions, such tools can predict behavior with unnerving specificity—in turn, conditioning our attitudes and conduct in a manner that is often hidden from users. As Ed Finn writes in *Slate*, "the ways in which computation is sidling up to the future reminds me of the old William S. Burroughs line: 'When you cut into the present, the future leaks out.'"

Dreams and Other Mutations

P-Orridge and the author first made contact in Great Britain in the early 1970s. One of the things Burroughs impressed on the young artist was the importance of using cutting-edge technology to maximize creative and or magical results. P-Orridge began to recruit other young people alienated by commercial society's empty promises. The connection to Burroughs' work is explicit: "Psychick Youth are a more exact version of *The Wild Boys*—they're like the contemporary update," P-Orridge said.[30] The band's armory included cassette recorders, Polaroid cameras, Xeroxes, and a device called "the Dream Machine." Part furniture, part objet d'art, the Dream Machine emits bursts of light and shadow in a manner thought to produce altered states. It's a relatively simple contraption: an arm's-length rod and lightbulb affixed to a spinning platform covered by a cylinder with cut-out patterns where the light shines through. Users sit close to the device, close their eyes, and let the flickering shapes work their magic.

Invented by Gysin and evangelized by Burroughs, the Dream Machine was also meant to be a cash cow; both men initially believed that the units, which look something like art-nouveau table lamps, would soon be in every home. But their entrepreneurial dreams were dashed when they failed to secure the necessary investment to mass produce the device. "You know it's never going to fly," said singer, actress, and one-time Rolling Stones muse Marianne Faithfull. "People prefer television."[31] Perhaps an ad on Fox News would have done the trick. "They should be on sale in supermarkets for fifty dollars each," P-Orridge said. "Because it really is a psychedelic drug with no drug. . . . It's a very marvelous anti-Control device as well as being a beautiful thing to look at."[32]

The Dream Machine still has its adherents, including several prominent musicians. "It's really like touching God in a way," said former Sonic Youth guitarist Lee Renaldo. "You're somewhere that you don't have access to in your daily life."[33] The idea is antediluvian; it is rumored that Nostradamus would wiggle his fingers in front of his face under sunlight in order to elicit visions of the future. A similar effect created by the Dream Machine lets users go "deeper into their heads," according to Renaldo.[34] Nick Zinner of the Yeah Yeahs said the device evokes "tranquil imagery, which is a good thing."[35] Although they failed to commercially manufacture Dream Machines, Gysin and Burroughs happily made the specs available to interested parties. "You can build one," said enthusiast Iggy Pop. "It's sort of like the Ark of the Covenant in the Bible, where they give these twenty-three pages of instructions."[36] (Twenty-three? We'll keep that number in mind for further consideration later.) Avant-garde turntablist DJ Spooky considers the Dream Machine a useful item in the Burroughs-Gysin reality-hacking toolbox:

These guys were kind of like, looking at the world as the particle physics of language, where if you had access to the right codes you could access all sorts of distant realms—interstellar space, cosmic realms, magnetic pulses . . . you name it. The Dream Machines were meant to tap into these magic code landscapes and let the subconscious become a kind of an open system.[37]

DJ Spooky should know: his sample-based music is hip-hop plunged into the cosmic void. His track "Fuse/The Five Steps" features Burroughs' bone-dry recitations interspersed with vast drones and in-determinate squelches. "To consolidate revolutionary gain, five steps are necessary," Burroughs intones. "Step number one: pro-claim a new era and set up a new calendar. Step number two: Re-place alien language. Step number three: Destroy or neutralize alien gods. Step number four: Destroy alien machinery of government control. Step number five: Take wealth and land from individual aliens.... Time to forget a dead empire and build a living republic."

With sampling, any snippet of text, sound, image, or video can be ripped from its source and altered or juxtaposed however a user sees fit. Sampling as a cultural phenomenon started with audio—first with tape-based experiments and later with digital devices. Control didn't always approve, and sometimes took action through one of its primary organs, the law.[38] But this was not a battle Control could win, even with an army of attorneys. When the Internet arrived, the floodgates opened further. These days, everyone sam-ples in some way, shape, or form. Borrow a lyric from a song for a Facebook post? You just sampled. Use a picture of that *Game of Thrones* character in a meme? You just sampled. Mash up dumb '80s videos on YouTube? You just sampled. Such activities technically make users copyright criminals, not that it's much of a deterrent. At least two generations have grown up remixing and sharing content on the Internet, and many of their favorite artists built their careers by sampling.

It is instructive to consider how artists sample, and why. In an essay for *Arcana V*—part of a book series compiled by avant-garde jazz maestro John Zorn—P-Orridge suggests that sampling is more than just a production technique; it is an occult action straight from the Burroughs grimoire:

It can be said, for me at least, that thee transformational impli-cations inherent in sampling, looping, cutting-up and/or there-after re-assembling both found data materials and infinite com-binations ov site specific sounds, is as probably equivalent to, and as socially significant and profound as, thee popularization and

mass proselytization ov LSD and thee splitting ov thee atom. . . .
All three are innately magickal processes giving thee initiate
practitioner tools to travel within their previously finite consensus reality container.[39]

P-Orridge goes on to explain how sampling has helped unleash the
"media virus" known as memes. Like Burroughs' vision of a coming
age where "very small units of word and image" would be commu-
nicated electronically, P-Orridge calls memes "individual cultural
items ov such precise metaphorical weight and resonance" as to be
capable of disrupting "any established political status quo," and encouraged their deployment to "splinter consensus reality."[40] Mission accomplished.

With an infinite smorgasbord of media available online, information is not only free, it has gone berserk. "Anything, in any medium
imaginable, from any culture, which is in any way recorded and can
in any possible way be played back is now accessible and infinitely
malleable and useable to any artist," P-Orridge said. "Everything is
available, everything is free, everything is permitted."[41] In genres
like industrial, permission is less important than precision—finding the right sample, even if by chance—and triggering it at the
appropriate time. Often, the goal is to subvert the original meaning of the sample through forced juxtaposition, resulting in a new
mutation with its own characteristics and connotations. This is the
Burroughs method.

In a 2014 dissertation on Burroughs and industrial music,
Jamie Vecchio advances the theory of "downward metamorphosis,"
whereby certain Burroughs characters—such as Bradley the Buyer in
Naked Lunch—undergo gruesome physical changes as they evolve
into new forms. Bradley the Buyer is an undercover narcotics agent
with such zeal for his work that he begins absorbing heroin users
into his body, in the process getting hooked on junkies. The addicts
that Bradley sucks in become part of an amorphous system lacking
distinguishing features—a chaotic, gelatinous mass. Vecchio sug-

gests this is similar to what happens to samples in industrial music tracks: "This de-contextualizing and de-centering process occurs because the media, whether it is on the page or aural, is physically manipulated and repurposed in ways in which the original authors did not intend. Control has never been fully subverted; it has only changed hands."[42]

There is also black humor evident in industrial artists' use of samples—the same kind of irreverence common to Burroughs' routines and vignettes. An industrial artist might, for example, play back audio or video clips of Margaret Thatcher or Ronald Reagan, then cut in pornographic sounds, air raid sirens, and explosions as a commentary on the leaders' obsession with sexual propriety and military might. "This sardonic, forced prostitution of popular media is part of industrial music's purposeful downward metamorphosis of popular culture into a biting commentary against itself," Vecchio argues. "Samples themselves become instruments. Electronic, programmed instruments replace instrumental virtuosity."[43] Burroughs was always adamant that anyone could perform a cut-up; no special training was required. Using the tools of the day, Genesis P-Orridge and colleagues took the methods of Burroughs and Gysin and weaponized them for an increasingly unstable future.

"Tell me about magick?" P-Orridge asked Burroughs upon their first meeting at his Duke Street flat back in 1971. It was quite an ask coming from a young punk barely old enough to buy a lager. More specifically, P-Orridge wanted to know if there was "a system, a way to adjust, control, break up and reassemble behavior, personality, creativity, and perception, so that novelty and surprise, the unexpected and improvisation could be applied to my identity, using myself as raw material, as malleable physically and mentally as any other medium?"[44] With wannabe gurus on every London thoroughfare, seeking out an aging solitarian for guidance on such matters might seem unusual. "In fact, it turned out to be exactly the right place to look," she said.[45]

P-Orridge was part of a broader community of young seekers who made the occult part of their everyday lives, but it was a lot different than the good vibes and fuzzy atavism of the American New Age. These kids came up in the shadow of punk, inheriting its confrontational attitude and suspicion of any and all authority. In the UK, so-called "council flats magick" became a prominent facet of the underground. British youths of lesser means had every reason to feel hopeless. The late 1970s and early '80s were a time of high unemployment, conditions exacerbated by ill-considered austerity policies advanced by a conservative government led by Margaret Thatcher. Music and the occult offered a way for young people to connect to something beyond the cheerless everyday—even if it was only their own imaginations—and to feel more powerful both individually and collectively.

Thee Temple Ov Psychick Youth—part fan club, part pre-Internet social network, part occult order—ran on a parallel track to the emerging "chaos magick" movement.[46] Borrowing heavily from writers and thinkers like Burroughs, Robert Anton Wilson, and Hakim Bey, chaos magick ditched the ceremonial trappings of Aleister Crowley for a more hands-on kind of spell-casting. As Matthew Levi Stevens writes in his book *The Magical Universe of William S. Burroughs*:

> Many chaos magicians clearly felt a debt to Burroughs and his peers, and shared many of the same concerns as Thee Temple Ov Psychick Youth: demystifying magick, yet at the same time distilling the best from Aleister Crowley and Austin Osman Spare, while taking advantage of the latest ideas emerging in computers, maths, physics and psychology. . . . William S. Burroughs was recognized as a definite pioneer and precursor.

Burroughs understood his place in this lineage and was even initiated into the Illuminates of Thanateros (IOT), the official organ of chaos magick, at some point in the early 1990s.[47]

P-Orridge initially encountered Burroughs as the Kerouac character Bull Lee in *On the Road*, recalling that "in those days, porn shops were the only place you could get this stuff."[48] P-Orridge wrote to Burroughs after coming across a request for images the author published in the back of a magazine called *File*. The letter made the outrageous claim that Burroughs was trying to boost his own cred by name-dropping P-Orridge as a way to get into parties. This tickled Burroughs, as did a care package with a homemade book called *To Do with Smooth Paper*. "Thanks for the smooth paper—William S. Burroughs," he replied by postcard. When an invite to visit Burroughs on Duke Street came, P-Orridge was excited and nervous. The meeting almost didn't happen, as she was not yet living in London and was therefore dependent on a friend who operated a studio on 10 Martello Street to relay messages. "Some idiot rang me up today and said he was William S. Burroughs," the friend told P-Orridge, "and I didn't fall for it!" As it turns out, the friend was a big fan and kicked himself when he learned he'd missed an opportunity to chat up the author.

P-Orridge eventually got Burroughs' phone number, and the two arranged a proper meeting. Upon entering his flat, the first thing visible was a life-sized cardboard cutout of Mick Jagger standing by his bookcase. "It was really a small place, just a small living room and bedroom," P-Orridge recalled.[49] Burroughs offered a drink, and soon enough, the two had consumed an entire bottle of Jack Daniels. P-Orridge's instruction had begun. "Reality is not really all that it's cracked up to be," Burroughs remarked, picking up a television remote control, a still-new technology P-Orridge had never seen in person. "He took the remote and started to flip through the channels, cutting up programmed TV," she said.[50]

> At the same time, he began to hit stop and start on his Sony TC cassette recorder, mixing in random cut-up prior recordings. These were overlaid with our conversation. . . . What Bill explained to me then was pivotal to my life and art: *everything is recorded*. If it

is recorded, it can be *edited*. If it can be edited, then the order, sense, meaning and direction are as arbitrary and personal as the agenda and/or person editing. This is magick.[51]

P-Orridge's takeaways are consistent with Burroughs' view of the true purpose of creativity: "It is to be remembered that all art is magical in origin—music, sculpture, writing, painting—and by magical, I mean intended to produce very definite results."[52]

Astral Disasters

When Throbbing Gristle broke up, P-Orridge formed Psychic TV, and Peter "Sleazy" Christopherson began a musical and romantic partnership with Geoff Rushton, whose nom de plume was John Balance. The pair would mine occult realms of sound in the intensely original Coil—a project that utilized ambient noise, spare industrial rhythms, and vocal incantations to produce powerful, trance-inducing soundscapes both enticing and unsettling. Coil's formation coincided with the arrival of digital sampling and computer-based music; the duo channeled what they'd learned from Burroughs through these emerging technologies. As Christopherson told *Fist* magazine in an interview about Coil's 1991 release *Love's Secret Domain*: "The original intentions of cut-ups were, if we go back to Burroughs and Gysin, to allow the future to leak through. They were spells, rituals, and magical maps with which to break up reality. That was their intention and their result. On *Love's Secret Domain*, we made a deliberate attempt to get back to magical cut-ups."[53]

Coil's Christopherson—also a partner at mega-hip UK design firm Hipgnosis, which produced classic album covers for Pink Floyd and Peter Gabriel—did the layout for the Dutch edition of Burroughs' collection of essays *The Electronic Revolution*, originally published in 1971 and later reprinted in *The Job*. Balance wrote the introduction, cementing the connection between Burroughs' ideas and the new breed of music-makers. The book was embraced by other industrial artists, including Richard H. Kirk of Cabaret Voltaire, who called it "a handbook of how to use tape recorders in a crowd ... to create a sense of unease or unrest by playback of riot noises cut in with random recordings of the crowd itself."[54]

Christopherson first met Burroughs in his Throbbing Gristle days. As a founding member of that seminal band, he would amass an arsenal of playback devices that served to enthrall and disorient audiences in equal measure. Ignoring instrumentation common to rock bands, Christopherson instead triggered different sounds with portable tape decks. He would also record and play back the band's performance as it happened, creating a kind of sonic time loop. Without Burroughs, it is unlikely that Christopherson would have explored aural cut-ups and fold-ins in such a way. The author's work and lifestyle also inspired Christopherson to fully embrace his homosexuality; he claimed that discovering *Naked Lunch* at age thirteen changed his life.[55] With his partner Balance, Christopherson explored power dynamics and kink in music both bracing and intimate.[56] Coil's 1986 LP, *Horse Rotorvator*, for example, boasts songs with titles like "The Anal Staircase" and "Penetralia"— neither of which would seem out of place in a Burroughs novel.

Coil's music is like entering a dark cave where time and space seem elastic. Their use of drones, sparse rhythms, and ambient noise dredges up insight and terror in equal measure. Christopherson described how Burroughs opened up strange vistas beyond the here and now: "Things that happen in his books happen in a spirit world where there isn't really any self-consciousness, intellectualization, or present time, really. The time they take place in isn't the annihilating reality of now. It is some other space altogether."[57] Despite Burroughs' enormous influence on Coil, the band chose not to sample him in their recordings. "To me, what's fantastic about William's work and voice and his performance, comes from the whole body of work and his whole view of life and sexuality and perversion and corruption, and all that stuff," Christopherson said. "So just to sample a few words is rather meaningless and not very interesting."[58]

Christopherson visited Burroughs in New York after the author returned to the States in 1974. "I remember getting very, very drunk with him . . . and it was one of those times where you could sit for a long time and not say anything and feel OK about it."[59] He recalled telling Burroughs he should put out an album of his audio cut-up experiments going back to the Beat Hotel. "We really wanted people to be able to hear what they actually sounded like," he said.[60] P-Orridge had encouraged Burroughs to release his tapes as early as 1973, but it wasn't until the next decade that the pair would make the trek to Lawrence to pore through the shoebox of old tapes provided by Grauerholz. "He just agreed to us taking the tapes away, fifteen hours of them, and editing them down to an LP," P-Orridge said. "It's a good job we got them, 'cause they were recorded over twenty years ago and the oxide was actually crumbling off the tapes as we held them."[61] *Nothing Here Now but the Recordings* was released in 1981, the final album on the Industrial Records label.

Coming Down the Mountain

From Burroughs' introduction to *Cities of the Red Night* (1981):

> This book is dedicated to the Ancient Ones, to the Lord of Abominations, Humwawa, whose face is a mass of entrails, whose breath is the stench of dung and the perfume of death, Dark Angel of all that is excreted and sours, Lord of Decay, Lord of the Future, who rides on a whispering south wind, to Pazuzu, Lord of Fevers and Plagues, Dark Angel of the Four Winds with rotting genitals from which he howls through sharpened teeth over stricken cities, to Kutulu, the Sleeping Serpent who cannot be summoned, to the Akhkharu, who suck the blood of men since they desire to become men, to the Lalussu, who haunt the places of men, to Gelal and Lilit, who invade the beds of men and whose children are born in secret places, to Addu, raiser of storms who can fill the night sky with brightness, to Malah, Lord of Courage and Bravery, to Zahgurim, whose number is twenty-three and who kills in an unnatural fashion, to Zahrim, a warrior among warriors, to Itzamna,

Spirit of Early Mists and Showers, to Ix Chel, the Spider-Web-that-Catches-the-Dew-of-Morning, to Zuhuy Kak, Virgin Fire, to Ah Dziz, the Master of Cold, to Kak U Pacat, who works in fire, to Ix Tab, Goddess of Ropes and Snares, patroness of those who hang themselves, to Schmuun, the Silent One, twin brother of Ix Tab, to Xolotl the Unformed, Lord of Rebirth, to Aguchi, Master of Ejaculations, to Osiris and Amen in phallic form, to Hex Chun Chan, the Dangerous One, to Ah Pook, the Destroyer, to the Great Old One and the Star Beast, to Pan, God of Panic, to the nameless gods of dispersal and emptiness, to Hassan i Sabbah, Master of Assassins.

To all the scribes and artists and practitioners of magic through whom these spirits have been manifested....

"NOTHING IS TRUE. EVERYTHING IS PERMITTED."

The above introduction is loaded with occult references. However, not all of them were written in blood on ancient parchment. Several of the names are ancient Mayan and Mesopotamian deities. Some come from the mythos of cosmic horror godfather H. P. Lovecraft. A few were pulled from *The Necronomicon*, a grimoire of supposedly ancient lineage that was put forward as the real deal in 1977 but later revealed to be a put-on. Last, but certainly not least, there is Hassan i-Sabbah, "the Old Man of the Mountain" who once controlled wide swaths of the Arab world with his cult of hashish-fueled mercenaries, the Assassins. Perhaps unsurprisingly, i-Sabbah is second only to Aleister Crowley in the short list of disreputable mystics beloved by musicians who also happen to be Burroughs fans.

P-Orridge points out the link between the philosophies of i-Sabbah and Crowley: "[Sabbah's] motto, 'Nothing is True, Everything Is Permitted,' recurs over and over, especially in Burroughs' books. It is not so far from the Thelemic precept 'Do What Thou Wilt Shall Be the Whole of the Law,' a theoretical concoction that Burroughs appeared to acknowledge towards the end of his life."[62]

In fact, Burroughs referenced Crowley early and often. Recall the 1959 kiss-off letter to his mother where he compared himself to the mage whom Victorian broadsheets once took to calling the "Wickedest Man In the World." Crowley even earned a reference in *The Place of Dead Roads* (1983): "He is into magic and has studied with Aleister Crowley and the Golden Dawn. They decide on a preliminary evocation of Humwawa, Lord of Abominations, to assess the strength and disposition of enemy forces. . . ." Grauerholz claimed that Burroughs' interest in Crowley was mostly a lark: "[He] considered Crowley a bit of a figure of fun, referring to him as 'The Greeeaaaaat BEEEEAST!' in that behind-closed-doors, queeny comic delivery he used sometimes: his voice rising straight up in pitch, into a hysterical falsetto."[63]

Conversely, Burroughs' fascination with Hasan i-Sabbah—whom he facetiously accused Crowley of plagiarizing—was both thorough and genuine. It may be that Burroughs maintained a fantasy image of himself as i-Sabbah; after all, he talked often about establishing an academy where male youths would develop martial skills and probe inner realms. The Assassins weren't just deadly with poison daggers: they were undercover operatives trained to blend in across the territories they controlled through influence and, where necessary, murder. They spoke a number of languages, could adapt to various religious beliefs, and were skilled in a range of trades that allowed them to pose as members of any community targeted for infiltration. One thing they weren't allowed to do, however, was play music, which was expressly forbidden by i-Sabbah.

Which makes an album like Bill Laswell's *The Road to the Western Lands* somewhat ironic. Taking inspiration from i-Sabbah and the Burroughs novel of the same name, Laswell's compositions evoke vast deserts whose shifting sands are stained red with blood. A bassist and producer whose prolificacy exceeds his popular renown, Laswell plays everything from funk and r&b to dub reggae to ambient electronica to extreme metal. (Whitney Houston recorded her first commercially released vocal track with Laswell's band Material.) He is also a Burroughs enthusiast who has toured the world with the "4,000-year-old rock 'n' roll band," the Master Musicians of Joujouka. This is in addition to collaborations with Herbie Hancock, Laurie Anderson, Mick Jagger, Sting, Carlos Santana, John Zorn, the Dalai Lama, Yoko Ono, John Lydon, Bootsy Collins, Buckethead, and George Clinton, to name just a few. Born in Salem, Illinois, in 1955, in the 1970s Laswell moved to New York, where he became a fixture in the avant-jazz scene. It was around this time that he advanced electronic dance music production on albums like Herbie Hancock's *Future Shock* (1983), including the smash hit "Rockit."

"I first heard about Hasan i-Sabbah through Burroughs," Laswell said.[64] "You know, there's many old Hollywood films that have the Assassins, with their black banner. Nothing is true, everything is permitted. . . . You can trace it back quite far. There's a dark kind of image there. I think it's just a feeling it brings to you." Like P-Orridge and others, he considers Burroughs a kind of spiritual teacher. "He's more of a sage than most anyone knows. And that will probably never be completely brought into the light, but that's kind of how I saw him. It was probably too hip or too subversive or just too real. And to me, in some sense, fundamental."

Laswell's recordings with Burroughs alternate between the hypnotic and the harrowing. "The road to the Western Lands is by definition the most dangerous road in the world, for it is a journey beyond death," Burroughs rasps on the title track. Laswell's bass line snakes through the arid soundscape like the River Nile, evoking dark pacts and hidden knowledge. "It is the most heavily guarded road in the world, for it gives access to the gift that supersedes all other gifts—the gift of immortality." An ominous clang heralds Burroughs' arrival on "Soul Killer," a song that trades trance grooves for the sonic equivalent of scorched earth:

Can any soul survive the searing fireball of an atomic blast? If human and animal souls are seen as electromagnetic force fields, such fields could be totally disrupted by a nuclear explosion . . . and this is precisely the ultrasecret and supersensitive function of the atom bomb: A soul killer, to alleviate an escalating soul glut. . . . This awesome power to destroy souls forever is now vested in farsighted and responsible men at the State Department, the CIA, and the Pentagon.

Burroughs goes on to equate the cowardice of Establishment hawks with the anti-human encroachment of technology. Humankind is kept in psychic and spiritual lockup, with agents of Control manipulating the masses through an endless bombardment of word, sound, and image—information viruses, as it were. As Laswell's track pulses on, Burroughs delivers the coup de grâce:

> Authority figures, deprived of the vampiric energy they suck off their constituents, are seen for what they are: dead empty masks manipulated by computers. And what is behind the computers? Remote control. Of course, look at the prison you are in, we are all in. This is a penal colony that is now a Death Camp. . . . Nothing here now but the recordings. Shut them off, they are radioactive as an old joke.

Laswell's compositions carry a hypnotic pulse, like a sonic Dream Machine. The bassist claims the key to making trance-based music is to allow the vibe to arise spontaneously. "Sound is everywhere—you know, it's like just slow down, take your time and that's your new record." Simply walking down the street arouses a flow of sensory input that comes at us in fragments, which is why Burroughs claimed that cut-ups are, in fact, the most accurate reflection of reality. Or, as Laswell puts it: "In everyday life, we experience non-tempered, non-syncopated, non-synced repetition that over time can induce a kind of trance state." Life is but a dream—a dream composed of ceaselessly interacting fragments, cut-up and reassembled as if by magick.

Bunkers, Punkers, and Junkies

Since music is registered with the whole body it can serve as a means of communication between one organism and another. . . . Agent attends a concert and receives his instructions.

WILLIAM S. BURROUGHS, *The Western Lands*

Nova Mob

"Where's Keith?" the kids shouted from the audience of the stately Entermedia Theater at 189 Second Avenue in New York, today known as Village East Cinema. Brion Gysin was onstage reading through every possible permutation of a single cut-up sentence, but only some in the audience were paying attention. The bridge-and-tunnel crowd wanted a real live Rolling Stone, like they'd been promised. Keith Richards had indeed been booked to appear at the 1978 Nova Convention—a three-day multimedia celebration of Burroughs' life and work—but he canceled at the last minute. Having recently been busted for heroin in Toronto, Richards and his minders thought it too risky for the rock star to attend a celebration for the Pope of Dope, as Burroughs was known to the denizens of the Lower East Side. Even if they'd never read a word, most attendees knew Burroughs by reputation—that ashen old junkie who shot his wife and wrote *Naked Lunch*. They were in for an interesting show, to say the least.

Like the man it celebrated, the 1978 Nova Convention was alternately impenetrable and enthralling. Rockers rubbed elbows with academics, authors, poets, performers, and provocateurs, including Susan Sontag, Timothy Leary, Robert Anton Wilson, Allen Ginsberg, Merce Cunningham, and John Giorno, to name a few. Burroughs himself gave lively readings, appeared in panel discussions, and held court backstage. The festivities wrapped up with a December 2 concert at the Ukrainian Theater that spilled over to Club 57 at Irving Plaza early the next morning. Performers included Blondie, Robert Fripp, Suicide, and the B-52s—a new wave party for the ages.

The convention proper also featured musical performances. Minimalist composer Philip Glass played a selection from *Einstein on the Beach*, an experimental theater piece cowritten with Robert Wilson (who would later collaborate with Burroughs and Tom Waits on the 1990 stage musical *The Black Rider*). Glass coaxed cascading waves of sound from his synthesizers, evoking exotic panoramas and languid, humid climes. With eyes closed, one could almost picture a younger Burroughs smoking kif under an arabesque archway in Tangier. In conversation with a *New York Times* reporter, Glass called Burroughs "the most important writer of our day," whose work helped set him on his own creative course. "Twenty years ago, the crucial events of my life were coming across his work and John Cage's work," he said. "They were both completely new and completely American, with no connection to European tradition. Burroughs really created a new American artistic tradition."[1]

Cage was also scheduled to perform, not that it mattered much to the rock 'n' rollers in the crowd. At least there was Frank Zappa, who had been hastily booked as a replacement for Richards. Zappa wasn't the only star on hand, however. Patti Smith arrived early and was hiding out backstage, nursing a bad cough. Smith's poetry reading at St. Mark's Church in February 1971, which Burroughs attended, was a defining moment for the East Village art scene and set Smith on a course for global stardom. Her debut album with the Patti Smith Group, *Horses* (1975), wowed critics and audiences alike, but she'd since hit a rough patch. Smith had only recently recovered from a devastating spinal injury resulting from a stage accident the year before and was still nursing wounds from the critical savaging and poor sales of her follow-up album, *Radio Ethiopia* (1976). By the time of the Nova Convention, things were looking up. Smith was basking in accolades for her third effort, *Easter*, which had arrived in March, and was happy to be celebrating her dear friend William.

As an emerging artist, Laurie Anderson got a boost from performing at the Nova Convention, though it would be a few years before her first appearance on a record—a 1981 collaboration with Burroughs and John Giorno called *You're the Guy I Want to Spend My Money With*. Anderson's esteem for Burroughs would also be on display on later releases, such as "Sharkey's Night" from *Mister Heartbreak* (1984). Here Burroughs' droll recitations are set against sparse but stirring dance-pop: "And Sharkey says: Deep in the heart of darkest America. Home of the brave. He says: Listen to my heart beat. Paging Mr. Sharkey. White courtesy telephone please." A couple of years later, Anderson copped a key Burroughs concept for "Language Is a Virus (From Outer Space)"—one of her better-known songs, which first appeared on *Home of the Brave* (1986).

Among the Nova Convention attendees was a young Thurston Moore, who would later gain notice as a member of noise-rock triumphalists Sonic Youth. What does Moore recall about the event? Among other things, Patti Smith's coat, which he referred to as "a black fur trench." All of nineteen years old at the time, Moore already recognized Burroughs' significance to the counterculture. "What I remember of the Nova Convention, in my teenage potted reverie, was a palpable excitement of the importance of Burroughs' return to NYC," Moore said in a 2014 text for a curated exhibit in London about the Nova Convention. "My awareness of the poets and performers on the Nova Convention bill was obscure, but I did realize everyone there had experienced a history in connection to the man."[2]

The event was to a large extent masterminded by James Grauerholz, who had only recently taken on the role of Burroughs' assistant and business manager. Grauerholz drew from his own connections in the art, music, and dance scenes, including Laurie Anderson, John Cage, and Merce Cunningham. He also leaned heavily on John Giorno's network and experience in staging events. The Entermedia was a hip venue, a movie theater turned burlesque house turned avant-garde performance space. It was a place where one could catch a set by the Talking Heads or onetime Burroughs protégé Daevid Allen. Filmmaker Howard Brookner—a young, gay, on-again, off-again junkie with a Burroughs obsession—was tapped to video the proceedings. Brookner was amassing footage for a documentary on Burroughs that did not see release until 1983, and then only after the BBC helped edit the many reels into what eventually became *Burroughs: The Movie*. It is a beautiful little film with touching interactions between Burroughs, Allen Ginsberg, Lucien Carr, and William Jr., along with other friends and family. Extra scenes from the 2014 restoration and re-release include a few brief Nova Convention shots where one can spot Jim Jarmusch—who would go on to become a major figure in independent cinema—working as an assistant cameraman.

Patti Smith was upset about having to follow Frank Zappa. Stuck with the spot vacated by Richards, she fretted about being a letdown. Grauerholz explained to Smith that Zappa was appearing as a favor, not to show her up. Zappa, whose complex and scathing music betrayed a general disdain for humanity, read an excerpt from the "The Talking Asshole" section of *Naked Lunch*. One of Burroughs' most blackly humorous routines, it was a good fit for the sarcastic rocker. "Alright, um, as you know, I'm not the kind of a person that reads books. I've said this before many times, I'm not fond of reading," Zappa confessed. "But I have in the past made exceptions, and uh, one of these exceptions was this part of the book that, I'm sure you know, called *Naked Lunch*, and I've received permission to read the part about the talking asshole." The original text remains both hilarious and provocative, not unlike Zappa himself:

> Did I ever tell you about the man who taught his asshole to talk? His whole abdomen would move up and down you dig farting out the words. It was unlike anything I ever heard.
>
> This ass talk had sort of a gut frequency. It hit you right down there like you gotta go. You know when the old colon gives you the elbow and it feels sorta cold inside, and you know all you have

to do is turn loose? Well this talking hit you right down there, a bubbly, thick stagnant sound, a sound you could *smell*.

This man worked for a carnival you dig, and to start with it was like a novelty ventriloquist act. Real funny, too, at first. He had a number he called "The Better 'Ole" that was a scream, I tell you. I forget most of it but it was clever. Like, "Oh I say, are you still down there, old thing?"

"Nah I had to go relieve myself."

After a while the ass start talking on its own. He would go in without anything prepared and his ass would ad-lib and toss the gags back at him every time.

Then it developed sort of teeth-like little raspy in-curving hooks and started eating. He thought this was cute at first and built an act around it, but the asshole would eat its way through his pants and start talking on the street, shouting out it wanted equal rights. It would get drunk, too, and have crying jags no-body loved it and it wanted to be kissed same as any other mouth. Finally it talked all the time day and night, you could hear him for blocks screaming at it to shut up, and beating it with his fist, and sticking candles up it, but nothing did any good and the asshole said to him: "It's you who will shut up in the end. Not me. Because we dont need you around here any more. I can talk and eat *and* shit."

After that he began waking up in the morning with a trans-parent jelly like a tadpole's tail all over his mouth. This jelly was what the scientists call un-D.T., Undifferentiated Tissue, which can grow into any kind of flesh on the human body. He would tear it off his mouth and the pieces would stick to his hands like burning gasoline jelly and grow there, grow anywhere on him a glob of it fell. So finally his mouth sealed over, and the whole head would have amputated spontaneous—(did you know there is a condition occurs in parts of Africa and only among Negroes where the little toe amputates spontaneously?)—except for the *eyes* you dig. That's one thing the asshole *couldn't* do was see. It needed the eyes. But nerve connections were blocked and infiltrated and atrophied so the brain couldn't give orders any more. It was trapped in the skull, sealed off. For a while you could see the silent, helpless suffering of the brain behind the eyes, then finally the brain must have died, because the eyes *went out*, and there was no more feeling in them than a crab's eyes on the end of a stalk.

Backstage, Zappa recalled his initial reaction to *Naked Lunch* when he first encountered the book as a high school student in Lancaster, California. "At the time, I said, 'How did he get away with that?' It was definitely an encouragement."[3] Zappa expressed interest in collaborating with Burroughs even after the Nova Convention was in the rearview. As the author reveals in the audio commentary to the 1991 film adaptation of *Naked Lunch*: "In 1979, Frank Zappa came to me with the concept of *Naked Lunch* as an off-Broadway musical. This struck me—and still does—as a pregnant idea, but it was not to be." The two iconoclasts remained friendly, however; Zappa even sent Burroughs a dozen roses for the author's seventieth birthday in 1984.

Poet Eileen Myles invited reprisal from other performers when they acted out the infamous William Tell scene where Burroughs killed Joan Vollmer. As Moore recounted, Myles was "hence persona non grata backstage and frozen out from the coterie of avant-lit celebrities shocked at [their] 'reminder' performance."[4] There is no record of Burroughs himself taking offense; Myles, at any rate, continued to promote Burroughs' work, and they read from *Naked Lunch* at a 2014 celebration that took place in Chicago.

Burroughs was a presence throughout the Nova Convention. He joined self-proclaimed "agnostic mystic" and *Illuminatus Trilogy* coauthor Robert Anton Wilson, psychedelic guru Timothy Leary, and Brion Gysin for a rambling conversation about time-space travel as the next stage in human evolution. He also delivered a short dispatch from one of his most notorious characters. "I'm sorry that Dr. Benway cannot be here in person," Burroughs deadpanned. "But he does send a message: 'I am a practitioner of medicine; I learn from my patients, and my patients learn from me. I am glad to report that everything is now well under control in Jonestown, and I have a few more calls to make tonight.'" Burroughs was referencing the mass suicides at Jim Jones' People's Temple in Guyana less than two weeks earlier, an incident that also saw US congressman Leo Ryan ruthlessly murdered by the cult, most of whose members were American citizens.

Burroughs' remarks made an impression on bassist and composer Bill Laswell. "Burroughs arrived the night of the festival right as it began," Laswell recalls. "He had to walk through the audience. . . . He had this huge cowboy-type hat and his notes were in a briefcase and there was a strange light around him coming up the stairs, from the front, and he walked up to this desk. I thought the Guyana thing was hilarious. I said, 'Wow, you know, this guy's got a sense of humor.'"[5] In a letter to Paul Bowles about the event, Burroughs describes an after-party beverage of Kool-Aid and vodka that was served out of a washtub, "just like Jonestown."

Following a rousing reading of "Roosevelt After the Inauguration," Burroughs offered an explanation on "what the Nova Convention is about." Whether his statement cleared up or further confused matters is debatable. "This is the space age, and we're here to go!" Burroughs declaimed.

> However, the space program has been restricted so far to the mediocre elite, who at great expense have gone to the moon in an aqualung. And they're not looking for space; they're looking for more time. . . . I can see all manner of spacecraft, some of them obviously lethal, preparing to take off. Only those who are willing to leave everything they've ever known in time need apply. It is necessary to travel; it is not necessary, and becoming increasingly difficult, to live.[6]

Patti Smith took the stage knowing many in the audience were still annoyed about the Keith Richards cancellation. "Keith wanted to come," she said.

But he ain't here. . . . He's on a plane somewhere . . . geographically, probably over Death Valley. Anyway, listen, I've been watching a lot of TV lately, and people seem to fall for the money-back guarantee thing, and we stand behind that. So right now, if anybody wants their money 'cause Keith Richards ain't gonna be here, I will personally pay you back. . . . I got twelve bucks.[7]

Smith proceeded to pull cash from her fur coat and wave it at the audience; nobody took her up on the offer. "You've seen the heroin, now see the heroine!" she exclaimed before launching into "Poem for Jim Morrison" with guitarist Lenny Kaye. "A fire of unknown origin took my baby away . . . swept her up and off my wavelength, swallowed her up like the ocean in a fire thick and gray," she spoke-sang over Kaye's minor-key chords. Several lines from the poem would later show up in the song "Fire of Unknown Origin" by Blue Öyster Cult, a band that counted Patti Smith's boyfriend Allen Lanier among its members.

Laurie Anderson used audio effects to pitch her voice below and above its natural register for her performance of the spoken word "America on the Move." John Cage traded his challenging compositions for "Writing for the Second Time through Finnegans Wake," a prepared text concerning his linguistic interest in James Joyce. This went right over the heads of many in the audience, who may have been more receptive to John Giorno's "Eating the Sky," a poem he wrote for the occasion and delivered with customary intensity. Allen Ginsberg and his partner Peter Orlovsky read "Punk Rock & Old Pond," which managed to capture the zeitgeist: "You want a revolution? You want apocalypse? Louder! Visciouser! Fuck me in the ass! Suck me! Come in my ears!"[8]

Robert Palmer covered the Nova Convention for the *New York Times*. "It was entirely in the spirit of Mr. Burroughs's work that the first musical performance on Saturday night, a solo organ piece by Philip Glass, left virtually nothing to chance," he wrote. "The piece was as conservative in its language and as rigorous in its organization as Mr. Burroughs's first novel, 'Junkie.' The evening's other musical performance, by Patti Smith, was more in the tradition of the cut-ups; it celebrated attitude, style, and the kind of 'holy accidents' that visionary artists have long cultivated." Palmer reserved most of his praise for the honoree, claiming that "Mr. Burroughs himself was the most appealing" and "his own most interesting character." The scenesters in the audience thought this character was interesting, too. And a few of them—including Thurston Moore—would go on to form bands as part of punk's first and second waves.

Back in NYC

The mid-to-late 1970s was an exciting, dangerous time in New York City. A new breed of rocker, all tatters and attitude, had taken over the East Village dive bar CBGB, where acts like Patti Smith, Television, the Ramones, Talking Heads, and Blondie thrilled audiences packed into the impossibly small room. While the musicians seethed and snarled on stage, Burroughs laid low in the Bunker— the windowless former YMCA not far from CBGB that he would call home for the rest of the decade. Here he entertained guests like Andy Warhol and Mick Jagger alongside the rising stars of the underground. "It was more of a small town in New York City in those days," Thurston Moore said. "Everybody knew each other. You would see all the people who were celebrated in that scene, such as those guys, and then the punk rock people like Tom Verlaine and Richard Hell and Patti Smith. Everybody lived in sort of the same area."[9] Just outside the heavily bolted doors of the Bunker was an endless parade of junkies, pushers, and hustlers. The Bowery neighborhood had long been known for its hard luck and harder drugs; now it was ground zero for punk.

Once again, Burroughs' timing was impeccable. Upon returning to the States in 1974, he found himself an unlikely—though mostly willing—participant in another major cultural shift. His years in the Bunker would cement his reputation as the "godfather of punk," a title he rejected even as he inspired key members of the scene. "It is no exaggeration to say that his books prophesied punk rock from *Naked Lunch* to *The Wild Boys*," friend and collaborator Victor Bockris said. "Burroughs believed in the efficacy of the youth revolt. He was all for it."[10] Blondie's Chris Stein agrees. "The guy had an aura," he said. "Burroughs was such an outsider, you know, on the fringe. He projected a personal energy and a sense of confidence that was maybe similar to your rock star type. . . . I think he definitely stood his own with all these people."[11]

Burroughs accepted Allen Ginsberg's offer to teach a course at New York City College, but the appointment was short-lived. It turned out he had little appetite for babysitting undergrad stoners and looky-loos. More satisfying were his occasional stints at Naropa Institute in Boulder, Colorado, founded by Tibetan Buddhist and dispenser of "crazy wisdom" Chögyam Trungpa. There Burroughs would give lectures and join Ginsberg, Gregory Corso, and Anne Waldman for talks on everything from dream logic to nuclear war to "creative reading." Some of these lectures were recorded and can still be accessed online at the Naropa Poetics Audio Archive. Though it was often nice to get out of the city, Burroughs overall enjoyed his new life in New York and the recognition he received from a new wave of confrontational performance artists, including Patti Smith, Richard Hell, and Jim Carroll.

Burroughs hadn't moved into the Bunker straightaway, having initially taken up residence in a loft on 452 Broadway and later an apartment at 77 Franklin Street. This was where he and Jimmy Page rapped about magick and Morocco. Not long after Burroughs got back to town, Ginsberg introduced him to James Grauerholz—a young man who would over the weeks, months, years, and decades to follow become his close friend, business manager, amanuensis, and estate executor. From 1974 until Burroughs' passing, Grauerholz helped Burroughs keep addiction at bay, advanced his reputation in American letters, and stoked interest among other artists and thinkers.

A University of Kansas dropout with an interest in music and literature, Grauerholz came to New York to experience the city that birthed the Beats. He first made a connection with Ginsberg, who

suggested to Burroughs that Grauerholz might make a suitable assistant. They had a fleeting romantic affair, but Grauerholz soon
found another partner—a recurring theme for Burroughs. Still, the
two achieved a strong and lasting bond as collaborators and com-
patriots. Grauerholz was top among Burroughs' chosen family; his
truest blue companion by a Kansas mile. When Burroughs eventually grew tired of New York, Grauerholz tapped his personal relationships and connections in Lawrence to establish a supportive
community for the author. For this, as well as his keen ability to
match Burroughs to creatively and financially rewarding opportunities, Grauerholz deserves praise.

Burroughs' first two years back in the States were enjoyable,
even enlivening, but his homecoming was soured by tragic news
from the UK. On February 5, 1976, his sixty-second birthday, he
received a telegram from Ian Sommerville that read: "HAPPY
BIRTHDAY. LOTS OF LOVE. LOTS OF PROMISE. NO REALI-
ZATION." A few short hours later, Burroughs got a second telegram
from Antony Balch with the news of Sommerville's death. Not long
after Burroughs left London, Sommerville moved to Bath, where
he took a job as a computer programmer. He soon found himself
in a public spat with Bill Levy, an American expat living in Holland
who published an underground magazine called *Suck*. Sommerville
allegedly had a heterosexual affair with Levy's partner, Susan Janssen. The infuriated Levy ran a piece called "Electric Ian: Portrait
of a Humanoid" while guest-editing another magazine called *The
Fanatic*. The piece excerpted Sommerville's love letters to Janssen
and even made fun of his genitalia. This, along with quotes from
acquaintances alleging halitosis (otherwise known as bad breath)
and financial frivolity, deeply stung Sommerville. Burroughs believed it caused his death. An inexperienced driver, Sommerville
was distraught and distracted on the way to send his birthday greeting. On the way back from the post office, he veered into another
automobile and was killed instantly.

Anguished, Burroughs hit the bottle. He attempted to reach
Sommerville in the Great Beyond, attending a séance that failed

to establish a connection. He then turned to Tibetan lama Dudjom Rinpoche, who came recommended by John Giorno. The guru told Burroughs that Sommerville was trapped in the second level of hell, unable to be reborn. As if to seal himself away from further catastrophe, Burroughs moved into the Bunker in June 1976. The fact that there were no windows didn't bother him. He enjoyed the security of living in a unit with three-foot thick concrete walls and four locked doors separating him from the outside world. "We must hold the Bunker at all costs," Burroughs said to Victor Bockris, who recalled how "Bill would on occasion reel around the room demonstrating for an astonished guest the effect of a steel spring cobra[12] on a box of cereal—WHACK!—cutting a great gash down its side. Or he might produce a bullet-riddled phonebook, growling, 'LOOK WHAT WE DID LAST NIGHT!' For the record, this was caused by extensive target practice with an air pistol. He never kept guns in New York."[13]

This did not prevent Burroughs from bringing along a small arsenal whenever he left the house that included a cane, a tear-gas canister, and a blackjack. He encouraged visitors to arm up, too, going so far as to form a gang with Bunker regulars called the Order of the Grey Gentleman. This intrepid group of lads (and one much older lad) set after muggers in the streets of Lower Manhattan, presumably intending to give them more than a talking to. "He taught me how to use a blowgun to inflict naturally optimal damage," Bockris said. "There were many enthusiastic discussions of plans and tactics."[14] No record of altercation between the Order and the Bowery's criminal element exists. Perhaps silence equals success.

Following the irritations and insults of Great Britain, Burroughs was having a fine old time in his new environs. Besides, who needs windows when one has company? "The best nights at the Bunker began sitting around Bill's big conference table on high-backed office chairs with orange cushions, consuming vodka and marijuana," Bockris recalled. Regular guests included Ginsberg and Orlovsky, as well as Debbie Harry and Chris Stein from Blondie, Joe Strummer of the Clash, and the painter Jean Michel Basquiat. "The conversation was always vigorous," Bockris said. "Bill was a great raconteur and had a large fund of hilarious tales from his storied life, but he also loved to hear other people's stories."[15] There were dinners with big names like Mick Jagger, whom Burroughs had first met years earlier in London. After one such occasion, Burroughs commented on transformations in underground and popular culture. "Now rock 'n' roll is a mass phenomenon performed before huge audiences and associated with a worldwide cultural revolution," he remarked. "The comparison of rock 'n' roll audiences and Nazi rallies is not at all farfetched. Anything that can get that number of people together is political. So Mick may be right on when he says he wants to go into politics."[16] That there has been no MP or PM Jagger shows which path the star ultimately chose. Not long after his dinner with Jagger, Burroughs was visited by David Bowie, who might have appreciated Burroughs' rant about rock stars as demagogues. Unlike Jagger, who acted aloof, Bowie "was the model of gentlemanly courtesy," according to Bockris.[17]

During this period, Burroughs explored cinematic adaptations of *Junky* and *The Last Words of Dutch Schultz*. Bowie, fresh from a starring turn in Nicolas Roeg's *The Man Who Fell to Earth*, was at one point floated as the lead for *Junky* (as was Jack Nicholson), but neither film was ever made. Burroughs considered taking up acting himself, telling Andy Warhol, "I can play doctors, CIA men and all kinds of things . . . a Nazi war criminal, I could play very well."[18] That these projects were even being contemplated was a testament to Burroughs' newfound cultural cachet. The Nova Convention, as well as public endorsement by the likes of Andy Warhol and influential cultural critic Susan Sontag, aided Burroughs' visibility in the mainstream. But it was the punks who cemented his status as an icon of the underground.

Society of the Spectacle

Punk's primary attributes can be debated; is it a lifestyle, a political movement, a fashion statement, a musical form, a commodity, or all of the above? Likewise, there is controversy regarding punk's exact origins. Some say it starts with Detroit acts like the Stooges and MC5, who lit up midwestern stages in the late 1960s and early '70s. Others point to Great Britain, where the Sex Pistols and the Damned terrorized the British Establishment and energized youths grown disaffected by high unemployment and crippling class divides. Still others single out the New York Dolls, who strutted out of Manhattan's red-light underworld like cross-dressing Frankenstein monsters. Burroughs' interactions with the original punk movement occurred largely within the New York scene, though he did once write the Sex Pistols a letter of support, and the Clash singer Joe Strummer was an enthusiastic guest at the Bunker. "Although he was an hour-and-a-half late, Strummer brought a bottle of whisky, a bottle of tequila, two six-packs of Heineken, and eight enormous joints," Bockris recalled.[19]

> He was bubbling over with eagerness to meet Burroughs, with whom he had a very relaxed and pleasant conversation about English policemen. William hauled out his arsenal of blackjacks, Japanese throwing stars and knives, while Joe took a series of Polaroids of him thwacking cardboard boxes and alternately emitting an extremely wide, malevolent smile. Strummer left completely satisfied.[20]

Punk's black leather heart was brought to beating life by the likes of Richard Hell, Jim Carroll, and Patti Smith. Hell bequeathed its look, Carroll its edge, and Smith its exuberance. Even the term "punk" came from the New York scene. Lenny Kaye, who would serve as Smith's guitarist for most of her performing career, referred to 1960s psychedelic garage bands as "punk-rock" in his liner notes for a 1972 *Nuggets* compilation. Rock writers such as Legs McNeil and Lester Bangs codified the emerging sound and attitude in magazines like *Punk* and *Creem*, just as the Beats were legitimized in the progressive literary journals of their day.[21] As Bockris later wrote, "The punks, led by Patti Smith and Richard Hell, adored the Beats and the Beats in turn were grateful to the punks for drawing fresh, renewed attention to their work."[22]

Often dismissed as nihilist posturing by the preceding generation, punk had, in its initial guises, both an intellectual streak and a social conscience. English acts such as the Sex Pistols borrowed heavily from the Situationist movement of the late 1950s, which put art through the critical-theory wringer in an attempt to awaken society from its mass-media induced stupor. American punks like Richard Hell and Patti Smith also embraced the nineteenth-century poets Baudelaire, Rimbaud, and Verlaine, and took something from the spirit, if not the sound, of free jazz. As was the case with the British Invasion of the 1960s, competition also helped to drive this new rock movement. American bands like the New York Dolls and the Ramones lit a fire under the asses of English acts like the Sex Pistols and the Clash, who in turn inspired West Coast groups like Black Flag and X.

It is impossible to overlook punk's connection to drugs, especially heroin. Borrowing from Burroughs' lexicon, Bockris described junk as the ultimate Control. "You have to buy the product, or else you're sick," he said.[23] Proto-punk stalwart Iggy Pop noted that Burroughs' investigations into the nature of addiction are actually helpful to users. "He opened a tunnel to a way out," Pop said. "'Cause if you're doing something and you wanna stop, you're not gonna stop until you figure out what it is you're actually doing."[24] Most music fans know about famous drug casualties like Sid Vicious and Nancy Spungen from punk's first wave. Another was Dee Dee Ramone (of the Ramones), a boisterously clever songwriter and raging addict who improbably managed to survive until 2002, when the needle finally did him in. He joined previously departed punk junkies such as Darby Crash, G. G. Allin, and Johnny Thunders, to name a few.

Kurt Cobain and Courtney Love became the king and queen of the Junkie Prom in the 1990s, their barbed crowns inherited from Sid and Nancy. Addiction was rampant in their scene. Love's original bassist in the band Hole, Kristen Pfaff, died of an overdose in 1994;

the band's drummer, Patti Schemel, recounted her own struggles with addiction in her autobiography, *Hits So Hard*. Heroin use remains a concern among today's punk musicians. Mish Barber-Way of contemporary act White Lung described the apathy of abuse in an essay for *Pitchfork*: "When you're on opiates, you don't give a shit about anything, whether that anything be good or bad. Everything feels blissful, even vomiting. Dope vomit is the most divine vomit you'll ever know. It just flows out of you as though God intended barfing to be heaven."[25]

Burroughs was adamant that his writing did not glamorize drugs. While it is true that his work depicts the ugliness of dependency, it also reveals the bliss of absorption, when the world dissolves into a gelatinous mass of natal warmth. In telling these truths, Burroughs no doubt enticed more than a few punks to experiment with narcotics. How far they went was up to them. Or was it? Perhaps they were just "soft machines" predestined to experience the needle and the damage done. In his novels, Burroughs frequently ruminates on individual agency—what it means to lose it, and how it might be regained, even against despairing odds. However unwise to imitate, Burroughs' unflinching examinations, rooted in personal experiences, afford his work an almost heroic quality. He dramatized the cruelties and humiliations of addiction as an epic battle against Control, just as his punk descendants externalized their own struggles through rudimentary musical assaults on society.

Hell Is for Children

Punk's image owes much to a single individual, Richard Hell, who was a member of more than one seminal underground act.[26] His early presence in the band Television alongside former schoolmate Tom Verlaine (who took his surname from the French poet) sent a jolt of spastic electricity through the stitched-together punk scene. Subsequent work with the Voidoids and the Heartbreakers helped shape the genre's perception among the greater public. This includes its sound—all slashing guitars, snarling vocals, and rapid-fire rhythms. Other groups would put their own spin on the genre, but punk's DNA comes straight from Hell. And emblazoned in the movement's genetic code is the by-now familiar "Burroughs gene" transmitted by Hell and fellow travelers.

Hell and Verlaine turned heads with their scruffy looks and torn clothes; soon kids across America and around the world would cop their style. Hell's unkempt hairdo was allegedly borrowed from the French poet Rimbaud, but his sardonic demeanor was all Burroughs. Of course, Burroughs, too, owes something to Rimbaud, who was a member of the Beat-like Symbolists in nineteenth-century France. "No influence that has affected Burroughs seems to me as important as Rimbaud," wrote Neil Oxenhandler in a 1975 critical analysis. "Even the most violent and aggressive outbursts have something childish about them."[27] The same could be said of punk.

Hell referred to himself as a member of the Blank Generation—a term he coined and used as the title of the Voidoid's movement-defining 1977 debut. By then the distinctions between Burroughs' fictional hooligans and the Lower East Side scene looked negligible. In fact, Burroughs' *Wild Boys* manifesto reads like a punk rock to-do list:

We intend to march on the police machine everywhere. We intend to destroy the police machine and all its records. We intend to destroy all dogmatic verbal systems. The family unit and its cancerous expansion into tribes, countries, nations we will eradicate at its vegetable root. We don't want to hear any more family talk, mother talk, father talk, cop talk, priest talk, country talk or party talk. To put it country simple we have heard enough bullshit.

To Beat scholar Jennie Skerl, the Wild Boys represent "an escape from a repressive civilization into a fantasy world of endlessly gratified desire."[28] This, too, could describe the emerging punk movement, as might Oxenhandler's observation that Burroughs' writing betrays "a purposeful ambivalence that never relents." A blankness, in other words. A dedicated consumer of Burroughs' ideas, Hell not only understood these parallels, but sought to amplify them through his own brand of hyper-charged rock 'n' roll performance art.

Born Richard Lester Meyers in October 1942, Hell grew up in the decidedly un-punk 'burbs of Lexington, Kentucky, where he played cowboy, spotted birds, and explored local caves. His father, who died when he was seven, was an experimental psychologist with a focus on animal behavior. After her husband's death, his mother went back to school and became a professor, which provided financial and social stability. Hell was extremely bright, though not academically inclined. "I probably peaked as a human in the sixth grade," he said. "My teacher that year, Mrs. Vicars, made a private special arrangement allowing me to write stories instead of doing the regular homework assignments."[29] Before long, his grades "plummeted from effortless excellence to C's, and D's and F's." In 1965 his mother took a teaching position at Old Dominion University in Norfolk, Virginia. Wanting no part of the local public school, Hell enrolled at Sanford Preparatory outside of Wilmington, Delaware. There he got hooked on the Rolling Stones and gulped codeine cough syrup—an early entrée to narcotics reminiscent of Burroughs' "knockout drops" from his Los Alamos days.

Hell was suspended for taking LSD at a school dance, shortly after which he and a friend named Tom Miller—later known as Tom Verlaine—ditched school permanently. The two made their way to New York City, where they fell quite deliberately into the wrong crowd. "Tom and I, partly out of interest in William Burroughs and Lou Reed, were curious about heroin, but we didn't know anything about finding it," he said. "We got lucky once and copped a couple of bags, but it made us both so sick, vomiting, that it destroyed most of our interest."[30] Hell's close friend and former Voidoids bandmate, the late guitarist Robert Quine, was also a Burroughs fan who owned an Olympia Press first edition of *Naked Lunch*. Burroughs people tend to find one another. And then they form bands.

Hell was not a member of Burroughs' regular crowd, though he did have dinner with him at Bockris' apartment one night in 1986 alongside Stein, Harry, Ginsberg, Basquiat, and Grauerholz. According to Bockris, the conversation covered such topics as Boy George's heroin habit, the brain tumor of then-CIA director William Casey, and the love affair between punk impresario Malcolm McLaren and actress Lauren Hutton.[31] Gossipy dinners notwithstanding, Hell claims Burroughs as a formative influence—and remember, this is the person who imbued punk with much of its perspicacity, as well as its basic look and sound. Shortly after the author's death in 1997, Hell penned an insightful tribute called "My Burroughs":

> His writing is beautiful and of course hilarious: meticulously seen, sawn, and nailed, deadpan, fearless, a matchless ear. He's among the most select (Joyce, Nabokov, Borges, Beckett) in having a style so refined that you can generally recognize him in a sentence. But just as great is that freedom from ties, from debts to, from vested interests in virtually anything.

This freedom from interest, or blankness, should not be confused with vacuity. After all, a blank page precedes the written word; magnetic tape is blank until someone presses record. Hell claimed that Burroughs "subverted any egoistic function of writing with his cut-ups . . . neutralizing horrors by revealing and describing them . . . he spent his workdays in the mines." Because it was the work itself that was of primary import: the author was just a vessel, and a knowingly imperfect one.

Collaborating with Burroughs was a sure sign that one had earned his trust. "The best way to relate to Bill was to work with him,"[32] Bockris said, pointing to the 1990 Burroughs album *Dead City Radio* as an example of his efforts in collaboration. That album, composed of various readings, features musician admirers like Donald Fagen of Steely Dan along with nearly every member of Sonic Youth—a band greatly inspired by the heroes of the original punk scene, especially Patti Smith.

High on Rebellion

Patti Smith's music doesn't sound much like punk as we know it to-day. In fact, it has more in common with classic rock—straightforward chords played at moderate tempos on guitars, keyboards, and drums, with passionate vocals and mostly intelligible lyrics. Still, some consider Smith's first single, "Hey Joe" b/w "Piss Factory"—released in 1974, the same year Burroughs returned to New York—to be the earliest punk track. (UK punkologists would likely disagree, pointing instead to "New Rose" by the Damned, which arrived two years later.) "Piss Factory" has none of the sonic hallmarks of the genre, but Smith's delivery possesses something of the rawness that came to characterize punk. She wrote the song about her experiences working in a baby buggy factory where she endured ugly conditions and uglier coworkers. "Piss Factory" isn't just an account of a lame job, however. It is a declaration of intent. With this aural invocation (a real Burroughs move), Patti Smith reinvented herself as the enfant terrible of the new underground:

I got something to hide here called desire
And I will get out of here—
You know the fiery potion is just about to come . . .
And I'm gonna go, I'm gonna get out of here . . .
I'm gonna be somebody, I'm gonna get on that train, go to New
*   York City,*
I'm gonna be so bad I'm gonna be a big star and I will never return
*   . . .*

The music itself is subdued, with loping piano chords and graceful guitar licks framed by Smith's almost coquettish vocal. With less pointed lyrics, it might have made a halfway decent pop song. Of course, punk has always been more of a spirit than a sound, and Smith had plenty of the former. Her fearless performances helped restore rock's primal drive, which had been diluted by musicians more concerned with their own instrumental virtuosity than connecting with listeners. This was the era of the double, triple, even quadruple album, when bands like Yes and Genesis were nearly swallowed by elaborate stage sets and their own pomposity. By contrast, Smith's show was stripped down, vital, communal. She gave herself up entirely to her fans, feeding on their energy and establishing a powerful bond between audience and performer. Women rockers were still rare in the 1970s, considered by the industry as sex kittens or supporting players—if they were considered at all. Smith's powerful presence, at once collegial and no-bullshit, helped evolve such perceptions. There was no doubt she had a brain, but her words carried the cadence of the streets. She certainly didn't want for confidence, which inspired others in her circle—including Robert Mapplethorpe, Richard Hell, and Jim Carroll—to be more confident. Smith proved that with the right attitude and plenty of determination, anyone could accomplish anything. Action creates reality, just like Hassan i-Sabbah taught his disciples.

Although Patti Smith didn't play punk music, she understood how her work helped inform the broader movement. "We were never really a punk band," she told writer Nick Tosches. "We were the predecessors of that; trying to create a space for people to express anti-corporate feelings. Rail against the big arena acts and the glitter bands. Bring it back to the streets, the garage."[33] Smith's greatest contribution to punk is not musical; it is folkloric. Like the Beats, she cultivated a mythic outlook and nurtured it with her creativity. Prone to hero worship, Smith gnashed teeth over lost icons like Jim Morrison and Rimbaud, preferring dead artists because they posed no competition. She also championed Burroughs, and still does. In an interview at the 2012 Louisiana Literature Festival, Smith shared some wisdom he imparted to her. "When I was really young and struggling, the advice that William Burroughs gave me was, build a good name, keep your name clean," she said. "Don't make compromises. Don't worry about making a bunch of money or being successful. Be concerned about doing good work, and make the right choices, and protect your work. If you build a good name, eventually, that name will be its own currency."

Smith began building her name as a regular performer at the St. Mark's Poetry Project accompanied by Lenny Kaye on guitar. It may seem strange that a poetry reading would serve as the opening salvo in a new fight against the Establishment. But that was also true of Ginsberg's "Howl," the Beat shot heard 'round the world. Smith's performance at St. Mark's was a galvanizing moment for a new generation of artistic renegades. And then, as if on cue, appeared that seemingly ancient entity called William S. Burroughs. "The first person who told me that Burroughs was in town was Patti Smith," Bockris said. "She announced his arrival from the stage of St. Mark's Poetry Project as if it were a move of military significance. 'Mr. Burroughs is back in town,' she whooped. 'Isn't that great!'"[34] Smith might not have even been onstage at all had it not been for the old man. "He encouraged me to sing before I sang publicly," she said.[35]

Girls and Boys

Born in Chicago in 1946, Smith grew up poor and religious, the first child of a Jehovah's Witness mother and factory worker father. In 1950 the Smiths moved to Philadelphia, settling in a rough neighborhood of Germantown. Her dad found work as a night machinist to support the family, which by then included Smith's two siblings, Todd and Linda. Money was always tight, but Smith's indomitable personality got her through. "I was very gawky and homely—real nervous and sickly and all that," she said. "But I was always happy. Really sort of brooding, but happy. Always optimistic, because I had this vision that I was going to do something. I always knew that I was more than what I seemed.... I was the class clown—I didn't care, because I knew that time would do right by me."[36]

The facts of Smith's childhood belie her rosy remembrance. She battled scarlet fever at age seven, an episode accompanied by intense hallucinations. Good fodder for the imagination, but a terrible strain on her well-being. Other members of the family bore their own burdens. "We had no money and my brother and sister were in the hospital with malnutrition," Smith said.[37] She was singled out for her appearance, including ratty clothes and a lazy eye that her parents couldn't afford the operation to fix. "Kids used to be scared of me because they thought I had an evil eye," she recalled.[38] Had she grown up in Saint Louis in the 1920s, she might have made friends with the "walking corpse," Billy Burroughs; it seems that childhood alienation is a prerequisite for great artists.

Smith was for the most part unfazed by her schoolmates' taunts. "I had this tremendous spirit that kept me going no matter how fucked up I was," she said. "I just had this light inside me that kept spurring me on. I was a happy child because I had this feeling that I was going to go beyond my body physical, even when I was in Philly. I just knew it."[39] Burroughs, too, was obsessed with escaping biological dichotomies, to be free from conditioning forces like pleasure and pain, addiction and lust. Smith and Burroughs both chose to "write their way out" of impulses and aversions embedded in their developmental years, and both did so in entirely unique ways.

Burroughs' childhood was shaped by an overbearing mother whose influence he sought to negate. Conversely, Smith adored her dad and took pains to curry his favor. "My father was very spiritual and intellectual," Smith said, crediting him for inspiring her own curiosity about the world. "He was always into developing the country of his mind . . . he hungered to read about everything."[40] Smith's identification with her father manifested in a variety of ways, from her favorite books and stories to her role within the family. The oldest child, she was often put in charge of her younger brother and sister. "Let's play mean father!" she'd say to Todd and Linda. "You be the kids and I'll beat you to death if you don't have the house clean."[41]

The embracing of masculine traits may have been Smith's way of relating to her father, just as Burroughs' rejection of the feminine was his way of escaping his mother. It should be made clear that gender identity and sexual orientation are not the same thing. Burroughs was a gay man and expressed himself sexually as such, though he had little tolerance for anything effeminate. Smith, for her part, loved men, perhaps even more than Burroughs, whom she admitted having a crush on. "He's a hard guy to get into bed. That's why I like him," she said.[42]

Burroughs understood the social and professional liabilities that came with open homosexuality. He wrote *Queer* between 1951 and 1953, but it wasn't published until 1985. Still, he professed little affinity for the gay rights scene. "I have never been gay a day in my life and I'm sure as hell not a part of any movement," he said.[43] Likewise, Smith's feminist image was complicated by her tendency to be subservient to men; she talked about how she wanted her partners "to make all the bread" and later dropped out of the music industry for more than a decade to support an alcoholic husband in down-and-out Detroit. But she made no apologies. "I like who I am," she told *Penthouse* in 1976. "I always liked who I was and I always loved men. The only time I ever feel fucked around by men is when I fight with a guy or when a guy ditches me. And that's got nothing to do with women's lib. That has to do with being ditched." To Lenny Kaye, Smith's stance was ultimately about freedom: "The whole point of Patti Smith was beyond gender, beyond politics, beyond, beyond," he said. "Any time you were defined, you were caught."[44] A perfectly Burroughsian mindset if there ever was one.

Smith's tomboy ways put her at odds with expectations for girls and women in the 1950s. She didn't so much reject the feminine as fail utterly to identify with it. "I was so involved with boy-rhythms that I never came to grips with the fact that I was a girl," she said.

> I was twelve years old when my mother took me inside and said, "You can't be wrestling outside without a t-shirt on." It was a trauma. In fact, I got so fucked up over it when my mother gave me the big word—that I was absolutely a girl and there was no changing it—that I walked out dazed on a highway with my dog, Bambi, and let her get hit by a fire engine.[45]

As a global star, Smith's androgynous look and attitude inspired countless young women and men to reject binary gender identities. It may also have endeared her to Burroughs. "Of course he was never too crazy about women, but I guess he liked me because I looked like a boy," she said.[46]

Visiting a Philadelphia museum with her father, Smith decided her own future on the spot. "I had never seen art up close before," she said. "From then on, I wanted to be an artist."[47] Art also helped her feel more secure in her looks. "I was real self-conscious about being skinny, and I had one teacher who said I shouldn't be," Smith recalled. "She took me to the school library and she showed me her art books and said I looked like an El Greco or a Modigliani. That was the first time I could relate to something physical."[48]

Smith's art obsession put her on a collision course with her religious mother, for whom creative expression was not just taboo, but a one-way ticket to damnation. "By the time I was about twelve or thirteen, I just figured, well, if that was the trip, and the only way you could get to God was through religion, then I didn't want Him anymore."[49] This anti-religious outlook would carry over to the first track on her 1975 debut, *Horses*. "Jesus died for somebody's sins but not mine," Smith taunts on "Gloria," an interpolation of an early song by Van Morrison from his old band Them. Her choose-your-own-adventure approach to spirituality got her through some tough spots. Barry Miles recalled visiting Smith while she was recuperating from her devastating stage fall in 1977. "What really struck me was her bedroom," Miles said. "She had a little altar by the window, just below the window sill. There was a low table with a cloth over it, on top of which was arranged a first edition of *Naked Lunch*—the original Olympia Press edition—a portrait of Rimbaud and Burroughs; some crosses, and a rosary."[50]

In 1956 Smith's family had recently relocated to New Jersey. At her new school she was given the assignment of picking a country on which to report over the course of the year. She chose Tibet, for which very little news was available due to an information blackout imposed by China. Her teacher tried to talk her into picking another country, but Smith held firm. Then came the 1959 Tibet uprising and subsequent Chinese army invasion that sent the Dalai Lama into exile. Now there was plenty of news, but at a terrible cost. She prayed fervently for the return of the country's spiritual leadership and remained involved in the cause of Tibetan independence over subsequent decades. "As unfortunately, I did live to see Tibet taken from the Tibetan people, I do hope that I will live to see it returned," she said at the close of a 1995 comeback performance. It could be a coincidence that several of Burroughs' musician admirers shared an interest in Tibetan Buddhism, including David Bowie, Genesis P-Orridge, and Richard Hell. But as Burroughs would say, "In the magical universe, there are no coincidences and there are no accidents."[51]

Philadelphia had already honed Smith's survival instincts, but New Jersey left its mark as well. "That's where I get my bad speech from," she said. "Even though my father was an intellectual, I wanted to be like the kids I went to school with, so I intentionally never learned to speak good."[52] She joined a jazz club where she got turned on to the likes of Miles Davis, John Coltrane, and Thelonious Monk, and improvisation later became a big part of Smith's performance style. She also swooned for the Rolling Stones, especially Brian Jones. (Jones, you recall, connects to the Burroughs mythos through the Master Musicians of Joujouka as well as the interests of Genesis P-Orridge.) Smith attended a Stones show and later described the tragic guitarist in the light of religious epiphany.

> He was sitting on the floor playing one of those Ventures electric sitars, and these girls kept pushing me and pushing me. They pushed me right onto the stage, and then I felt myself going under and I was gonna be trampled, and out of total desperation I reached up and grabbed the first thing I saw: Brian Jones' ankle. I was grabbing him to save myself. And he just looked at me. And I looked at him. And he smiled. He just smiled at me.[53]

A transcendent moment, however fleeting. Smith also grappled with more earthly passions, including awkward attempts to win attention from the opposite sex. "I was really crazy about guys," she said. "But I was always like one of the boys. The guys I fell in love with were completely inaccessible."[54] Passionate desire unrequited by the males in her social group. Burroughs could no doubt relate.

In the summer of 1966, while working in the "piss factory" to pay her way through Glassboro State Teacher's College, Smith discovered she was pregnant. "The boy, who was only seventeen, was so inexperienced he could hardly be held accountable," Smith said.[55] Since the father was in no position to support her, Smith and her parents determined it best that she give the child up for adoption. It was no doubt an agonizing decision, but one that demonstrates the extent to which she made her art a priority. "For a brief moment I felt as if I might die; and just as quickly I knew everything would be all right," Smith recalled. "An overwhelming sense of mission eclipsed my fears. . . . I would be an artist. I would prove my worth."[56] Some might consider Smith's decision—or Burroughs' absentee fatherhood—to be fundamentally selfish, but this ignores the deep distress that accompanies such a choice. Smith endured intense feelings of shame and isolation while waiting to give birth in a temporary foster home. Then she was humiliated during a difficult delivery. "Due to my unwed status, the nurses were very cruel and uncaring," Smith said. "They left me on a table for several hours before informing the doctor that I had gone into labor. They ridiculed me for my beatnik appearance and immoral behavior, calling me 'Dracula's daughter,' and threatening to cut my long black hair."[57] Even after all that, she managed to summon the strength to part with the infant she had only just delivered.

Burroughs' quasi-abandonment of William Jr. was exacerbated by the grim facts of Joan Vollmer's death; imagine the deep shame and regret the older Burroughs must have felt around his son. While no one would give Burroughs a Father of the Year award, he was deeply affected by his boy's steady decline in young adulthood. In a review of the book *Cursed From Birth: The Short, Unhappy Life of William S. Burroughs Jr.*, Tom Bowden describes the elder Burroughs' sense of helplessness:

We find a father doing everything he can—within the realm of letting his son take responsibility for his own behavior—to help his son through hard times, who sobs uncontrollably at the hospital when his son undergoes the liver transplant that could kill him (not that Billy had many options at that point in his dissolute life), who is angrily frustrated by his son's steadfast insistence on blaming everybody else but himself for his troubles.

It is impossible to guess what the outcomes would have been had Burroughs or Smith made different choices at key junctures in their lives. But anyone who considers either of their paths to be regret-free should have their head examined by Doctor Benway.

A Punk Is Born

Smith pursued her creative expression with the fervor of a religious convert, remixing her mother's religion with her own saintly pantheon, which included writers and artists like Rimbaud, Burroughs, and Bob Dylan. Upon arriving in New York City in 1967, she took a job as a Christmastime cashier at F.A.O. Schwartz before finding more suitable employment at Scribner's on Fifth Avenue and, later, Strand Books on Broadway, a gig she kept right up until she entered the studio to record *Horses*. Her early days in the city were a struggle, but the kind that she embraced. She was in the world, ready to do whatever it took to become a famous artist. Her spirits were further buoyed by nineteen-year-old art student Robert Mapplethorpe, with whom she fell madly in love. The two moved into a small apartment on Hall Street in Brooklyn, where they would spend long nights talking, sketching, writing, and staring at one another, as neither could afford a television set. Mapplethorpe would eventually embrace his homosexuality, causing a period of intense heartbreak for Smith, but the two remained close until Smith left for Detroit in 1979. They lived together from 1967 to 1972, during which time Smith largely supported Mapplethorpe through her work at the bookstore.

Her awakening to the power of punk as a musical form came when she saw Richard Hell's original band, Television. That group started out as a flailing, abrasive mess that soon coalesced into a highly musical unit with deft instrumental interplay and lyrical double entendres. Smith liked Hell a lot—all that leaping around was intense and also adorable—but it was his former schoolmate Tom Verlaine who set her heart alight. (The two dated off-and-on during this period as it became clear that her relationship with Mapplethorpe was destined to be platonic.) Victor Bockris—who with publishing partner Andrew Wylie put out Smith's first book of poems, *Seventh Heaven,* in 1972—described her seeing Television perform at CBGB as nothing short of a revelation:

> First, there was the magnificent front line of Tom Verlaine, Richard Lloyd, and Richard Hell; then there was the music—jagged, awkward, and spiky, but still mesmerizingly beautiful. A thrill like a series of electroshocks ran through Patti that night, the same feeling she'd had when she'd first heard Little Richard when she was a child, or the Rolling Stones when she was a teenager. It was so moving, so raw, so exposed and alive that she could hardly stop herself from bursting into tears.[58]

The buzz around Smith increased with each poetry reading, accompanied by guitarist Lenny Kaye, then keyboardist Richard Sohl. Soon after, drummer Jay Dee Daugherty and bassist Ivan Kral joined, officially inaugurating the Patti Smith Group. The switch to rock 'n' roll didn't happen overnight. In the months before she became a bandleader, Smith found her writing taking precedence over drawing and painting, which may have been motivated by an unconscious desire to define herself apart from Mapplethorpe's emerging genius. The best part about writing is that it didn't have to stay on the page, completely unlike a painting, which is dead to improvisation—the stuff of creative mercury—as soon as it is complete. Poems, and especially songs, could evolve based on intuition and energy from the crowd. She just had to figure out how to draw one. Besides being seen at hip bar Max's Kansas City with Mapplethorpe, Smith felt the best way to get attention was to have a bold and unique voice, like Burroughs or her songwriting idol Bob Dylan. "I felt the people we could learn from were the rock 'n' roll stars," she said. "I like people who are bigger than me. I don't like meeting a bunch of writers who I don't think are bigger than life. I'm a hero worshipper."[59]

Among her biggest heroes was Burroughs, whom she initially encountered as a visitor to the infamous Chelsea Hotel, where the older writer would stay while in town. "Burroughs showed me a whole series of new tunnels to fall through," Smith said. "He was so neat. He would walk around in this big black cashmere overcoat and this old hat. So of course, Patti gets an old black hat and coat, and we would walk around the Chelsea looking like that."[60] Smith would go on to sprinkle Burroughs references in her work, including "Land," which features a character named Johnny on loan from *The Wild Boys*. Smith and Burroughs developed an affectionate relationship. "I had the biggest crush on William," she said. "Really, a big one."

> And I used to even daydream about, you know, he would fall in love with me and we'd get married. . . . When the two of us were alone, he'd say, "Well, my dear, it's the end of night. Let's hear a little Bobby Shafto." And I would sing him the little song: "Bobby Shafto's gone to sea, silver buckles on his knee, one fine day he'll marry me, pretty Bobby Shafto." And there was another one: "Oh dear, what can the matter be? Dear, dear, what can the matter be? Oh dear, what can the matter be? Johnny's so long at the fair."[61]

When not crooning to Burroughs at the Chelsea, Smith slunk through the streets with junkie poet Jim Carroll, who would achieve literary notice with the publication of *The Basketball Diaries* in 1978. Carroll's rock 'n' roll debut, *Catholic Boy* (1980), is a revved-up rant-a-thon full of street-smart bravado with a pinch of pathos. The song "Nothing Is True" borrows a well-worn Burroughs maxim originally attributed to Hasan i-Sabbah. Carroll rap-sings over bed-of-nails guitars and a relentless beat:

You get nothin' back for all you've saved
Just eternity in a spacious grave
She said, "Nothing is true, everything is permitted"

Things just go from bad to worse
Starts like a kiss and ends like a curse
But nothing's true, she said everything is permitted

Much as Ginsberg, Burroughs, and Kerouac form the Beat triumvirate, Carroll, Smith, and Hell are punk's original troika. This new breed of underground artist was especially informed by Burroughs, and none more than Smith, who tends to his spirit to this day. As she wrote in *Just Kids*:

> William S. Burroughs was simultaneously old and young. Part sheriff, part gumshoe. All writer. He had a medicine chest he kept locked, but if you were in pain, he would open it. He did not like to see his loved ones suffer. If you were infirm he would feed you. He'd appear at your door with a fish wrapped in newsprint and fry it up. He was inaccessible to a girl but I loved him anyway.

> He camped in the Bunker with his typewriter, his shotgun, and his overcoat. From time to time he'd slip on his coat, saunter our way, and take his place at the table we reserved for him in front of the stage. Robert, in his leather jacket, often sat with him. Johnny and the horse.

Thurston Moore bore witness to Smith's comeback performances in April 1977 following her terrible injury in a stage fall earlier that year. It was also the first time he laid eyes on Burroughs. "He was sitting in the audience at CBGB when Patti Smith was playing," Moore recalled.

> I remember it being jam-packed and sitting tightly up against this little round wooden table, and all of a sudden people who worked

there came into the middle of the room and just started yelling, pulling people out of the chairs and pushing people away. They slammed down a table right in the middle of the room and threw some chairs around it. Everybody was really upset while this was going on. Then they escorted William Burroughs and a couple of his friends in and sat them down very diplomatically at this table. I remember sitting there thinking: "Oh my God, it's like William Burroughs." He was this old, grey eminence in a tie and a fedora. He sat there and looked around at us. . . . I remember that was probably the most fabulous Patti Smith performance I ever saw. She was on fire, knowing that William Burroughs was sat right in the middle of the room watching this concert.[62]

Burroughs recognized something powerful in Smith's performances. "By the time he comes to know Patti, he has come through the whole show of *Boujloud*, and the boy dancers to a thousand *rhaitas* swirling," Grauerholz said.[63] (*Boujloud* is a Moroccan festival similar to Halloween, with parades and ritual performances.) Burroughs had admired Smith's shamanic display going back to when he first saw her perform at St. Mark's. "[Burroughs] was very aware that under the pancake makeup, you may be having a holy experience," Grauerholz said. "And the holiness is the interaction between what you're enacting and the audience who is with you."[64]

Smith's return to the stage followed months of convalescence in the wake of her stage accident in Tampa, Florida, on January 26, 1977. At the time, set staple "Ain't It Strange" featured an extended middle section in which Smith whirled about the stage taunting God to "c'mon and make a move." On that night, a change in stage layout caused Smith to misjudge the distance and fall backward over a monitor. She plunged fifteen feet headfirst to the concrete floor of Curtis Hixen Hall, shocking audience, band, and crew. "It was like a Bugs Bunny cartoon," Smith later said. "When he walks over a cliff into midair and just keeps on walking until he realizes there's nothing there."[65] With two cracked vertebrae in her neck, doctors thought she'd be lucky to ever walk again, to say nothing of performing. She was given one of two daunting options: risky surgery with an uncertain outcome or a long and arduous rehabilitation. Smith opted for physical therapy.

During her recovery, Smith broke it off with Tom Verlaine of Television for good. She would soon move on from her regular live-in boyfriend Allen Lanier of Blue Öyster Cult and vanish from the New York scene entirely. But first came the comeback performances at CBGB, which kicked off on Easter Sunday and included punk rockers Dead Boys and the Damned. Around this time, Smith appeared with Burroughs and Ginsberg at a joint signing in the Gotham Book Market, shortly after which she entered the studio to begin work on what would be a well-received comeback record, *Easter* (1977). She scored a monster hit in 1978 with a lyrically modified version of "Because the Night" by Bruce Springsteen. Producer Jimmy Iovine offered the song to Smith, who was recording *Easter* next door to Springsteen's sessions for *Darkness at the Edge of Town*; it would reach number 13 in the United States and number 5 in Great Britain. This success meant more pressure from the suits for a follow-up, though the royalties surely helped during the lean years in Detroit. Smith's next LP, *Wave*, arrived 1979 and was not received with the same elation as *Easter*, but by then it didn't really matter. She had already made the decision to quit the band that bore her name and decamp to Detroit with her soon-to-be-husband, Fred "Sonic" Smith, a former guitarist for proto-punk revolutionaries MC5. She would remain almost entirely out of the public eye for more than a decade.

Ditching the cultural capital of the world for down-and-out Detroit seems as perplexing as Burroughs' own decision to trade New York for humble Lawrence, Kansas. Both had their reasons for wanting a fresh start. "To leave New York was a very tough thing," Smith said in a 1979 interview with Burroughs, eventually published by *SPIN* in 1988. "But it was a great joy, too—you know, like a pioneer." Smith did much of the talking throughout their interview, which would come as no surprise to those who knew her then. Burroughs

was more like a psychic acupuncturist, waiting patiently to in-
sert a needle. Or maybe a Scientology auditor equipped with pre-
cision-honed prompts. "Now it's '79 and I'm still involved in this
thing, but it's come to a point in my life that, like you said, I have to
stop and say, 'What am I doing?'" Smith said. "'Cause I didn't start
doing what I was doing to build myself a career. And I find myself at
a time in my life when, if I'm not careful, that's exactly what's gonna
be built for me."

Burroughs tried to boost Smith's spirits by noting her influence
on the new music scene. "You have the whole punk generation, es-
sentially, who are anti-heroes," he said. "See, they're rejecting the
old values, because having been woken up, they realize that all this
nonsense that they've been brought up on *is* nonsense. And all these
standards. And they're rejecting those standards. So we could re-
gard them, if you will, as something that you have been instrumental in creating." Smith was exasperated by the comparison. "I don't
give a fuck, I don't agree with these kids," she said. "I believe in
heroes. See, I love these kids, but I think that I've spawned a lot of
little monsters, though, sometimes. Because I don't feel the same
way they do. I don't think it's cool to shoot yourself up with heroin
at 21 years old and die. I don't think it's cool to die at 21, you know."

Throughout their conversation, Smith seemed to be searching
for justifications for her decision to leave New York and quit the
business. "I never think that anybody should do art unless they're
a great artist," she said. "I think that people have the right to express themselves in the privacy of their own home, but I don't think
they should perpetuate it on the human race unless they've really
decided that it was something that would help in the advancement
of the human race." Setting the bar that high, she gave herself permission to not even bother to meet it.

Burroughs was also looking for an exit. New York was changing
rapidly by the end of the 1970s. Rising rents and aggressive policing
had erased the character of many neighborhoods, sometimes to the
benefit of public safety, always at the expense of underground culture. Although Burroughs' respectability among the literary elite

remained on an upward trajectory, skyrocketing real estate prices and the economics of his craft made staying in New York untenable. There was another, perhaps more compelling reason to split: he had picked up another junk habit. This was probably inevitable given that he lived in the middle of a heroin supermarket. It was also a side effect of the stature he enjoyed in the punk world. Many on the scene were users. And they all wanted to shoot up with the Pope of Dope. Bockris suggests other contributing factors resulting in relapse. "William had started using heroin again in October 1978 in Los Angeles," he said. "By the beginning of 1979 he was addicted for the first time in ten years. . . . It must be emphasised that Burroughs went back on heroin because he had a severe writer's block. As soon as he got onto dope his typewriter sounded like thunder once again."[66]

Grauerholz decided to return home to Lawrence and managed to convince Burroughs that his survival depended on joining him. "James was worried that if Bill did not get out of New York soon he was going to die there," Bockris said.[67] The only bright spot was that addiction inspired new routines that could be put in his books. Actually, addiction was the ultimate routine, something that could be done—and described—over and over again in much the same way. When Burroughs had a habit, the world, or at least his apartment, was a stage. Among the cast on many a New York evening was author and screenwriter Terry Southern, a prodigious drinker with equally prodigious wit. His banter with Burroughs injects Bockris' *With William Burroughs: A Report From the Bunker* with morbid levity, especially one scene in which Southern dumps out a table's worth of pharmaceutical samples for Burroughs to inspect and, if deemed suitable, ingest. Any similarities between Burroughs and a certain fictional man of medicine are purely coincidental:

BOCKRIS: Here's a diuretic.
SOUTHERN: A diuretic may contain *paregoric*—and you know what *that* means!
BURROUGHS: No, no . . .

SOUTHERN: I say a diuretic is chock-a-block full of a spasm-
relieving nerve-killer ... definitely a coke-based medication!

BURROUGHS: A diuretic ...

SOUTHERN: I'll cook it right up, Bill.

BURROUGHS ... is something to introduce *urination*, my dear—
that's *all* that it is.

SOUTHERN: Is that all a diuretic does? Induce urine?

BURROUGHS: Yes.

SOUTHERN [*GRAVELY*]: Well, Doctor, I suppose we're in for another damnable stint of trial-and-error.

BURROUGHS: Yes, I'm afraid so. Such are the tribulations of the
legitimate drug industry.

BOCKRIS: Nicotinic acid! What's that like?

BURROUGHS: That's *vitamins*, my dear.

Burroughs' reasons for leaving New York were not the same as
Smith's, and neither was their level of output after departure. Burroughs not only continued to make his work publicly available, he
also gave talks and lectures and collaborated on numerous audio
and film projects. He published three novels in the new decade: *Cities of the Red Night* (1981), *The Place of Dead Roads* (1983), and *The
Western Lands* (1987). Smith spent the 1980s and early '90s completely out of the limelight, raising a son and daughter with Fred
Smith and rarely venturing beyond her suburban Detroit neighborhood. Before her husband's death in 1994, the two collaborated on
Dream of Life (1988), a long-in-the-works album that fared poorly
in the marketplace and among critics. Like Burroughs, Smith suffered a string of loved ones dying: in addition to her husband, she
lost Robert Mapplethorpe in 1989, her longtime keyboardist Richard Sohl in 1990, and Burroughs himself in 1997. Before he passed,
Smith visited the old man in Kansas; a home movie from 1996 shows
her sweetly singing at his kitchen table.

Here to Go

> *Musical intelligence, information and directives in*
> *and out through street singers, musical broadcasts,*
> *jukeboxes, records, high school bands, whistling*
> *boys, cabaret performers, singing waiters, transistor*
> *radios . . . red sails in the sunset, way out on the sea.*
>
> WILLIAM S. BURROUGHS, *The Western Lands*

Books of the Dead

In October 1979, a couple of weeks before Halloween, Burroughs made an appearance at the opening of Plan K in Brussels, Belgium—a former sugar refinery that had recently been refashioned as a performance space by an avant-garde theater troupe of the same name. Plan K specialized in stage adaptations of Burroughs' works and had invited the author to speak. Rounding out the bill were musical acts Cabaret Voltaire and Joy Division. The latter gained notoriety with taut, downcast numbers like "She's Lost Control Again" and "Interzone," which takes its name from the seedy no-man's land in *Naked Lunch*. The band's front man, Ian Curtis, was a major Burroughs fan. He would commit suicide only a year later on the eve of what would have been Joy Division's first US tour. But on this night, Curtis had reason to be cheerful; he was meeting a personal hero.

Curtis had discovered Burroughs as a lad on the prowl for anything interesting in the dismal Manchester of the 1970s. The owner of one of the bookstores he frequented, Mike Butterworth, told the website Reality Studio: "He came in every couple of weeks, sometimes more often. Ian bought second-hand copies of *New Worlds*, the great '60s literary magazine edited by Michael Moorcock, which was promoting Burroughs and J. G. Ballard. My friendship with Ian started around 1979: we talked Burroughs, Burroughs, Burroughs."[1] This obsession is winked at in Anton Corbijn's film version of Curtis' short life, *Control*. In one scene the camera pans across the singer's bookshelf, with copies of Burroughs' *Naked Lunch* and *Ah Pook* enjoying pride of position.

The Plan K gig came off well, with Joy Division's doomed front man belting out grim lyrics in a hollow baritone while his bandmates carved out skeletal riffs and rhythms. After Burroughs' reading, Curtis made a beeline for the author. Accounts differ, but the consensus is that he was somehow rebuffed. Curtis asked for a free copy of *The Wild Boys*, as he already owned a few of Burroughs' other titles. Burroughs, whose manners would never permit unwarranted rudeness, likely didn't know with whom he was speaking and dismissed Curtis as an impertinent freeloader. Richard Kirk of Cabaret Voltaire remembers a slightly more lengthy exchange: "My one enduring memory from Plan K was of sitting around a table with Ian, William, and other band members of Joy Division and Cabaret Voltaire. Ian asked William what he thought of Suicide (the New York 'no-wave' band); William thought he meant the act of suicide, and I think he said he disapproved."[2]

It is not known whether Burroughs ever heard about Curtis taking his own life, or if he would have even remembered a rock band that happened to play at the same event where he was booked to speak. A letter to Allen Ginsberg way back in 1956 included the lines, "The English boy was talking about suicide, life not worth living. This seems incredible to me. I think I must be very happy." Coincidence or the future leaking out? With Burroughs, one never knows for sure.

Burroughs may not have entirely achieved happiness—who does?—but in the later years of his life he enjoyed a calm that offered opportunity to reflect on his past and final destiny. A supportive network of friends from James Grauerholz' Lawrence social circle helped Burroughs indulge his interests: cats, shooting, painting, and writing, in that order. The Lawrence years were very productive and included the publishing of new books and collections, gallery showings, and collaborations with an array of music-makers. Friends old and new paid regular visits, including Kurt Cobain and members of Sonic Youth, R.E.M., Hüsker Dü, and Ministry. Burroughs appeared to grow more comfortable in his role as countercultural elder statesman. He traveled far less frequently, but in the early 1980s, he returned to Europe for a series of events that cemented his own reputation as a performer.

In the spring of 1981, Burroughs was in Amsterdam for the One Word, One World Poetry Convention, also attended by Jim Carroll. The Grateful Dead, beatific heroes of the 1960s psychedelic scene turned grizzled road dogs, were currently traipsing through Europe on a tour that saw leader Jerry Garcia getting further hooked on Persian White—a heroin varietal he preferred to smoke rather than shoot. In those days, much effort was spent tending to Garcia's deepening addiction, with entire tours routed around the availability of narcotics. (Garcia would clean up and relapse several times in the years leading up to his death from a heart attack in 1995.) Though he was most associated with Ken Kesey's infamous acid tests, during which the Dead indulged in epic musical freakouts for audiences that often included Beat jester Neal Cassady, Garcia was intimately familiar with the grip of junk. "If drugs are making your decisions for you, they're no fucking good," he told *Rolling Stone* in 1991. "With drugs, the danger is that they run you. Your soul isn't your own."[3] And yet, like Burroughs, he made no apologies for his own indulgence. "Death comes at you no matter what you do in this life, and to equate drugs with death is a facile comparison," he said.[4]

A lifelong Beat obsessive who thrilled to the writing of Ginsberg, Kerouac, and Burroughs, Garcia leapt at an opportunity to meet up with the latter in Amsterdam, a city well known for its drug tourism. Accompanied by then–road manager Rock Scully and bandmate Bob Weir, Garcia met Burroughs at a small Gothic hotel downtown. Scully described the scene:

Burroughs, in porkpie hat and raincoat, looking like a ghost, is checking out as we arrive. He says the hotel is not seedy enough for him. It makes him nervous. I introduce them—although they've met many times before, Burroughs doesn't have a great memory for rock stars. "Mr. Burroughs, do you remember Jerry Garcia from the Grateful Dead?"

"I've always liked the name of your band," said Burroughs. He repeats the words "the Grateful Dead" solemnly. . . . "wonderful occult ring to that. Never heard your music, though." Jerry offers him a tape, which he politely pockets, but you know he'll never play. In his esotero-pedantic strange midwestern way, Burroughs wants to know does the name come from the old folk tale or is it from the Egyptian ship of the sun? "Well, we always thought of it more as, uh, the death of the ego than any specific legend," says Garcia. "Good," says Burroughs like an intelligent tutor of occult sciences. "That is the way Jung would interpret it, too."[5]

Garcia and Burroughs had more in common than it might appear at first blush. Both found themselves at the center of a social and professional phenomenon they had no interest in dominating. Though neither embraced being in charge, both men expressed their creative intent in such a manner that others were inspired to follow. The Grateful Dead in many ways operated as a cult absent a cult leader; Burroughs' cult was (or is) probably smaller in sheer numbers, but it too functioned without much encouragement from its cardinal figure. Despite being identified with the sixties' counterculture, Garcia was avowedly anti-political, in part because he recognized the corrupting influence of power. "For me, the lame part of the Sixties was the political part, the social part," he said. "The real part was the spiritual part."[6] Burroughs had no love for hippies, but he shared Garcia's outlook on politics. "All political movements are basically anti-creative—since a political movement is a form of war," he said in a 1960 interview with Gregory Corso and Ginsberg. His opinion of leaders was equally low. "We must all face the fact that our leaders are certifiably insane or worse," he remarked.[7]

The "leaderless leadership" practiced by Garcia within the Dead organization looks a lot like Burroughs' "do easy"—a path of least resistance based on doing what one wants in the moment in the most relaxed manner possible. In addition, both men saw collaboration as a means of invoking a kind of creative intelligence beyond what an individual could access on their own. Burroughs tapped into this phenomenon through his routines with friends, whereby a concept, idea, or riff would take on a new life when introduced to other minds in the mode of spontaneous creative play. Kerouac, Ginsberg, Kells Elvins, and Terry Southern were among his favorite partners. The skits and scenarios that came out of these collaborative improvisations formed the basis of much of Burroughs' work; pound-for-pound, routines are as important to his oeuvre as cut-ups.

Improvisation in a group context was also important to Garcia, as well as to the Dead fans who trailed the group from city to city, drawn to music that was often so amorphous as to defy conventional description. "It's like the study of chaos," Garcia said. "It may be that you have to destroy forms or ignore them in order to see other levels of organization."[8] Or, as Burroughs stand-in Bill Lee would put it, "exterminate all rational thought."[9] The Grateful Dead's fan community of "tapers" extended the band's legacy by capturing its live performances, much as Burroughs' associates and admirers such as Genesis P-Orridge, Patti Smith, Bill Laswell, Thurston Moore, and others advanced his work and ideas through audio preservation and reconfiguration.

Burroughs and the Dead are also connected through the audio collages of John Oswald, who, directly inspired by Burroughs' own experiments with tape, produces "plunderphonics"—recombinant compositions that draw from pre-recorded sources. "In the early '70s I spent an inordinate amount of time constructing some miniature tape pieces, which I call 'Burrows,' based on texts as read by Bill Burroughs," Oswald said. "My first attempt at audio publishing, in 1975, was not vinyl or cassette but a set of ten of these 'Burrows' on reel-to-reel."[10] In the mid-1990s, Oswald was approached by members of the Grateful Dead to create plunderphonics based on the band's epic, largely instrumental jam "Dark Star"—a song that was never performed the same way twice—using tapes recorded from

1968 to 1993. "At that point, I hadn't listened to any Grateful Dead music in about twenty years," Oswald said. "I do think it's often a good idea to come into a project without a lot of prior knowledge and get kind of an alien's overview of what the music seems to be."[11] The project, called *Grayfolded*, was released as two separate volumes in 1994 and '95. It sounds alien, indeed; a sprawling array of tones and rhythms layered on top of one another in a kind of aural kaleidoscope. It is demonstrative of the collective intelligence that so fascinated Burroughs and Garcia—a creative outcome that could not have been realized but through collaborative processes.

All of the above might have made good conversational fodder for Garcia and Burroughs, but unfortunately, their connection was too brief to result in anything more than what Rock Scully recalled. Burroughs had grown accustomed to exchanging pleasantries with music-world ambassadors he knew next to nothing about. Though such meetings were often amusing, he remained deeply skeptical, even wary, of fame. Celebrities could be used to advance Control's agenda, perhaps without the stars even being aware. Scientology took this approach, and Burroughs had rejected it as a cult. He also loathed the obsequious nature of fame. Burroughs split the world into two camps: Johnsons and Shits. Johnsons were reliable, trustworthy, and minded their own business. Shits had no respect for privacy and always wanted something—the epitome of a psychic vampire.

Burroughs had no way of knowing about Garcia's own struggles with fame, nor was he inclined to ask. If he had, he might have sympathized. During his lifetime (and certainly after) Garcia became an almost religious figure to many Dead fans. The aural fractals spun from Garcia's guitar, along with his persona—something like the Cheshire Cat combined with Eastern sage—invited worship even as Garcia himself rejected it, much as Burroughs' own aura attracted plenty of freaks and hangers-on. By 1981, Garcia had to deal with kids sprawled out in the hallways of his hotel suite hoping to get high with their rock 'n' roll Buddha, along with endless hassles from law enforcement, who saw Dead shows as a miracle ticket to drug busts. Unlike Burroughs, who now had a fortress of solitude in Lawrence, Garcia remained on the touring treadmill until his death, just two years before Burroughs made his final departure to the Western Lands.

Interzone to Eurozone

Burroughs again crossed the Atlantic in 1982 for the Final Academy —a series of UK events co-organized by Genesis P-Orridge and billed as a convening of "like minds who share the common ground of The Third Mind—located at the intersection point of cut-ups, where the future leaks through—where logic is short-circuited, deprogramming Control."[12] That's a lot to fit on a show poster. Taking place at various venues in London over four days between September 29 and October 2, the shows placed Burroughs' work in context with the emerging "occulture." Sharing the bill were Brion Gysin, John Giorno, and post-punk acts Psychic TV, Marc Almond, 23 Skidoo, Last Few Days, and Cabaret Voltaire. Film showings, readings, and experimental music sets split the difference between multimedia art installation and tribal ritual.

Burroughs' original concept for the Final Academy was a bivouac in the tradition of Hassan i-Sabbah's mountain fortress Alamut, where youths—male ones, at least—would be taught "a true and different knowledge."[13] When Burroughs was unable to find the money to purchase Aleister Crowley's Loch Ness estate, which instead ended up with Jimmy Page, he published a series of articles in *Mayfair* and various underground magazines as a kind of virtual syllabus. Burroughs intended to compile this work in a volume called *Academy 23*, which never saw the light of day (though portions would appear in other collections such as *The Job*). The Final Academy shows were hardly a substitute for the metaphysical-martial training camp Burroughs had long envisioned. Still, the events reflected an ongoing interest in Burroughs' methods and ideas, which offered a conceptual and practical framework for a new breed of sonic experimenters like Psychic TV, Coil, and others.

Adjunct events took place in Manchester and Liverpool on October 4 and 5, respectively, and featured much the same lineup plus Marc Almond of leather-clad synth-poppers Soft Cell, whose 1981 album *Non-Stop Erotic Cabaret* occasioned outcries among England's polite society. The band's best-known single, "Tainted Love," cracked the US Top Ten a couple months before Almond's appearance at the Final Academy, adding a dose of pop legitimacy to the proceedings. Matthew Levi Stevens, author of *The Magical Universe of William S. Burroughs*, describes what it was like to attend:

> September, 1982, and William S. Burroughs is in town for The Final Academy. Psychic TV are prime movers, and thanks to Genesis P-Orridge I have a ringside seat. Everybody wants to get their books signed, or have their photo taken with "Uncle Bill" as he is affectionately known. I choose to do neither, deliberately . . .
>
> Eventually I am in just the right place at just the right time. . . . When I get a chance to speak to William in person, I ask him about Magic, and whether he would care to recommend any books on the subject? Without hesitation he mentions Dion Fortune's *Psychic Self-Defense*, even though he qualifies it as "a bit old-fashioned." Then, without prompting on my part, he begins to talk of Black Magic and Curses in Morocco, travelling with Medicine Men up the Amazon, and Astral Projection and Dream Control. I realise that for Burroughs all this is UTTERLY REAL, the "Magical Universe" in fact.[14]

The musical performances at the Final Academy were alternately entrancing and assaultive. John Giorno delivered poetic harangues backed by a live band featuring members of other acts on the bill. Brion Gysin read cut-ups and sang songs, accompanied by French guitarist Ramuntcho Matta. P-Orridge's new group, Psychic TV, pushed the envelope with an intense mixed-media set that sent some straight for the exits. Though only a teenager at the time, Stevens had the presence of mind to take notes:

> TV monitors flank the stage, where Genesis P sits in near darkness, intoning a carefully prepared Statement to pre-recordings of soundtrack music, ritual ambience and holographic 3D sound effects. Tinkling bells and the moaning of Tibetan thighbone trumpets: the sound of souls in torment. A squeaking bicycle wheel. "Are you asleep, or do you want to wake up?" asks a pre-recorded, nasal voice.... Meanwhile, the visuals: symbols of Control—"sex, power and magick"—I am amused to see that it's clearly more than a lot of the hard-core Punks can take. The atmosphere is almost religious, for all that the images on screen are transgressive: bloodletting, genital piercing, initiation rites—something sexual, even if it isn't clear exactly what. Glancing across to where William Burroughs sits, flanked by the Psychick Youth faithful, he seems captivated.[15]

Burroughs himself made the biggest impression, much as he did at the 1978 Nova Convention. "When Mr. Burroughs climbs onto the stage and takes his place behind the wooden desk, shuffling his papers and stretching awkwardly—like a doctor about to give a particularly unpleasant diagnosis—you could hear the proverbial pin drop," Stevens wrote.[16] Artist and designer John Coulthart had a similar takeaway: "I'm not sure now what I expected from his reading but I remember being surprised at the degree of humour involved. What might seem cold and dead on the page came to life dripping with satiric vitriol under the stress of that snarling delivery."[17] The Final Academy shows anticipated a future where live concert audiences routinely record performances on personal electronic devices. "I have never been to an event that is so obviously being documented for posterity—it seems as if every other person has a camera or tape-recorder of some kind," Stevens perceptively noted.

In 2012, Joe Ambrose—writer, musician, and unofficial tender of the Burroughs legacy—took steps to bring Final Academy–inspired performances to contemporary audiences. "I'd just moved back from Tangier after ten years in and out of Morocco and I knew the anniversary of the original event was coming up," Ambrose said.[18]

> People in London were whingeing that there was nothing going on, by which they meant that there were no countercultural events happening anymore. I'd done hundreds of Burroughs/Moroccan Trance/hip-hop events in London with my group Islamic Diggers. We did shows with Anita Pallenberg, with Lydia Lunch, with the Master Musicians of Joujouka, that kind of shit. So, having so much respect for what the original creators of the Final Academy had done, having heard so much about it, I decided, why not? It was a gas to do and I was especially chuffed that Genesis P-Orridge sent one of the participants, Matthew Levi Stevens, a message of support, saying she was glad that her efforts were being appreciated. It was a wonderful night which didn't in any way try to ape the original.

In the final two decades of his life, Burroughs continued to receive requests to speak at events around the world. Such offers often came from outside literary and academic quarters. "There came a time in the late '70s, when it was apparent to me that there was an opportunity to do shows in clubs, actual entertainment venues more usually used for music—rock music or punk music," Grauerholz said.[19] Burroughs and Grauerholz would choose whether to accept an offer by balancing enthusiasm with economics. Sometimes it simply came down to whether the gig seemed fun. Burroughs certainly had a great time with Laurie Anderson reading from *Cities of the Red Night* on her Home of the Brave tour a few years later. "They had a natural kinship," Grauerholz said. "He was very fond of Laurie."[20]

In 1983, Burroughs and Giorno embarked on a brisk tour of Scandinavia that took them to Sweden, Norway, Finland, Amsterdam, and Denmark. Once again the shows combined readings and musical performances. Denmark's the Sods, who would soon change their name to Sort Sol, appeared at the Copenhagen gig. That band's debut, *Minutes to Go*, took its title from a collection of cut-up poems by Burroughs, Gysin, Gregory Corso, and Sinclair Beiles and is considered the first Danish punk record. Burroughs more than held his own alongside the younger artists. His ability to capture a crowd's attention with nothing more than his speaking voice was a talent Giorno watched develop from readings at St. Mark's and Max's Kansas City alongside Patti Smith. "He was confronted by this energy," Giorno said. "And he began for the first time—though he had it in him, it's not like it came out of the blue—this great style of performing. He figured out on some subliminal or unconscious level, how to be a great performer. . . . One of the greatest performers in the world."[21]

The Scandinavian tour, which filmmakers Lars Movin and Steen Møller Rasmussen memorialized in the 2007 documentary *Words of Advice: William S. Burroughs On the Road*, shows an aging Burroughs in top form. He delivers some of the best bits from the yet-unpublished *The Western Lands*, such as the scathing mummy routine:

> The most arbitrary, precarious, and bureaucratic immortality blueprint was drafted by the ancient Egyptians. First you had to get yourself mummified, and that was very expensive, making immortality a monopoly of the truly rich. And then you had to reserve your tomb in a *reputable* necropolis . . . like a good country club. Then your continued immortality in the Western Lands was entirely dependent on the continued existence of your mummy. That is why they had their mummies guarded by demons and hid good.

Burroughs' trek across northern Europe demonstrated his blossoming influence outside the English-speaking underground. Back in the States, his icon was only growing larger among a new horde of punk acts rebelling against the trickle-down tackiness of the Reagan years.

This Is Hardcore

In America, punk had metastasized into an imposing movement that belied its humble beginnings as a disaffected writers' circle in New York City. Now the scene took increasingly aggressive stances against the system, with music that was meaner, faster, louder. The new sound was called hardcore, and it aimed to take no prisoners. No wonder then that its adherents looked to Burroughs for inspiration. "Punk rock was influenced by Burroughs because punk rock was this huge, international, anti-authoritarian, cultural rediscovery, and recreation revolution," said V. Vale, publisher of *RE/Search*, a celebrated underground magazine that in January 1982 featured Burroughs on the cover.[22] "In the sense that punk was all about trying to tell the truth and be anti-authoritarian, and the black humor, I think Burroughs was totally punk rock and a role model," Vale said.

"A lot of the pioneers of punk had read Burroughs extensively,"[23] said Jello Biafra, the brainiac former front man of San Francisco's Dead Kennedys. "Some of the ideas kind of trickled into peoples' work, and other people absorbed that work not knowing how much had come from Burroughs." Biafra recalled using cut-ups to power through a case of writer's block while composing lyrics for "The Man with the Dogs," the b-side to an early Dead Kennedys single. "The lyrics were not coming together. I couldn't figure out how I wanted to tell the story, or what belonged where.... It was kind of a big mess," Biafra said. "And so I finally threw up my hands and figured, what have I got to lose? I'm gonna try the Burroughs method and I'm gonna cut up every line of this song and move it around until I get something I like. And sure enough, it worked."[24]

Iggy Pop of the Stooges—a band that influenced pretty much every punk and hardcore act that came after—also dipped into the Burroughs bag: "I wrote a song called 'Gimmie Some Skin,' which is one of my most depraved-sounding numbers, apparently, and I talk about [Burroughs] in it," he said. "The second verse is 'Billy Billy Lee ain't no fool / All the junkies think he's cool.'"[25] Sonic Youth guitarist Lee Ranaldo smartly noted that the Burroughs connection goes back even further. "Certainly someone like Dylan took a lot of inspiration," he said. "A very sort of modern approach to language, and using it to uncover different truths. I think that's why people in the music community have responded to William's work—because there were a lot of ideas that you could take off from."[26]

Punk-rockabilly trailblazer Tav Falco is a dyed-in-the-wool Burroughs fan. Enduring on the underground since 1979, his band Panther Burns enjoy a cult following on multiple continents, though they are by no means a household name. In 2012, Falco wrote a well-informed article for *Vienna Review* previewing an exhibit called "Cut-ups, Cut-ins, Cut-outs: The Art of William S. Burroughs," which showed at the Kunsthalle Wien in Vienna. Five years later Falco made an impassioned—and wordy—case for Burroughs' appeal:

> Any underground musician alive knows the writings of Burroughs and has fallen under overarching effluvia that spewed from the unruly, unhinged, unsavoury, incurable, uncalculated, unapologetic, uncompromising, unstable, unconscious, unbridled, unmerciful, non-linear, incongruous dagger called a pen. . . . [They] have subliminally absorbed his habits of heightened sensory perception within their own lives as a built-in. For them Burroughs is a byword for the uncanny, the queer, the unholy, the unexpurgated, the epitome of art damage.[27]

One reason punk was able to absorb Burroughs' influence is because it is a stylistically amorphous genre where intent is more important than technique. As noted in chapter 6, the first wave of punk lacked musical signifiers besides the songs being loud and easy to play. The 1980s hardcore acts were more go-for-the-throat, but they maintained the do-it-yourself attitude that powers the scene to this day.

Punk is all about adaptability, making use of the tools right in front of you—whether it's a typewriter, scissors, or a cheap pawn shop guitar. No surprise, then, that Burroughs would become an inspiration for musical malcontents on both American coasts and points in-between.

In the early 1980s, Burroughs visited Los Angeles and the Bay Area, where his name was already legend in a West Coast scene that included acts such as Dead Kennedys, Off!, and Black Flag. These bands cranked up the venom well beyond their New York and UK predecessors. In San Francisco, Burroughs was interviewed by Raymond Foye, writing under the pseudonym Ray Rumor for *Search and Destroy* (which took its name from a Stooges song). As Foye noted in his intro, "William Seward Burroughs has been mentioned by more bands interviewed in *Search and Destroy* than any other thinking writer—to punk rock, he is something of a major provocateur."[28] Burroughs also posed for Bay Area punk photographer Ruby Ray. "I was a nervous wreck and only had about 10 minutes to shoot him and I had to make do with the location where he was attending a party," she said.

> We brought the guns that were the props and I chose the garden to contrast the guns with. I kept praying the whole time that the film was exposed properly, and prayed again when I had to develop it. It wasn't like with digital cameras where every photo comes out perfectly exposed; you really have to think when using film and natural light. Bill was at ease with me and I love the way the pictures came out.[29]

Hüsker Dü was an American hardcore band that formed in Saint Paul, Minnesota, in 1979. Powered by creative and personal tensions between guitarist-songwriter Bob Mould and drummer-songwriter Grant Hart (they both sang lead, with Mould taking the lion's share of vocals), Hüsker Dü elevated hardcore to the level of art. Fusing speed and aggression with melodic sensibility and affective lyrics, the band was a powerful influence on the acts who came in their wake, with albums like *Zen Arcade*, *New Day Rising*, and *Flip Your Wig* inspiring a whole new genre offshoot known as emo. Hüsker Dü was also notable in that its co-leaders, Mould and Hart, were (respectively) gay and bisexual men working in a genre known for tough-guy posturing. Studiously non-swishy, Burroughs represented a kind of masculine homosexuality that defied stereotypes. Similarly, Hüsker Dü boldly challenged prevailing attitudes in the hardcore scene with a string of albums and tours before calling it quits in 1988. Reasons for the band's dissolution included their manager's suicide, along with Hart's addiction to heroin. He eventually kicked for good, but years of abuse would contribute to his death in 2017 due to complications from liver cancer and hepatitis C.

Hart, whose songwriting gifts exceeded that of most punks, was a lifelong Burroughs fan and a personal friend. "I met him during the Giorno Poetry Systems photoshoot for *Diamond Hidden in the Mouth of a Corpse*, and he showed a mutual interest in me," Grant said.[30]

> I've always been a bit sympathetic to the Greek method of like, you learn from an older person. In the case of William and me, there was nothing sexual, but there was a very strong affection.... You know, being sweet to people who deserve some sweetness. I think people like him end up being so lonely because of their intellect. To have had the honor of even meeting him.... Here's a man who was one of the people responsible for knocking censorship out of the American reality, hopefully never to return.[31]

Grant hung out with Burroughs around ten times in the last two decades of the author's life. Unlike those who turned up at the Bunker or in Lawrence hoping to boost their own hipness through association, Grant seemed genuinely attuned to Burroughs' emotional well-being. As he said in 2000:

> I'd like to think, and I know, that I contributed to some happy moments in his life. He had made a comment to me during the

third-to-last time we spent together. He said, "Why do you tell me jokes? You're the only person who ever comes around here with a joke." And I told him, "Well, I hear a good joke and I tell it." But people thought they had to have a thick skin when they came to visit William, or put their best foot forward, trying to be something that they might very well be, but not all the time, you know? I think a lot of people put on a show for William when they were in contact with him, and eventually he was deprived of that much humanity. I think he got a lot of it living in Lawrence, doing a lot of his own shopping, that sort of thing. Here's a man, a French legionnaire, a member of the American Academy of Arts and Letters, and nobody's telling him jokes! That's pretty sad. So, from that point on, whenever we'd talk, I'd keep my ears out for one that William would like.[32]

Hart's post–Hüsker Dü band, Nova Mob, took its name from the Control addicts in *Nova Express*. That group, which ran from 1989 to 1994, performed edgy pop-rock songs with smart and seedy subject matter. "Shoot Your Way to Freedom," from the band's 1994 self-titled release, taps a Burroughs vein for sure:

Beyond these iron stalls
Beyond these iron walls
You've got to shoot, shoot, shoot
Your way to freedom

From cradle to the grave
A man is but a slave
You've got to shoot, shoot, shoot
Your way to freedom

Hart made extensive use of randomness in his compositions. "I defer to chance operations very, very often," he said. "At its worst, chance will mimic a bad decision, and bad decisions are made all the time in art. When looking for one word out of a billion that works, you gotta allow the word to find you. And it's only gonna happen if you open up the possibilities of chance."[33]

Grant's final solo album, *The Argument* (2013), is a take on John Milton's *Paradise Lost* as initially adapted by Burroughs (and expanded considerably by the songwriter). "There were about two pages that were dedicated to a real brief treatment of *Paradise Lost*," Hart said. "I thought, 'This is an interesting project, who's doing music for it? Really? I could do better than that.'"[34] The album also draws musical inspiration from fellow Burroughs admirer David Bowie. Like Bowie's *Blackstar*, released just a few days before his death, reviews for *The Argument* were glowing. Better still, Grant had a little time to enjoy them. Unfortunately, he was unable to deliver a follow-up before his own untimely death. Perhaps Hart is keeping Burroughs entertained in the Western Lands.

William S. Burroughs Superstar

Burroughs' music world notoriety was also amplified by his old friend, the poet John Giorno. A steady supply of albums released by Giorno Poetry Systems featured Burroughs alongside the likes of Tom Waits, Lydia Lunch, David Johansen, Arto Lindsay, Swans, COIL, Diamanda Galas, Hüsker Dü, Sonic Youth, Cabaret Voltaire, Einstürzende Neubauten, Butthole Surfers, Nick Cave, and more. LPs such as *Better an Old Demon than a New God*, *A Diamond Hidden in the Mouth of a Corpse*, and *Smack My Crack* cemented Burroughs' reputation among edgy bohemians and still hold value in today's collectible vinyl market.

Giorno Poetry Systems, a bastion of independent media in the 1970s and '80s, owes its very existence to Burroughs. "In 1965, even before founding Giorno Poetry Systems, I began recording my friend William Burroughs, starting with tape experiments at his Centre Street loft and with Brion Gysin at the Hotel Chelsea," Giorno said.[35] "We taped the riotous Democratic National Convention in the summer of 1968, and presented the results that September at New York's Central Park Bandshell. Three months later

I featured William in the inaugural installation of Dial-A-Poem at the Architectural League of New York."[36] Launched in 1969, Dial-A-Poem was a telephone number that people could call to hear poems taken from recordings that Giorno had made. (Dial-A-Poem no doubt inspired Dial-A-Song, a service operated by brainy pop duo They Might Be Giants from 1985 to 2006.)

Giorno remains a Burroughs booster; to this day he lives on the third floor of 222 Bowery and keeps Burroughs' beloved Bunker much as it was when the author lived there. As Nate Friedman wrote in a 2015 article in *The Observer*:

> [Giorno] took over the Bunker from Burroughs after he died, and he hasn't touched it, so when you walk up from the once-demonic promenade of the Bowery now outfitted with clubby restaurants and juice bars, and then pass through the iron gates and two bulletproof doors and up a flight of stairs you can come into his bedroom and see everything kept the same: the target poster riddled with BB gun shrapnel, the typewriter, the sunglasses on a bedside table, the NRA membership flyer hung proudly on the wall, the bed still made, the desk still set for someone to sit and write.[37]

Burroughs' visibility in pop culture was further advanced by filmmaker and musician Gus Van Sant. Van Sant became infatuated with the author as a youth and based his 16 mm film from 1977, *The Discipline of DE* (aka "do easy"), on a story from Burroughs' 1973 collection *Exterminator!*. The ten-minute movie endorses Burroughs' Zen approach for domestic living. "DE simply means doing whatever you do in the easiest most relaxed way you can manage which is also the quickest and most efficient way," says Van Sant's narration, taken from Burroughs' original text. "You can start right now tidying up your flat, moving furniture or books, washing dishes, making tea, sorting papers. Don't fumble, jerk, grab an object. Drop cool possessive fingers onto it like a gentle old cop making a soft arrest."[38]

Van Sant sought out Burroughs for his blessing to make the movie. He got a lot more than that. "I found him listed in the New York telephone book," the filmmaker said.

> I was under the impression that if I visited him and asked his permission in person that I would have more of a chance. And that may have been true—he did give me an okay—but also I was able to ask a few questions about the ideas in the story. One of the things he said during our visit, not in the film or story, was, "Of course, when anyone knocks something over, or trips over something, or breaks anything, they are at that moment thinking of someone they don't like." This was illuminating.[39]

Van Sant's work behind the lens is steeped in Burroughs' ideas and methods. "I believe the properly manipulated image can provoke an audience to the Burroughsian limit of riot, rampant sex, instantaneous death, even spontaneous combustion," he said in a 1991 interview.[40] Heavy stuff. Less so was the 1985 audio collaboration *William S. Burroughs: The Elvis of Letters*, which features Van Sant's guitar, bass, and drum machine providing cheerful accompaniment to Burroughs' wry recitations. The EP's four cuts—"Burroughs Break," "Word Is Virus," "Millions of Images," and "The Hipster Bebop Junkie"—could even be described as charming, which would probably annoy the album's authors.[41]

A few years later, in 1989, Burroughs appeared in Van Sant's breakthrough film *Drugstore Cowboy*, which starred Matt Dillon and Kelly Lynch as hapless addicts who commit a string of robberies to support their habit. Burroughs played the role of an elder junkie who dispenses wisdom to Dillon. Van Sant described how the character evolved during pre-production:

> I sent [the script] to Burroughs to see if he wanted to be in the film. He liked it quite a bit, but he didn't like the kind of down-and-out-had-nothing-going-on quality of this aging character. He thought

he could have something going. He also turned him into a priest, which was a character he had written about, various priests in his books.[42]

Burroughs' role as a junkie priest cemented his icon among movie-goers in the emerging alternative generation, as did his appearance on countless commercially released recordings in pop, rock, hip-hop, alternative, and experimental genres. By the late twentieth century, Burroughs had become an emblem of an America that not only tolerated but willingly embraced strangeness.

Dead City Radio hit shelves in 1990 and showcased Burroughs with musical accompaniment from John Cale, Donald Fagen, Lenny Pickett, Chris Stein, and Sonic Youth. The album was the brainchild of Hal Wilner, a music producer who had previously worked for *Saturday Night Live*, where he booked Burroughs for an appearance in December 1981. At the top of the show, cameras revealed Burroughs sitting at a large, starkly lit desk with a vintage typewriter on his far right. He introduced Dr. Benway to 100 million television viewers across the country as patriotic music played in the background—a counterculture icon beamed into American homes much like trusted news anchor Walter Cronkite.

Wilner later visited Burroughs at the Bunker, where he engaged in a foolhardy effort to keep up with the old man's day drinking. "Within an hour or two, we were getting on to some insane subjects," Wilner recalled.[43] "One of them was our mutual love of Marlene Dietrich. And he starts singing 'Falling in Love Again' to me in German at the table." It was at that moment that Wilner decided to make a record with Burroughs as the featured performer. Standout tracks on *Dead City Radio* include "Thanksgiving Prayer," which Burroughs recited in a dry croak over sweeping strings that conjure images of amber waves of grain:

For John Dillinger in hope he is still alive
Thanksgiving Day, November Twenty-eighth, 1986

Thanks for the wild turkey and the passenger pigeons
Destined to be shit out through wholesome American guts
Thanks for a continent to despoil and poison
Thanks for Indians to provide a modicum
Of challenge and danger
Thanks for vast herds of bison to kill and skin
Leaving the carcasses to rot
Thanks for bounties on wolves and coyotes
Thanks for the American dream
To vulgarize and to falsify until the bare lies shine through
Thanks for the KKK
For nigger-killing lawmen feeling their notches
For decent church-going women with their mean, pinched, bitter,
*   evil faces*
Thanks for "Kill a Queer for Christ" stickers
Thanks for laboratory AIDS
Thanks for Prohibition
And the war against drugs
Thanks for a country where nobody's allowed to mind their own
*   business*
Thanks for a nation of finks
Yes, thanks for all the memories, all right let's see your arms!
You always were a headache and you always were a bore
Thanks for the last and greatest betrayal
Of the last and greatest of human dreams

"Ah Pook the Destroyer/Brion Gysin's All-Purpose Bedtime Story"
is a short treatise on Control backed by John Cale's effervescent
viola. "A New Standard by Which to Measure Infamy" tells the tale
of a male passenger on the Titanic who dressed in drag in order to
secure passage on a lifeboat; Steely Dan's Donald Fagen provides
sparse piano embellishments. Burroughs imagines a Control-free
future on "No More Stalins, No More Hitlers," another track featuring John Cale:

We have a new type of rule now. Not one-man rule, or rule of aristocracy or plutocracy, but of small groups elevated to positions of absolute power by random pressures and subject to political and economic factors that leave little room for decision.

They are representatives of abstract forces who have reached power through surrender of self. The iron-willed dictator is a thing of past.

There will be no more Stalins, no more Hitlers.

The rulers of this most insecure of all worlds are rulers by accident. Inept, frightened pilots at the controls of a vast machine they cannot understand, calling in experts to tell them which buttons to push.

Wilner's instincts about how to best present Burroughs on record were canny. "I heard him and saw him in a very traditional light," he says. "I saw him as true Americana; a product of this country.... That he should be right up there in front of a map or a railroad track or a flag, as you might see John Wayne or Johnny Cash. He was one of *those* . . . and a true natural at it."[44]

Another interesting project that Burroughs participated in toward the end of his life was *The Black Rider: The Casting of the Magic Bullets*, a stage musical collaboration between Burroughs, playwright Robert Wilson, and avant-rock rapscallion Tom Waits. A Brechtian riff on the Faust legend, based on the German folktale "Der Freischütz," *The Black Rider* also evokes the tragic death of Joan Vollmer. The story concerns a bookkeeper named Wilhelm who becomes smitten with the daughter of a local woodsman. He asks permission to marry the girl, which the father refuses based on Wilhelm's ineptitude as a hunter. Dejected, he heads into the forest, where he intends to teach himself to shoot. There Wilhelm encounters Pegleg, who offers seven magic bullets guaranteed to hit their mark: six for Wilhelm, one that the devil gets to steer. It's no spoiler to say that things don't turn out well for our hero. *The Black Rider* comes off like a Burroughs routine set to music, with semi-autobiographical parables striking notes of desperation and mordacity. Wilson explained how the show came together:

> I had read the 17th century German ghost story and thought to ask Tom Waits to write the music, as Tom and I had been talking about making a work together. I had asked Tom to write the songs and the lyrics, and to write a book based on Der Freischutz. Tom said he didn't feel comfortable writing a book, but would write the lyrics and the music. Allen Ginsberg had been saying to me for years that I should work with Burroughs. He even wrote to Burroughs after Allen and I did the opera Cosmopolitan Greetings in Hamburg, so I thought to ask William if he would be interested. He asked me to go to Lawrence, Kansas, to discuss it with him. We had previously been on several programs together at St. Mark's Church and Judson Church. I went with dramaturg Wolfgang Wiens to Lawrence and spoke to William about a collaboration; showed him drawings of an outline that I had made of the visual book. He immediately said yes, in fact we made recordings of him speaking and singing during the few days I spent in Kansas.[45]

The trio workshopped together in Hamburg, and Wilson says that, at the end of the day, it's difficult to know precisely who contributed what. "Tom was very much obsessed with Bill's work, but I'm not so sure of Bill's familiarity with Tom," Wilson says. "We sent Bill recordings of Tom's music and he gravitated towards it very strongly." Given the talents involved, it's no wonder that the musical has stood the test of time. "I think it was a very strong collaboration between Burroughs, Waits and myself," Wilson says. "We were all very different, and it was a unique piece of theatre that played for nine years in repertory at the Thalia theater in Hamburg. It's a classic story and was a perfect fit for the three of us."[46]

The Black Rider continues to be performed around the world to great acclaim. Following the debut in Hamburg in 1990, it subsequently showed at the Edmonton Fringe Festival in Canada in 1998 and the New York Fringe Festival the following year. A 2004 touring version starred Marianne Faithfull in the role of Pegleg, the Mephisophelean trickster who gets Wilhelm "mixed up in the magic bullets that lead straight to the devil's work ... like marijuana leads to heroin," to quote Burroughs' lyrics. Recent productions of *The Black Rider* in Sydney, Australia, and Oakland, California, in 2017 delighted audiences and critics, who commended Burroughs' dialog as well as the creepy, carnivalesque music composed by Waits.

The Black Rider owes its longevity in part to the Waits album of the same name, which features a delightful version of the standard "T'ain't No Sin" creakily sung by Burroughs himself. Released on Island Records in September 1993, the album finds Waits at the peak of his carnival barker powers. Standout cut "Crossroads" aims for the Burroughs sensibility and ably sticks its mark:

The more of them magics you use, the more bad days you have without them
So it comes down finally to all your days being bad without the bullets
It's magics or nothing
Time to stop chippying around and kidding yourself,
Kid, you're hooked, heavy as lead

It's a shame that Wilson and Waits did not have the opportunity to collaborate with the author again before his death in 1997; after all, there were at least five more bullets left to be fired. Perhaps the devil got the first shot.

Burroughs also made a mark in the world of hip-hop. Improbable as it may seem, Burroughs' use of urban noise in his recordings has something in common with the streetwise collages of rap's fiercest guerilla intellectuals, Public Enemy. Front man Chuck D's lyrical assaults on Establishment powers are set against sonic elements that wouldn't be out of place on one of Burroughs' tape curses:

sirens, alarms, gunshots, and other "trouble sounds." To be sure, the privileged Burroughs had little in common with the inner-city black kids making this music. Still, his vision of militant youths bum rushing Control is in keeping with the spirit that characterizes some of the best hip-hop, classic or contemporary. The genre loves its outlaws, and Burroughs was certainly that.

Burroughs captured the imaginations of the Disposable Heroes of Hiphoprisy, who in 1993 collaborated with the author for the album *Spare Ass Annie and Other Tales*—a buoyant, beat-happy affair built around such classic routines as "The Talking Asshole" and "Dr. Benway." Burroughs recorded his parts separately, with producer Hal Wilner threading everything together. The author is toasted by MC Zulu, who boasts, "Check dis out. From Lawrence, Kansas, reading from *Naked Lunch* and weighing slightly over 100 pounds, Uncle Bill." The record doesn't sound as awkward as one might imagine, and that's probably because Burroughs' fragmented oratory fits well over repetitive rhythms. The overall effect is one of trancelike invocation, in keeping with the Burroughs aesthetic.

In 1993, rapper, musician, and producer Justin Warfield dropped *My Field Trip to Planet 9*, a record loaded with verbal bullets fired with gleeful precision. "Burroughs has a special rhythm all his own, his literary style is a big influence on me as a hip-hop lyricist," Warfield said. "I don't think most people in the rap world are hip to the cut-ups, but if they checked out Burroughs and Gysin they'd certainly see the connections between the two."[47] It wasn't the last time that Warfield—who achieved mainstream recognition in the 2000s with alt-rockers She Wants Revenge—would dip into the Burroughs bag. Joining forces with UK producers Bomb the Bass, Warfield delivered the *Naked Lunch*–inspired "Bug Powder Dust" in 1994. The track's lyrics read like an inventory of Burroughs-isms: "I'm like Bill Lee writing when he's in Tangiers / And now I'm on a soul safari with my Beatnik peers," Warfield raps. Another verse features the lines "Like an exterminator running low on dust / I'm bug powder itchin' and it can't be trussed / Interzone trippin' and

I'm off to Annexia / I gotta get a typewriter that's sexier." Following references to William Tell and Jimmy Page, Warfield drives it home with an explicit hook:

Bug powder dust an' mugwump jism
The wild boys runnin' 'round Interzone trippin'
Led into control about the Big Brother
Tryin' like hard to not blow my cover

And so, with approximately zero effort, Burroughs became an MC. His laconic delivery was readymade for sampling, as borne out by Material's *Seven Souls*, Bill Laswell's *The Western Lands*, and DJ Spooky's *Rhythm Science*—three recordings whose hypnotic grooves benefit from Burroughs' distinctive drawl. Numerous other acts have sampled Burroughs, including El-P, Dälek, Cut Chemist, and Kool Keith, to name a few. Burroughs' influence on hip-hop is subliminal and evolving, with new generations of artists and producers weaned on the dope beats and brash banter of their Burroughs-admiring antecedents.

Cutting into the Future

In 1982, Burroughs sat down with members of the band Devo for a rollicking conversation published in the February 1982 edition of *Trouser Press*. Formed in 1973, Devo set a Burroughsian course right out of the gate. Their name referred to the concept of "de-evolution"—a persistent theme in Burroughs' work. The band's surreal-yet-sprightly pop-rock injected absurdist satire into the mainstream charts. Devo scored an improbable hit in 1980 with "Whip It" but seemed entirely unconcerned with repeating their success, choosing instead to double down on their mocking image and deadpan music. Their *Trouser Press* back-and-forth with Burroughs is notable in part because it may be the first time the author had been thrown together with artists whose intellects came close to matching his own. Burroughs' conversation with Devo's Mark

Mothersbaugh and Jerry Casale covers a dizzying array of topics—from Jordache jeans to religious fundamentalism to the likelihood of America becoming a fascist state. It's also laugh-out-loud funny:

JOHN CASALE: William, you and David Bowie had a discussion in *Rolling Stone* in 1974 about whether to use sonic warfare on-stage. Bowie said he was not interested in doing that to people. He said he would never turn it on a crowd and make them shit their pants. I suppose we would. . . .

WILLIAM S. BURROUGHS: In a sense, if any artist is successful, he would do exactly that. If you wrote about death completely convincingly, you'd kill all your readers.

JC: What's going too far, though? Making them shit their pants?

WSB: Would it be going too far to kill them? I'll ask that question.

JC: Well, I suppose there's still some liberalism left in Devo; we'd say yes. We want 'em to come back and shit again.[48]

The entire interview is prescient. "If there's anything important about history," Casale said, "it's that stupidity wins. We're paranoid for good reasons: hundreds of years where assholes take over, knowledge is lost, and things go backwards." Burroughs didn't need much convincing. "There's something behind the whole scene—any scene," he said. "If you see chaos, ask yourself who profits in this. Somebody does. Of course, in a situation of chaos, one group who are going to profit are the very rich. Not the fairly rich—I'm talking about a very, very select club. They can weather anything." Casale wasted no time on the rebound:

It's ridiculous; all you have to do is look at Jerry Falwell and Ronald McDonald and Ronald Reagan and start putting it all together. What we see then, are born-again Christians dressed in double-knit pilgrim suits with particle guns that look like blunderbusses gettin' in station wagons and searching out people who aren't Christian enough to eat Thanksgiving turkey.

Devo didn't see humanity as destined for uplift, but rather the opposite. The reason? There's simply too much money in keeping people dumb.

Burroughs didn't consider himself a futurist, but he was embraced by other forward-looking thinkers. William Gibson, the science-fiction author whose visions inspired the tech-centric movement known as cyberpunk, first encountered Burroughs at age thirteen. "Burroughs was like an electric guitar player who invented effects pedals," Gibson said. "He could do things in prose, in the late '50s or early '60s, that no other writer on the planet could do. I bought a paperback anthology of Beat writing—I hid it from my mother because of bad words and the excerpts from *Naked Lunch*, which I'm sure I initially found almost completely unreadable—but I kept the book and over time, I sort of cracked the code."[49]

Code was about to take on a whole new primacy in everyday reality. All it took was the right device for Burroughs' concept of a language virus to reach the level of global contagion. The arrival of the personal computer opened up new possibilities for cutting into and reassembling media. As author, futurist, and critic Douglas Rushkoff says, "The first time I hit the Edit menu on my Mac and saw Cut Copy Paste, I thought 'William!'"[50] Advances in consumer technology put playback devices in the hands of the masses, starting with the Sony Walkman. But it was the Internet that changed everything. Much like the atomic blast at Los Alamos, the arrival of the World Wide Web sent shockwaves through the broader culture. And music was among the first media to be swept up in the maelstrom.

The Internet thoroughly transformed, and by some reckonings nearly destroyed, the music industry. At the turn of the millennium, legions of file-sharers would log on to sites like Napster, Kazaa, and Limewire to download immense catalogs of music for free. What was once scarce was now abundant. Those who lived through this shift remember the thrill of discovering popular hits and obscure nuggets that could be purloined with the click of a mouse. It didn't matter if you were in London or Los Angeles, Texas or Tangier—if you were online, you could mainline as much music as you wanted. What users did not realize at the time, however, is how this free-for-all would alter people's behavior. Downloading music became as addictive as junk, and perhaps more insidious given the sheer availability. James Jackson Toth, chief songwriter for the band Wooden Wand, recalled the heady days of file-sharing in a 2018 article for *NPR Music*:

> Shortly after we'd purchased our first desktop PC, my then-girlfriend downloaded the file-sharing program Audiogalaxy. In an intense sleep-deprived delirium bordering on narcotic, I downloaded every private press/weirdo/garage/psych/folk/prog/punk record I'd ever heard about throughout my years of fanzine-and-catalogue-trawling and conversations with other musicians and collectors. I challenged Audiogalaxy by plugging into the search engine the most obscure records I could think of, but it couldn't be stumped. It was incredible. . . .
>
> When Audiogalaxy vanished, another peer-to-peer program, Soulseek, took its place; same dealer, different street corner. . . . Music everywhere. Music every day. Music every minute.[51]

The new era of connectivity was not a one-way street: it was every which way at once. In short order, users began to cut up and re-combine whatever media they could get their hands on, giving birth to meme culture. "As cyberpunk fiction became the cybercultural reality of the 1990s with the birth of the 'Net, Burroughs became a patron saint of early hackerdom," says author Gareth Branwyn, who helped foreground digital culture as a writer for *Mondo 3000* and *WIRED*. "In his bold rejection of social and intellectual norms, he gave the rest of us permission to play."[52]

In fact, the Internet is probably the most fully realized cut-up tool ever devised. "Do it yourself until the machine comes," prophesied Burroughs and Gysin's *The Third Mind*. Well, the machine came, and it was every bit as metamorphic as the pair could have imagined. "They seemed to predict the 'nothing is true and everything is permitted,' and conversely 'everything is true and nothing is permitted' ethos of today's digitized social and reportage media," says Tav Falco.

> We even have a presidency administered by Twitter. The speed of digital media disgorges a spew of opinions, memes, photos, videos, instant reports, and life experiences that appear to be reading down the screen like a rippling linear newspaper column, but actually have the impact of an electronic mosaic imprinted on our memory banks—all the information all at once—yet often forgotten in a flash.[53]

The relentless pace of the Information Age has posed challenges for creators. The old gatekeepers are still there, and now there are new ones like Google, Amazon, Apple, and Spotify. Any artist can get on these platforms, but that's hardly a guarantee of being heard. Would a Burroughs or a Bowie even manage to get traction in such a saturated media environment? "For all the problems of the old guard media Establishment and the humdrum squares vs. freaks, our current situation is vastly more challenging for outsiders to break through," says author and musician Jamie Curcio. "There are niches within niches online, and the challenge is not platform but rather signal vs. noise.... Where is the counterculture?"[54]

We are every day bombarded with fragmentary words, sounds, and images shot through the digital ether. Sometimes this information gains incredible traction. When a "small unit of information" captures our collective attention—however briefly—we say it "went viral": Burroughs' parlance has become everyday slang. Never mind who's behind the curtain; memes require no attribution. In fact, virality depends on a kind of de-authoring that would be quite familiar to Burroughs, whose cut-ups often made use of material from undisclosed sources. Digitized media—including pre-recorded music—

are finally liberated from the tyranny of origination. Anything that can be cut up *is* cut up, with no attribution or deference given.

De-authoring is prevalent among participants in remix—an umbrella term that covers a range of cut-up-like activities. To remix something is to take its original form and alter it by removing, adding, or obscuring elements taken from pre-existing sources. This phenomenon builds on the sampling techniques pioneered by the likes of Throbbing Gristle and Public Enemy, which makes remix a clear descendant of cut-ups. A great deal of online activity is humorous or irreverent, but remix sometimes aims for the profound. Artists such as James Leyland Kirby, aka the Caretaker, are at the forefront of an approach that has come to be known as "hauntology." Kirby takes 1920s and '30s ballroom pop—music far more familiar to Burroughs than rock 'n' roll—and digitally degrades it to achieve something like the gauze of fading memory. The British label Ghost Box explores "the misremembered musical history of a parallel world" according to its website.[55] Bands on the imprint, such as Pye Corner Audio and the Focus Group, remix so-called "library music" (stock sounds used in 1960s and '70s public service broadcasts) in "a varied program of musical activities for educational and ritual use." Recall Burroughs' remark at the 1962 International Writers' Conference: "This method is of course used in music where we are continually moved backwards and forward on the time track by repetition and rearrangements of musical themes."[56] In other words, recorded sound makes past, present, and future entirely malleable.

The Western Lands

Knowing you might not make it . . .
in that knowledge courage is born.

WILLIAM S. BURROUGHS

Home on the Range

When Burroughs first settled in Lawrence in 1981, he stayed in an apartment near the University of Kansas, in a building on Oread Avenue, where Grauerholz also resided. Initially he intended to test the waters while working on *The Place of Dead Roads* (1983), the second book in his *Cities of the Red Night* trilogy. "I was sick of New York," he told biographer Ted Morgan. "It had no advantages for me. There was no reason to stay there." Burroughs adapted well to the liberal college town, which was very different than other parts of Kansas, where the religious right held sway. "I detest Bible Belt Christianity—dead, suffocating under layers of ignorance, stupidity, and barely hidden bigotry and vicious hate," Burroughs wrote in *Last Words*, a collection of journal entries published by Grove Press in 2000.

The gentle, sloping hills of Lawrence are in contrast to the flat horizon lines of much of the Midwest; its downtown is charmingly quaint, though Burroughs bemoaned the lack of decent restaurants. He took most of his meals at home, prepared by a rotating cast of local friends. Burroughs was now happily able to indulge in target practice pretty much whenever he felt like it. The next place he rented was a two-story stone house just outside of town that came with a fish pond and a big barn that was great fun to shoot at. Burroughs did not have a car at that point, so he relied on a group of Grauerholz pals—including Wayne Propst, Bill Rich, and Susan Brosseau—to assist with errands and the like. Propst, a talented artist, became particularly close to Burroughs and served as a kind of handyman. Rich was also a great chum; a notable in the local music scene, he played in bands and promoted shows at the Outhouse, where Nirvana performed before stardom set Kurt Cobain on his tragic course.

Burroughs became a cat lover in Lawrence. It all started with Ruski—a stray Russian Blue who happened by one night when Burroughs was smoking a joint on the back porch. Other furry friends soon joined the family, which led to Burroughs keeping a "cat journal" that was published in 1986—with drawings by Brion Gysin—as *The Cat Inside*. "I prefer cats to people," Burroughs said. "Most people aren't cute at all, and if they are cute, they rapidly outgrow it."[1] When not tending to his furry menagerie, Burroughs made good progress with *The Place of Dead Roads*, a book greatly influenced by British author Denton Welch, whose fastidiously observant prose Burroughs had long admired.

Burroughs also took up painting, which brought in additional revenue and extended his reputation into an entirely new arena. Always receptive to chance, Burroughs' "shotgun paintings" initially happened by accident. While trying out a new firearm, he aimed at a piece of plywood and noticed how his shot stripped away layers in an interesting pattern. He decided to add collage elements such as photos taken from magazines before pulling the trigger on the next piece of wood. Burroughs initially had no intention of making these works available for sale, but then Timothy Leary visited and offered $10,000 for a single painting. Another breakthrough occurred when Burroughs realized that he could aim at a can of spray paint, adding a new dimension of color and chaos to his readymade canvases. After Brion Gysin died, he took up proper painting, though his approach remained intuitive. "In painting, I see with my hands, and I do not know what my hands have done until I look at it afterward," he said. "Very often it turns out to be illustrative of my writing, or what I am thinking about writing."[2]

In February 1983, Burroughs' brother Mort died, leaving him with no immediate blood relatives. Grauerholz would be his closest family from there on out. Not long after, the landlord of the stone house decided to raise the rent, which inspired Burroughs and Grauerholz to cobble together $28,000 to put down on the place on 1927 Learnard in southeast Lawrence. Built in 1929 from a Sears and Roebuck kit, the modest bungalow would be Burroughs' home for the remainder of his life. The single-story house was originally white, but Burroughs had it repainted a bold red. It had a nice front porch, a big storm cellar, and a detached garage. Burroughs' room was near the back, where he would often sit at a small wooden desk reading or banging out ideas on an electric typewriter. The backyard had a garden, which he would patrol for vermin with a small, hand-held cattle prod. Burroughs was not allowed to shoot his guns within city limits, so he would either go over to friend Fred Aldrich's place about fifteen miles outside of town or blast away in the basement using a long tube constructed by friend George Kaull that acted as an oversized silencer. When he went for a walk, he was sure to bring his cane sword. "I have to be prepared," Burroughs said. "Look at what happened to Lennon."[3] In lieu of celebrity dinner companions, there were his local buddies.

Grauerholz did not live with Burroughs on Learnard Ave but was nevertheless close by and visited the red bungalow at least a few times a week. He enlisted a rotating cast of friends to cook meals, help out around the house, and keep Burroughs company. It's important to recognize the great kindness Grauerholz extended to Burroughs by providing the first truly nurturing support system of his already long life. Grauerholz initially considered making a clean break when he moved back to Kansas in 1980. He figured he could work on growing his own music career from Lawrence, a hip enough place for a singer-songwriter to come from. "The problem that I had in New York, and which forced me to leave and get a little perspective on it, is that I could neither accept William's dependence on me and my dependence on him," Grauerholz said in 1982.

> I could neither accept our relationship nor reject it, and say, "William, I'm gonna wrap it all up and go off and be a rock 'n' roll star"

or whatever I could be, I supposed. That was the schizophrenic situation.... And I must say, after two-and-a-half years of living in Lawrence and working for William, it has resolved itself, and I accept it. I'm proud of it. And as far as my destiny ... this is a pretty great destiny.[4]

It's tempting for some to see Grauerholz as a kind of Svengali figure or puppet master. To be sure, he had a talent for keeping Burroughs' name in circulation and a business manager's tenacity to make sure deals got done. But according to Victor Bockris, it was not in Burroughs' nature to do things he didn't want to. "I want to try to clear up once and for all the idea that William was manipulated into anything," he said.

It was James' job to handle all the offers and requests that poured in equally from businessmen and old friends. As Bill got into his later 70s, he was less inclined to travel and more aware of using what time he had left to finish his work.... When James had to turn down this invitation or that deal, he earned the resentment of the people he refused.... What seems inexcusable to me is that when these same people, who claimed they cared so much for Bill, caterwauled about how his life was completely manipulated, they seemed not to recognize how much that would have hurt the man they claimed to adore.[5]

Making Lunch

Though Grauerholz was an able gatekeeper, Burroughs was hardly shut off from the world. Friends old and new regularly came to Lawrence to pay a visit. Some, including members of Sonic Youth, R.E.M, and Ministry, were from the music world. Others, like filmmaker David Cronenberg, were longtime fans looking to create adaptations of his work, which is how *Naked Lunch* finally became a motion picture. Apart from *Finnegans Wake* by James Joyce and

Gravity's Rainbow by Thomas Pynchon, *Naked Lunch* was considered the most unfilmable major work of twentieth-century literature. Nevertheless, several attempts were made as far back as the 1960s to turn Burroughs' most well-known novel into a movie. Mick Jagger was set for the lead when Burroughs' close friend and collaborator Antony Balch worked on the project. Plans fell apart due to tensions between Balch and Jagger, after which Dennis Hopper signed on to direct, with Terry Southern producing the screenplay. That version was doomed in part because most of the funding went up Hopper's nose. Frank Zappa wanted to make a musical version of *Naked Lunch*, but that never proceeded past the idea stage, though he did take Burroughs to see *The Best Little Whorehouse in Texas* for inspiration. Television bigwig Chuck Barris of *The Gong Show* and *The Dating Game* was also interested, but ultimately nobody could get the project off the ground; that is, until Cronenberg proposed his ideas for *Naked Lunch* while chatting up Burroughs at his seventieth birthday party at the Limelight in New York City in 1984. The director's breakthrough film, *Videodrome*, had been released the previous year and costarred Burroughs' friend Debbie Harry. The movie depicted grotesque mutations triggered by broadcast and playback technology, making Cronenberg a solid contender to helm the long-proposed *Naked Lunch* adaptation. Burroughs had only recently struck a $200,000 seven-book deal with Viking, greatly easing his financial concerns. A movie, should it actually make it through development, could be another big payday.

It would be six more years before *Naked Lunch*—starring Peter Weller in the William Lee role—arrived in theaters in December 1991. Cronenberg struggled to produce a script Burroughs would approve, making several trips to Lawrence in an attempt to get on the same page. Eventually they settled on a metatextual riff on the author's life that was more fevered impression than direct adaptation. The death of Joan Vollmer is a major theme, even though she is not so much as alluded to in the book. Perhaps it was destiny forcing a reckoning; maybe Burroughs' self-protective emotional shell was becoming thinner with age. Whatever the reason, for the first time in his life he began to publicly confront the shooting of his wife—initially in his introduction to *Queer*, the centerpiece of the Viking deal, and then by allowing Cronenberg's vision for *Naked Lunch* to incorporate elements of the tragic event that had for so long haunted his private hours.

Cronenberg described the motivations of the movie's William Lee character, a stand-in for Burroughs that he also used in his books. "It's Joan's death that first drives him to create his own environment, his own interzone," Cronenberg said in a joint interview with Burroughs published by *Esquire* in 1992. "And that keeps driving him. So in a sense, that death is occurring over and over again." As one might expect, Burroughs was not entirely comfortable with Vollmer's death being depicted in the film. "I was dismayed, naturally, to see the scenes that David wrote in which 'Bill Lee' shoots his wife, 'Joan'; but on reflection, I feel that the scenes in the script are so different from the tragic and painful episodes in my own life from which he drew his inspiration that no intelligent person can mistake the movie for a factual account."[6]

Before filming began, Burroughs and Grauerholz joined Cronenberg and a couple of associates in Tangier to scout shooting locations. The place wasn't at all like Burroughs remembered; his favorite haunts were gone, and so were his friends from the freewheeling expat days. Ultimately, Cronenberg was forced to abandon the idea of a location shoot when the Gulf War broke out in 1991, even though Morocco was some 7,500 miles from Kuwait. The movie was instead filmed in the director's native Toronto.

The music for *Naked Lunch* was composed by Howard Shore and prominently featured the free-jazz saxophone skronk of Ornette Coleman, who had accompanied Burroughs to Tangier in 1973 to perform and record with the Master Musicians of Joujouka. When the movie finally arrived in theaters, it enjoyed decent notices from critics but did limited box office. It made its biggest impression as a VHS tape championed by a new generation in the word-of-mouth manner common to the pre-Internet era. Once again, it's safe to assume that more than a few of these kids formed bands—the author of the book you're reading among them.

Magick and Loss

By the mid-1980s Brion Gysin's health began to seriously deteriorate. In July 1986 he was diagnosed with lung cancer and informed that he had mere days—not weeks, or months—to live. Burroughs booked a flight for Paris. Alas, Gysin passed before the date of departure, and Burroughs never made the trip. He eulogized his old friend in the introduction to *The Last Museum*, a work of speculative fiction composed by Gysin and published posthumously:

> Brion Gysin died of a heart attack on Sunday morning, July 13, 1986. He was the only man I have ever respected. I have admired many others, esteemed and valued others, but respected only him. His presence was regal without a trace of pretension. He was at all times impeccable.

Burroughs was devastated by the loss. Gysin wasn't just a collaborator and companion, he was a guru and a muse. "Meeting Brion was one of the most significant events of my life," Burroughs remarked in 1990. "He taught me everything I know about painting, he brought the cut-up method to writing, he introduced me to Moroccan music and the Pipes of Pan—I'd say he was the most important single influence."[7] With his own end approaching sooner than later, Burroughs became ever more preoccupied with death, though he retained his sense of humor. In a conversation with punk scribe Legs McNeil for a 1991 edition of *Spin*, Burroughs described a recurring dream: "Everyone I see is dead. The only thing that bothers me about the Land of the Dead dream is that I can never get any breakfast. That's typical of the Land of the Dead."

Burroughs' friend and occasional intellectual sparring partner Timothy Leary died in May 1996. Leary's son Zach telephoned Burroughs at the very end, saying that his dad would like to speak with him. In and out of a coma, Leary managed to get on the phone and asked Burroughs, "Is it true?" Burroughs didn't know what he was talking about, but decided to play along. "Well, I guess it's true," he said. "It's true, Tim." To which Leary replied, "Well, I love you, Bill." Burroughs answered, "I love you too, Tim."[8] Leary died just a handful of hours later; his last words: "Why not?"

Allen Ginsberg was a frequent visitor to Lawrence, where he would stay in a guest bedroom at the bungalow. Burroughs' local friend David Ohle remembered, "One unforgettable moment was seeing William and Allen early one morning in their pajamas trying to chase raccoons out of William's kitchen with a walking cane." Ginsberg had always been staunch. In 1984 the poet had finally succeeded in lobbying the American Academy of Arts and Letters to elect Burroughs as a member. That the snobby institution would accept someone with such a checkered history, whose books many still considered abhorrent, was a testament to Ginsberg's tenacity. This was made possible by his passionate belief in Burroughs' deservedness and the desire to see his friend recognized as one of the most important authors of his time—or any, for that matter. Despite Burroughs' distaste for the literary intelligentsia, he happily accepted and proudly wore the Commandeur de l'Orde des Arts et des Lettres insignia, which was pinned to the jacket in which he was buried.

Over the next decade, Ginsberg's health deteriorated. Sometime during the summer of 1996 he began complaining of increased fatigue due to a range of maladies including Bell's palsy, diabetes, high blood pressure, and heart issues. In March 1997, Ginsberg's doctor, upon hearing the symptoms, advised immediate hospitalization. Results confirmed both hepatitis C and cancer of the liver, the latter of which had reached an untreatable stage. The prognosis was just three to six months, which Ginsberg pushed back on, saying, "That sounds too long."[9]

Burroughs was informed immediately. Ginsberg's internal clock was more accurate than the oncologist's; on April 5, 1997, he drifted into a coma, passing shortly thereafter.

Losing Gysin had been agony. Ginsberg's death was unbearable.

The *New York Times* ran a short statement from Burroughs in which his midwestern reserve barely masks the pain he felt in losing his friend of more than half a century. "Allen was a great person with worldwide influence," Burroughs said. "He was a pioneer of openness and a lifelong model of candor. He stood for freedom of expression and for coming out of all the closets long before others did. He has influence because he said what he believed. I will miss him."

Burroughs kept going as best he knew how. His writing continued to be published, and his paintings were shown internationally. In the early 1990s, Burroughs' artworks were exhibited at prominent galleries in Madrid, Marseille, Venice, Lyon, San Francisco, and New York. In 1996 he had the biggest showing yet, with more than 150 works in solo display at the Los Angeles County Museum. Curated by Robert S. Sobieszek, *Ports of Entry: William S. Burroughs and the Arts* established Burroughs as a legitimate figure in the fine arts world. Since his death, his work fetches collector prices and now enjoys permanent exhibition in Germany, Austria, Slovenia, and the UK.

Ports of Entry gave Burroughs a much-needed mood boost. With the University of Kansas Spencer Museum of Art next in line to host the show, the decision was made to offer additional programming to coincide with the exhibit. That resulted in the Nova Convention Revisited, an event that drew many of the same performers from the original, including Patti Smith, Laurie Anderson, Philip Glass, and John Giorno. Debbie Harry and Chris Stein also made an appearance. Frank Zappa, who so graciously subbed for Keith Richards back in 1978, had died in 1993. Filling the rock star void this time around was R.E.M.'s Michael Stipe, who joined the Patti Smith Band onstage. There were also readings—including an excerpt from *Queer* recited by Smith—as well as video clips of Burroughs from his own performances. Burroughs said he would not be attending the Nova Convention Revisited, but he nonetheless made an appearance toward the end of the event, giving a brief reading that earned him a standing ovation.

Youth Movement

Burroughs enjoyed his quiet life of semi-anonymity. Though he did welcome a number of famous well-wishers in his final decade, it was nowhere near the volume of callers to the Bunker. Besides Cobain, who made a real impression on Burroughs, most of the drop-bys meant more to the company than the host. That is no doubt the case with Sonic Youth, who visited more than once. Then married, the two recalled time spent with Burroughs with the same warmth one might extend a beloved grandparent.

Sonic Youth's first pop-by happened while on tour opening for R.E.M. Grauerholz was a fan of both acts and set up the visit. Thurston Moore was moved by both the hominess of the bungalow and the graciousness of their host. "I always remember walking into his little house, which was one of those houses that Sears and Roebuck had sold during the '50s do-it-yourself, build-your-own-house deals," he recalled. "[Burroughs] was extremely welcoming. He was elderly. He had magazines and books everywhere about knives and guns. That was a little off-putting. I didn't know what to think of that because that was the last thing I was interested in. . . . We visited his Wilhelm Reich orgone machine in the backyard. I sat in it and it was full of cobwebs."[10]

Sonic Youth returned a few years later, not long after Cobain's suicide. "I always remember William talking to me about it," Moore said.

> He had this look in his eye like: "Why would anybody take their own life?" He couldn't make sense of it. Why would you do that? Why would you disturb your energy and your cosmic soul like that? You don't do that. You protect it. You have to fight for it. You can do whatever you like, you can take heroin your entire life, you can be an alcoholic or you can be a creep, but you don't eradicate yourself. You don't kill yourself purposefully.[11]

Kim Gordon felt a familial connection right out of the gate. "That day, all I could think about was how much Burroughs reminded me of my dad," she said. "They shared the same folksiness, the same dry sense of humor. They even looked a little alike."[12] Adding to the family vibe was Gordon and Moore's infant daughter, whom the couple had brought along on tour. As Gordon recalls, "At one point when she started crying, Burroughs said in that Burroughs voice, 'Oohhh—she *likes* me.'"[13] Burroughs didn't spend a lot of time around children, but he nonetheless had a way with the baby. "She was in my arms and she was whining," Moore said. "He put his hand up towards her face. I thought: 'Uh oh! I need to stand tall here' but basically, he just did this little hand movement and she immediately quieted up. It was like this magician's hand movement."[14]

As Sonic Youth's chief composer, Moore borrowed some of Burroughs' magic for his own. "The cut-up process was definitely something I used, and I do that not only with literary language, but with music as well," he said.

> I've always been interested in what happens if you take things and move them around. In a way, that was always the modus operandi of Sonic Youth. There was always talk of Sonic Youth being this experimental band in terms of guitars or other things, but actually the most experimental thing about the band was song structure. How we took traditional song structure and would try techniques with it. One of those techniques was certainly the cut-up.[15]

Sonic Youth broke up in 2011 with the dissolution of Moore and Gordon's partnership, which dated back to 1981. Both have gone on to make records and tour—Moore more prolifically. Gordon's music with Body/Head and Glitterbust is experimental and often improvised. Moore tends to favor wild and wooly rock, with lyrics that continue to make use of the cut-up method. His band Chelsea Light Moving—named after an actual moving company established by Philip Glass to earn money to rent a concert hall—represents the fulfillment of Moore's desire to "to form a band that played Burroughs rock."[16] Their debut single was actually called "Burroughs"; influential music site Stereogum said of the track, "The lyrical theme is, yes, author William Burroughs, and the music sounds, yes, a lot like Sonic Youth. These are all very good things."[17]

Moore would lend his name and enthusiasm to events commemorating what would have been Burroughs' one-hundredth birthday in 2014. This included an exhibition in the UK focused on the original Nova Convention, featuring photographs taken by James Hamilton, who covered the 1978 convening for *Village Voice*. "For me, it was very personally exciting, because as a nineteen-year-old, I was there," Moore said.

> I think William Burroughs was always able to sort of look at the world as something far more than meets the eye. His interest in different systems of Control in both the physical world and the metaphysical world brought these ideas that were steeped in reality and these ideas that were almost science fiction to a new place. . . . He was definitely one of the most esoteric and far-out writers, in one sense very personal and in another sense, very political.[18]

Or, as Columbia University's Ann Douglas said, "He traveled outside of the human condition imaginatively, or as far outside it as a very human person could go and report it back to us."[19]

Just One Fix

Members of the band Ministry visited Burroughs in 1993. Led by junkie provocateur Al Jourgensen, Ministry had, over their career, gone from being a synth-laden goth act to full-metal-jacketed terrors, with albums like *The Land of Rape and Honey*, *The Mind Is a Terrible Thing to Taste*, and *Psalm 69* delighting misanthropes around the world (that is, if misanthropes can be delighted). The band's music comes on like a swarm of saw blades, or perhaps the

Jaws of Life programmed to do the opposite. Burroughs surely would not have enjoyed listening to Ministry, but he might have appreciated the band's contribution to the weaponizing of sound.

Jourgensen discovered Burroughs in high school after he got in a brawl with some kids who smashed his guitar, which was just about the only possession he cared about. When authorities discovered a veritable pharmacy on his person, he was shipped off to a mental hospital for twelve months. "It was one of the best years of my life," Jourgensen said.[20] "First of all, they gave me free drugs that I had previously been paying for—Tuinal, Seconal Sodium, Valium. They did everything they could to keep patients sedated back then.... So I was high all the time, and while I was there I had this tutor assigned to me who turned me on to books by William Burroughs."[21] Like so many other artists, it was *Naked Lunch* that initially got under Jourgensen's skin. "I mean, if you want incentive to either start or stop doing heroin, you can find it in that book," he said.

> It was a total mindfuck to me, man. There were junkies everywhere, and there's this character, Dr. Benway, this sicko motherfucker who does this demented surgery. There are Mugwumps, these homo amphibians whose jizz gets you high, and there are all these orgies and decapitations and totalitarian regimes and brilliance and total nonsense. It's fucking unbelievable.... I seriously couldn't get enough.[22]

Jello Biafra, Jourgensen's bandmate in the side project Lard, described a true believer in the Burroughs catechism: "For a while [Jourgensen] attributed his longevity to heroin itself because William Burroughs convinced him it had these healing properties. Who knows? Maybe it does, because Al is still here."[23]

Burroughs also influenced how Jourgensen worked in the studio. "I would edit the tape for twelve to fourteen hours," he said. "I would have razor cuts all over my hands from that much editing.... But it was really invigorating because I was using the same cut-up method that William Burroughs used, only I was doing it with music, which is why he and I hit it off a few year later when we met to work on the song 'Just One Fix' from *Psalm 69*."²⁴ Jourgensen was keen to present Burroughs within the context of his own Control-smashing music, but he ran into legal snags. As he describes in his autobiography:

> I got all these cool spoken-word parts from William Burroughs, from readings and speeches he had done. We were all set to release the album, but it got delayed two months because Warner Bros. told me Burroughs wouldn't give me permission to use his stuff. At the time everyone was all nervous about getting sued for illegal sample usage, and getting clearance for all this shit became more important to the labels than the music itself. I told *Rolling Stone* that our album was delayed because Burroughs wouldn't let us sample him. . . . James Grauerholz saw that and called me up and told me, "Nobody asked us. We never said you can't use that stuff. As a matter of fact, why don't you come to Lawrence, Kansas, where Bill lives, and we'll do new stuff."²⁵

Jourgensen made a quick phone call to Howie Kein at Warner Bros. to call him an asshole, after which he set out for Kansas from Ministry's home base in Chicago. Well, sort of. "We had instructions on how to get to the house, but we showed up three days late without telling anyone," Jourgensen said. "Keeping William Burroughs waiting for us for three days was probably a bad move."²⁶ His excuse managed to incorporate the 23 Enigma, which Burroughs himself researched and promoted. "I was supposed to fly out on the twenty-third of that month, but I don't fly on the twenty-third, because I am very superstitious," he said. "If you travel on the twenty-third, you're toast. That goes back to the wagon-trail days of the Wild West. If you set out on the twenty-third to go from Missouri to Oregon in a wagon, you are sure to die."²⁷ How could the old man argue with such logic?

Eventually, Jourgensen and a junkie friend found their way to Learnard Avenue. "I have to admit that it's not exactly what I expected," Jourgensen recalled. "It was modest and looked more like the home of a small store owner than a legendary writer." Jourgensen and company arrived around 2 p.m., shambled to the porch, and knocked on the door. "Bill answers, and the first thing he says is, 'Are ya holding? Where is it? I can smell a junkie from a mile away,'" Jourgensen said. Burroughs' guests only had enough heroin on them for maintenance—to keep from getting sick, not for getting high. Besides, Burroughs was supposed to be off junk anyway. Jourgensen replied in the negative, "and before I had the chance to say anything else, Bill slammed the door in our faces."

Heading back to Kansas City—nearly two hours round-trip—Jourgensen managed to acquire a quantity of heroin. "We went back to Bill's house, and he opened the door and said, 'Oh, it's *you* again,'" Jourgensen remembered. "He knew he had to do a video with us, and he had already agreed to it. But he wouldn't do it without drugs, so we said right away, 'No, no, we scored.' So he said, 'Come on in.'"[28] Burroughs at that time was on methadone, and Grauerholz kept a close eye on his treatment and use of legal stimulants like alcohol. But according to Jourgensen, Grauerholz was sick in bed with the flu:

> When the cat's away, the mouse will play. We take out the baggies of heroin and Bill comes downstairs with this 1950s leather belt and these big, thick hypodermics and needles from the same era, all of which he'd lovingly wrapped up. . . . When I woke up, I saw there was a letter on the living room table that had a seal from the White House. I noticed it was unopened. Bill woke up and I said, "Hey Bill, you got a letter from the White House." And he said, "Eh, so what? It's junk mail."[29]

Despite the shaky start, Burroughs and Jourgensen hit it off. After they had wrapped up shooting for the "Just One Fix" video, Jourgensen took the old man to see a performance by Jim Rose, who led a modern-day freak show that had toured with the original Lollapalooza festival. Burroughs appreciated the gesture but was unimpressed by the performance. Jourgensen recalled him saying, "I once knew a man in Morocco who could simultaneously swallow three snakes, all different colors. Then you'd pay him a dollar and you'd tell him what color snake you'd like him to regurgitate. That guy must have made a hundred dollars a day regurgitating snakes. Now *that's* impressive. You guys eating glass and putting nails in your head—seen it."[30]

Burroughs and Jourgensen remained close. "Right away I was on Bill's friend list—and it was a short list," Jourgensen said. "Up until the time of his death he would call me about once a week and we'd talk. But the real reason for his call was to bitch at me for doing coke. His exact quote was: 'Why would a person do a drug that keeps you up all night twitching? Keep to heroin, kid.'"[31]

Space Oddities

In addition to cats, Burroughs developed an abiding interest in UFOs during his final years. He'd long been drawn to fringe science—from Wilhelm Reich to Scientology to ESP to the "bicameral mind"[32]—but the idea of little green men (or gray ones, more precisely) held particular fascination. He was drawn to the work of Whitley Strieber, whose book *Communion* is a first-person account of abduction by space aliens. Burroughs recognized the parallels between the violations Strieber experienced and the Ugly Spirit that had colonized him long ago. He reached out to Strieber not to hear further abduction accounts, but rather to ask for tips on getting on the aliens' radar. Burroughs was highly annoyed that he hadn't already been contacted. "I think I am one of the most important people in this fucking world and if they had any sense they would have manifested," he said. "It may mean it was not propitious for them to come and pick me at this particular time. It may mean that they would contact me at a later date, or it may mean that they look upon me as the enemy. . . . They may find that my intervention is hostile to their objectives. And their objectives may not be friendly at all."[33] Burroughs went so far as to allow the lawn to grow unkempt in order to cut a patch in the shape of a penis—a kind of erotic crop circle meant to attract space aliens to his little red bungalow.

Burroughs' UFO research took place in the middle of the original

TV run of *The X-Files*. That show helped bring extraterrestrial in-quiry back into the public consciousness at a level not seen since the 1950s, when the Roswell crash and rash of subsequent UFO sight-ings excited and terrified Americans in equal measure. Burroughs fingered one race of aliens—the Grays—as likely agents of Control. At one point, he suspected Strieber of working with them. After a few conversations, Burroughs concluded that Strieber wasn't the brightest bulb, and therefore a prime target for manipulation by superior intelligences. "Why are abductions and contacts always to mediocre and inferior minds?" Burroughs wrote in a journal entry dated February 3, 1997. "Why don't they come and see ME? Because they don't want to, are afraid to contact anyone with advanced spir-itual awareness. The Grays want to make people stupider. Anyone with real perception is a danger to them. A deadly danger."[34]

It would have been interesting if Burroughs had lived to meet musician Tom DeLonge, ex of pop-punk numbskulls Blink 182, who is currently an outspoken pitchman for UFOlogy. Frustrated with government secrecy around extraterrestrial visitation, DeLonge founded the organization To the Stars, "to be a powerful vehicle for change by creating a consortium among science, aerospace and entertainment that will work collectively to allow gifted research-ers the freedom to explore exotic science and technologies with the infrastructure and resources to rapidly transition them to products that can change the world."[35] DeLonge claims to be working directly with the US government to help clear up decades of misinformation and obfuscation by authorities. This all may seem crazy, but emails exposed by Wikileaks confirm contact between DeLonge and John Podesta—Democratic operative and confirmed extraterrestrial en-thusiast. DeLonge also solicited the help of former Air Force major general William N. McCasland to establish an advisory committee to assist with his investigations.

In 2017, the *New York Times* ran a lengthy piece on the US gov-ernment's current role in investigating the UFO phenomenon. The article revealed a secret Pentagon cloister called the Advanced Aerospace Threat Identification Program run by Luis Elizondo, a military intelligence official who had only recently resigned due to brass ignoring "the many accounts from the Navy and other services of unusual aerial systems interfering with military weapon platforms and displaying beyond-next-generation capabilities."[36] Supposedly, the program receives $22 million of the Department of Defense's $600 billion annual budget. If Burroughs were alive today, he might very well be a consultant for the DOD, or at least a member of DeLonge's advisory board.

The Western Lands

Burroughs' final novel is among his best. In some ways, *The Western Lands* is like a greatest hits record: it's got all the stuff you love—with none of the filler. Burroughs said the book was about "the possibility of hybridization, the crossing of man and animals."[37] Perhaps, but it is also a heart-rending look back at friends and lovers lost, families abandoned, and the author's own probing of the meaning of existence and possible paths to immortality. The latter is addressed through Burroughs' fictive analysis of the "seven souls"—a spiritual cosmology prevalent in Ancient Egypt. The gist is that human beings actually have seven distinct souls, each subject to immutable laws that govern the continuation of being in the afterlife. Death, as it turns out, is just the beginning of an even bigger journey, one fraught with peril and uncertain promise. *The Western Lands* is a jump-cut travelogue through the Land of the Dead, where characters struggle with new space-time conditions as they battle against, you guessed it, Control. At least this time, there is help. Burroughs invented a secret service called Margaras Unlimited to address the crisis of migratory souls. The group, whose only loyalty is to its mission, supports space exploration, the simulation of space conditions, and the expansion of human awareness. *The Western Lands* contains elements of biography, but its scenes and characters are presented in a random-access panoply of observations, remembrances, and routines. "Any writer who hopes to approximate what actually occurs in the mind and body of his characters cannot confine himself to such an arbitrary structure as logical sequence," Burroughs said.[38]

Perhaps this is why the book made such great material for Bill Laswell's 1998 album of the same name, which features Burroughs' bone-dry recitations over twisting grooves and ancient-sounding melodies. The music captures the essence of the book, which Burroughs boiled down to a single sentence about its main character: "So William Seward Hall sets to write his way out of death."[39] And that not only includes his own death, but that of the magical universe, which is threatened by a conspiracy of dogmatic, authoritarian agents who want to impose a reality that is "controlled, predictable, dead."

The book's ending is one of the greatest bow-outs of all time, right up there with David Bowie's final album, *Blackstar*:

> I want to reach the Western lands—right in front of you, across the bubbling brook. It's a frozen sewer. It's known as the Duad, remember? All the filth and horror, fear, hate, disease and death of human history flows between you and the Western Lands. Let it flow! My cat Fletch stretches behind me on the bed. . . .

> How long does it take a man to learn that he does not, cannot want what he "wants"? . . .

> The old writer couldn't write anymore because he had reached the end of words, the end of what can be done with words. And then? . . .

> In Tangier the Parade Bar is closed. Shadows are falling on the Mountain.

> "Hurry up, please. It's time."[40]

On May 22, 1997, Burroughs made his last public appearance in the video for U2's "Last Night on Earth." Amid a jumble of cut-up visuals, Burroughs can be seen flashing an oversized spotlight and waving his cane sword around. He referred to the band as "You Too" in his journals, having never seen their name in print. The following month, Burroughs went on what would be his final shooting session at Fred Aldritch's place. When he came home, he discovered the body of his cat Fletch sticking out from under his Toyota, which the beloved animal had crawled under to die. Three days later Burroughs had a heart attack. Friend and household helper Tom Peschio discovered him at 4 p.m. in the throes of cardiac arrest. He had managed to take a nitroglycerin tablet and was fully conscious when Grauerholz arrived, followed shortly thereafter by paramedics. Pat Connor, a local man who was scheduled to dine with Burroughs that evening, rushed out of his car and asked Burroughs, "What's goin' on?" Burroughs' reply: "Back in no time."[41] Those were the last words he would speak.

William Seward Burroughs II died at 6:50 p.m. on August 2, 1997. Longtime friend Patricia Elliott recalled Grauerholz clasping Burroughs' hand and sobbing uncontrollably. "I had never seen James more beautiful," she said. "The love and respect that I had observed between those two over the years flashed through my thoughts like a bursting series of light."[42] Burroughs was buried in a white shirt and blue necktie, a Moroccan waistcoat given to him by Brion Gysin, and the black shoes he would wear for performances. Placed inside his dark green sports jacket were his reading glasses, a ballpoint pen, some top-shelf marijuana, and a small packet of heroin. A five-dollar gold piece was also included as fare for Burroughs' journey to the Western Lands. At his side were his beloved cane sword and .38 Special snubnose, fully loaded.

At a dinner shortly before he died, Burroughs exclaimed, "I don't want to be cremated, I want to go down into the ground and ROT!"[43] And so his body was brought back to Saint Louis for interment in the family mausoleum at Bellefontaine Cemetery—block 37, lot 3938. A service was held at 7 p.m. on August 6, at which Grauerholz offered closing remarks. Burroughs was laid to rest the following day. Patti

Smith flew in from Detroit; Grant Hart also traveled to pay his respects. Attendees at Burroughs' burial found themselves wishing Ginsberg were there. He would have known just what to say to comfort the grieving.

Burroughs' influence on other artists should by now be clear. Though he may not have personally been a big appreciator of music, he understood quite well how his ideas and methods encouraged others to innovate in the medium. He disliked imitation, but took pride in the fact that fellow travelers took inspiration from his work; the point was to do something, anything, to break out of the sterile, conditioned world foisted upon all of us. Burroughs' writing, interviews, recordings, performances, and paintings will live on. So will the friendships he cultivated with many of the people referenced within these pages. William S. Burroughs remains in the hearts of those who knew him best—John Giorno, Victor Bockris, and James Grauerholz chief among them. Those who only know the icon have the opportunity to become better acquainted by delving into Burroughs' voluminous body of work. In doing so, we may also discover something of ourselves—our fears, desires, longings, aversions, and hopes for the future. That's what happened to this author anyway. And I'm not alone. "One of my favorite aspects about Burroughs is that he encourages your own mind travel," said Beat scholar Regina Weinreich. "You have to become a traveler with him."[44]

It makes sense to give the final words of this book to Grauerholz: "It's like the old writer says: 'Whenever you read these words, I am there.' [Burroughs'] immortality is in his readers. . . . He lives there in them."[45]

Acknowledgments

This book was a journey for its author, one that could not have been undertaken or completed without the encouragement and support of my wife, Faith Rebecca Swords. Not only did she help me think through ideas and themes, she assisted mightily with edits, reviews, and revisions on the long road to publication. And we had a blast doing it; I often think of our relationship as being something like William and Joan's minus the drug addiction, sexual incompatibility, and tragic fatality—which leaves the repartee and genuine affection. The best it gets in this brutal old world.

Riley Greene played the role of intrepid assistant with aplomb, keeping me on top of deadlines, arranging interviews, and offering an executive editor's eye for detail. She did it all with customary diligence and humor; I thank her tremendously for her contributions.

I am greatly indebted to Victor Bockris and James Grauerholz, who provided a direct link to the life and times of William S. Burroughs. When I first reached out to Bockris, I thought he might brush me off. After all, he had first dibs on the topic and had already contributed mightily to Burroughs' legend, especially among the art punks of 1970s New York. Instead, he provided me with a wealth of observations and insights. His books, such as *Beat Punks: New York's Underground Culture from the Beat Generation to the Punk Explosion* and *With William Burroughs: A Report from the Bunker*, along with an array of existing interviews, helped shape my understanding of Burroughs in an evolving cultural context.

Bockris' biographies of Lou Reed and Patti Smith also proved useful, as did his gentle correction of erroneous apocrypha relating to Burroughs' icon.

Grauerholz challenged me to go beyond the icon to capture something of the man within. I don't know whether I accomplished that, but if I was successful to any degree, it is due to Grauerholz, who provided penetrating, touching, and often uproarious insights into Burroughs' personality and character. Having never met the author, this was crucial. I also came to appreciate Grauerholz' commitment to Burroughs, which included both his business savvy and profound personal investment in the author's well-being. Grauerholz saved Burroughs' life. He also kept him at the forefront of popular consciousness during the era in which I first encountered him. Thank you, James.

I would also like to thank Genesis P-Orridge, Chris Stein, Alex McLeod, Bill Laswell, Tav Falco, Robert Wilson, Douglas Rushkoff, Joe Ambrose, Jamie Curcio, and Gareth Branwyn for their insights on some pretty arcane topics. My gratitude also extends to the many musicians whose stories populate these pages; it wasn't just their connection to Burroughs that inspired me, but also their music. My vintage vinyl collection grew considerably in the course of writing this book, as did my respect for the artists who put their own masterful spins on the Burroughs doctrine.

Acknowledgment is also due Burroughs' many biographers. Without Ted Morgan's pioneering *Literary Outlaw: The Life and Times of William S. Burroughs*, the world would be bereft of many quotes and insights attributed to El Hombre Invisible—which brings me to Barry Miles, who wrote not one but two books about Burroughs, the latest of which, *Call Me Burroughs: A Life*, may be the definitive chronology of the author's long and storied existence. I also appreciate the work of Matthew Levi Stevens, author of *The Magical Universe of William S. Burroughs*; David S. Willis, author of *Scientologist! William S. Burroughs and the "Weird Cult"*; and Jennie Skerl, whose scholarly collection *William S. Burroughs at the Front: Critical Reception* proved indispensable in my reinvestigation of Burroughs' themes and obsessions. My kudos also extend to the lay researchers at such websites as Reality Studio and Beatdom. The estate website, williamsburroughs.org, also proved a wonderful online haunt with a treasure trove of reminiscences and ephemera.

My agents, William LoTurco and David Kuhn, were instrumental in helping me take a concept that I'd been pondering for some time and hammer it into a proper outline, offering support and encouragement as I fleshed it out into an actual book. My deep gratitude extends to Casey Kittrell and everyone at the University of Texas Press for working closely with me to develop the manuscript, and also for bringing the work to the public. And a huge debt is owed to my earliest editors—my mom, Matthew G. Paradise, and Pamela Polston. This is all your fault.

Not to end on a downer, but composing this book had me thinking a lot about my own mortality. Of course, that's nothing new. What is new is how, in telling the story of William S. Burroughs— along with several now-departed artists like David Bowie, Lou Reed, Daevid Allen, Peter Christopherson, John Balance, Grant Hart, and others—I came to better terms with my own inescapable journey to the Western Lands. Perhaps it also has something to do with the birth of my daughter, Ruby, who arrived at the midway point in the writing. (She is, and will remain, the greatest thing I have ever coauthored.) The point is, I had something of an epiphany. The gist of it is that, although we all expire—many of us without a shred of public recognition—it is what we love in this life that defines us, which is why I would like to close these acknowledgments by thanking my dear friends Mark Cooley and Stephen Balgooyen—my old musical mates who nearly thirty years ago dumped me at the front door of the metaphysical Beat Hotel with nothing but a headful of acid and my wits to guide me. It is due to their love and encouragement that I became myself; consider this book my humble effort at reciprocity.

Notes

Nirvana the Hard Way

1. Barry Miles, *Call Me Burroughs: A Life* (New York: Twelve, 2015), p. 623.

2. Frank Morris, "William S. Burroughs And Lawrence, Kansas: Linked Inexorably," *KCUR*, February 5, 2014, accessed April 12, 2018, http://kcur.org/post /william-s-burroughs-and-lawrence-kansas-linked-inexorably.

3. William S. Burroughs, *The Adding Machine: Selected Essays* (New York: Grove Press, 2013), p. 49.

4. Telephone interview by author, February 5, 2017.

5. Miles, *Call Me Burroughs*, p. 580.

6. Morris, "William S. Burroughs."

7. Telephone interview by author, February 5, 2017.

8. Ibid.

9. Steve Knopper, "The Grunge Gold Rush," *NPR*, January 12, 2018, accessed April 12, 2018. https://www.npr.org/sections/therecord/2018/01/12/577063077 /the-grunge-gold-rush.

10. In 1992, Cobain told a Singapore publication, "Rebellion is standing up to people like Guns N' Roses"; the same year, Axl Rose called Cobain "a fucking junkie with a junkie wife" during a Guns N' Roses performance. Things came to a head with a testy scene backstage at that year's MTV Video Music Awards, where Axl threatened physical violence against Cobain, though no blows were exchanged. https://www.rollingstone.com/music/news/guns-n-roses-vs-nirvana -a-beef-history-20160411.

11. Burroughs, *The Adding Machine*, p. 59.

12. Burroughs attended one of Korzybski's seminars in 1939, and in 1974 he recalled being "very impressed by what [Korzybski] had to say. I still am. I think that everyone, everyone, particularly all students should read Korzybski. [It would] save them an awful lot of time." "William Burroughs Press Conference at Berkeley Museum of Art on November 12, 1974," *Archive*, November 12, 1974, accessed April 12, 2018. http://www.archive.org/details/BurroughsPressConf.

13. Blake was also a noted influence on Ginsberg who mentions him in "Howl."

14. "Hoodlums and riff-raff of the lowest caliber filled the highest offices of the land. When the Supreme Court overruled some of the legislation perpetrated by this vile route, Roosevelt forced that honest body, one after the other on threat of immediate reduction to the rank of congressional lavatory attendants, to submit to intercourse with a purple-assed baboon so that venerable honored men surrendered themselves to the embraces of a lecherous, snarling simian while Roosevelt and his strumpet wife and veteran brown-nose Harry Hopkins, smoking a communal hookah of hashish, watched the immutable spectacle with cackles of obscene laughter." William S. Burroughs, James Grauerholz, and Ira Silverberg, "Roosevelt After Inauguration," *Word Virus: The William S. Burroughs Reader* (New York: Grove Press, 1998), p. 333.

15. William S. Burroughs, *The Western Lands* (London: Penguin Classics, 2010), p. 116.

16. In his introduction to *Queer*, written in the 1950s but not published until 1985, Burroughs opined on the death of his wife Joan Vollmer, killed by a bullet fired from Burroughs' pistol during a drunken game of William Tell: "I am forced to the appalling conclusion that I would never have become a writer but for Joan's death, and to a realization of the extent to which this event has motivated and formulated my writing. I live with the constant threat of possession, from Control. So the death of Joan brought me in contact with the invader, the Ugly Spirit, and manoeuvred me into a lifelong struggle, in which I have had no choice except to *write my way out*" (emphasis added).

17. Telephone interview by author, October 28, 2017.

18. Ibid.

19. Telephone interview by author, February 3, 2017.

20. Matthew Gilbert, "The Life and Times of William S. Burroughs," *Boston Globe*, January 25, 2014, accessed April 12, 2018. https://www.bostonglobe.com /arts/books/2014/01/25/the-life-and-times-william-burroughs/NdXpBePEr ha2VEwsdnzUmN/story.html.

21. Telephone interview by author, October 28, 2017.

22. "William S. Burroughs & Kurt Cobain—The Priest They Called Him," *Genius*, July 1, 1993, accessed April 12, 2018. https://genius.com/William-s -burroughs-and-kurt-cobain-the-priest-they-called-him-lyrics.

23. "Nirvana—In Bloom," *Genius*, November 30, 1992, accessed April 12, 2018. https://genius.com/Nirvana-in-bloom-lyrics.

24. Burroughs, *The Adding Machine*, p. 61.

25. "William S. Burroughs and Kurt Cobain—A Dossier," *RealityStudio*, February 18, 2007, accessed April 12, 2018. http://realitystudio.org/biography /william-s-burroughs-and-kurt-cobain-a-dossier/.

26. Ibid.

27. Sarah Smarsh, *It Happened in Kansas: Remarkable Events That Shaped History* (Guilford, CT: Globe Pequot, 2010), p. 109.

28. Telephone interview by author, February 3, 2017.

29. Ted Morgan, *Literary Outlaw: The Life and Times of William S. Burroughs* (New York: W. W. Norton, 2012), p. 311.

30. Ibid.

31. Ibid.

32. Wayne Propst offers a touching and humorous account in the 2007 documentary *Words of Advice: William S. Burroughs On the Road*.

33. Jason Louv, "The Scientific Assassination of a Sexual Revolutionary: How America Interrupted Wilhelm Reich's Orgasmic Utopia," *Motherboard*, July 15, 2013, accessed April 12, 2018. https://motherboard.vice.com/en_us/article /mggzpn/the-american-quest-to-kill-wilhelm-reich-and-orgonomy.

34. Mary Bellis, "Why Did the U.S. Government Want This Device Destroyed?," *ThoughtCo*, April 9, 2017, accessed April 12, 2018. https://www.thoughtco.com /wilhelm-reich-and-orgone-accumulator-1992351.

35. "William S. Burroughs and Kurt Cobain—A Dossier," *RealityStudio*.

36. "Noise Poetry: An Interview with Thurston Moore," *Beatdom*, August 8, 2016, accessed April 12, 2018. http://www.beatdom.com/noise-poetry-an -interview-with-thurston-moore/.

37. Jim McCrary, "When Hunter S. Thompson Visited William S. Burroughs," *William S. Burroughs*, May 21, 2014, accessed April 12, 2018. http://www.williams burroughs.org/features/category/guns.

38. Brenda Knight, *Women of the Beat Generation: The Writers, Artists and Muses at the Heart of a Revolution* (Berkeley, CA: Conari, 2010), p. 54.

39. Jack Kerouac, *On the Road* (London: Penguin, 2000), p. 146.

40. Telephone interview by author, October 28, 2017.

41. James Grauerholz, "The Death of Joan Vollmer: What Really Happened?," *Fifth Congress of the Americas* (2012), accessed April 12, 2018. http://docplayer .net/7574805-The-death-of-joan-vollmer-burroughs-what-really-happened .html.

42. Jack Black, *You Can't Win* (Chico: Nabat Books, 2001).

43. In addition to Burroughs, musicians Sonny Rollins, Chet Baker, and Elvin Jones submitted to the heroin treatment program at Lexington.

44. The CIA's notorious MKUltra project was a sprawling covert research operation that, among other things, engaged in dosing Americans with experimental mind-altering substances—often without their knowledge. Among its goals was to "render the induction of hypnosis easier" and "enhance the ability of individuals to withstand privation, torture and coercion." Kat Eschner, "What We Know About the CIA's Midcentury Mind-Control Project," *Smithsonian Magazine*, April 13, 2017, accessed April 12, 2018. https://www.smithsonianmag

.com/smart-news/what-we-know-about-cias-midcentury-mind-control-project -180962836/.

45. Grauerholz, "The Death of Joan Vollmer."

46. *Burroughs: The Movie*, directed by Howard Brookner, performed by William S. Burroughs, Allen Ginsberg, Lucien Carr, and John Giorno (United Kingdom: Criterion, 1983). DVD.

47. Grauerholz, "The Death of Joan Vollmer."

48. William S. Burroughs and James Grauerholz, *Last Words: The Final Journals of William S. Burroughs* (New York: Grove, 2001). Kindle.

49. Morgan, *Literary Outlaw*, p. 252.

50. Victor Bockris, "King of the Underground," *Gadfly Online* (August 1999), accessed April 12, 2018. http://www.gadflyonline.com/home/archive/August99 /archive-burroughs.html.

51. "William S. Burroughs and Kurt Cobain—A Dossier," *RealityStudio*.

52. Telephone interview by author, October 28, 2017.

53. "William S. Burroughs and Kurt Cobain—A Dossier," *RealityStudio*.

Subterranean Homesick Burroughs

1. Simon Warner, *Text and Drugs and Rock 'n' Roll: The Beats and Rock Culture* (London: Bloomsbury, 2013).

2. Telephone interview by author, October 28, 2017.

3. Ibid.

4. Ibid.

5. *William S. Burroughs: A Man Within*, directed by Yony Leyser, performed by William S. Burroughs, Patti Smith, and Iggy Pop (United States: Oscilloscope Laboratories, 2010). DVD.

6. William S. Burroughs and Daniel Odier, *The Job: Interviews with William S. Burroughs* (New York: Penguin, 1989), p. 42.

7. Ibid., p. 14.

8. James Henke, "Jerry Garcia: The Rolling Stone Interview," *Rolling Stone*, October 31, 1991, accessed April 12, 2018. https://www.rollingstone.com/music /news/jerry-garcia-the-rolling-stone-interview-19911031.

9. Burroughs, *The Adding Machine*, p. 132.

10. Telephone interview by author, October 28, 2017.

11. Burroughs, *The Adding Machine*, p. 36.

12. "Burroughs' Statements at the 1962 International Writers' Conference," *RealityStudio*, February 21, 2008, accessed July 12, 2018. https://reality studio.org/texts/burroughs-statements-at-the-1962-international-writers -conference/.

13. Morgan, *Literary Outlaw*, p. 52.

14. Telephone interview by author, October 28, 2017.

"If not for you / Winter would have no spring / Couldn't hear the robin sing / I just wouldn't have a clue / Anyway it wouldn't ring true / If not for you." "Bob Dylan—If Not For You," *Genius*, October 19, 1970, accessed April 12, 2018. https://genius.com/Bob-dylan-if-not-for-you-lyrics.

15. Compare to: "Therefore all seasons shall be sweet to thee / Whether the summer clothe the general earth / With greenness, or the redbreast sit and sing / Betwixt the tufts of snow on the bare branch / Of mossy apple-tree." Samuel Taylor Coleridge, "Frost at Midnight," *The Rime of the Ancient Mariner and Other Poems* (Grasmere, Cumbria: Wordsworth Trust, 2006).

16. Morgan, *Literary Outlaw*, p. 61.

17. Michael Limnios, "Interview with Poet, Musician and Artist Daevid Allen of Psychedelic Rock Groups Soft Machine and Gong," *Blues.Gr.*, April 1, 2014, accessed April 12, 2018. http://blues.gr/profiles/blogs/interview-with-poet -musician-and-artist-daevid-allen-of.

18. Oliver Hall, "William S. Burroughs on the Cut-up Technique and Meeting Samuel Beckett & Bob Dylan," *Dangerous Minds*, March 22, 2018, accessed April 12, 2018. https://dangerousminds.net/comments/william_s._burroughs_on_the _cut-up_technique_and_meeting_samuel_beckett_bob.

19. Cameron Crowe, liner notes, *Bob Dylan: Biograph* (Columbia Records, 1985).

20. Sean Wilentz, *Bob Dylan in America* (London: Vintage, 2011), p. 49.

21. Crowe, *Bob Dylan: Biograph*.

22. Ibid.

23. Ibid.

24. James Adams, "Brother Bill: How William S. Burroughs Influenced Bob Dylan," *RealityStudio*, May 8, 2016, accessed April 12, 2018. http://realitystudio .org/scholarship/brother-bill-how-william-s-burroughs-influenced-bob-dylan/.

25. Oliver Harris and Ian MacFadyen, *Naked Lunch @ 50: Anniversary Essays* (Carbondale: Southern Illinois University Press, 2009).

26. Adams, "Brother Bill."

27. Crowe, *Bob Dylan: Biograph*.

28. Alan Faena, "Cut Up: The Creative Technique Used by Burroughs, Dylan, Bowie and Cobain," *Faena Aleph*, April 1, 2015, accessed April 12, 2018. http://www.faena.com/aleph/articles/cut-up-the-creative-technique-used-by -burroughs-dylan-bowie-and-cobain/.

29. Adams, "Brother Bill."

30. Ibid.

Here, There, and Everywhere

1. Richard Metzger, *Book of Lies: The Disinformation Guide to Magick and the Occult* (New York: Disinformation, 2003).

2. Sinclair Beiles, William S. Burroughs, Gregory Corso, Brion Gysin, and Claude Pélieu, *Minutes to Go* (San Francisco: Beach Books, Texts & Documents, 1968).

3. Macy Halford, "Patti Smith's Levels of Reality," *New Yorker*, November 18, 2010, accessed July 12, 2018. https://www.newyorker.com/books/page-turner /patti-smiths-levels-of-reality.

4. Miles, *The Beat Hotel: Ginsberg, Burroughs, and Corso in Paris, 1958–1963* (New York: Grove, 2001), p. 156.

5. Ibid.

6. Miles, *Call Me Burroughs*, p. 301.

7. Burroughs, Grauerholz, and Silverberg, *Word Virus*, p. 272.

8. William S. Burroughs, "The Conspiracy," *Interzone* (New York: Viking, 1989), p. 108.

9. William S. Burroughs, *Naked Lunch* (New York: Grove Press, 1959), p. 6.

10. Burroughs, *The Adding Machine*, p. 11.

11. Ibid.

12. "Dr Benway's House," Sonic Youth website, accessed July 12, 2018. http:// www.sonicyouth.com/mustang/sy/song423.html.

13. This is also the basic schematic for King Crimson guitarist Robert Fripp's collaboration with sound sculptor Brian Eno, which produced music as captivatingly alien as Burroughs' best writing.

14. Burroughs, *Naked Lunch*, p. 104.

15. Oliver Harris, "The Frisco Kid He Never Returns: Naked Lunch and San Francisco," *RealityStudio*, November 20, 2009, accessed April 12, 2018. http:// realitystudio.org/scholarship/the-frisco-kid-he-never-returns-naked-lunch -and-san-francisco/.

16. "Rub Out the Words: Letters from William Burroughs," *Granta*, June 26, 2017, accessed May 22, 2018. https://granta.com/rub-out-the-words-letters -from-william-burroughs/.

17. Burroughs, *Naked Lunch*, p. 46.

18. Derek Jones, *Censorship: A World Encyclopedia* (London: Fitzroy Dearborn, 2001).

19. Ibid.

20. Morgan, *Literary Outlaw*, p. 368.

21. Ibid.

22. Barry Miles, *Paul McCartney: Many Years from Now* (New York: H. Holt, 1997), p. 242.

23. Ibid.

24. Ibid, p. 241.

25. Bockris, "Burroughs," email to author, April 9, 2017.

26. Ibid.

27. Genesis P-Orridge, "Brian Jones' Visit to Jajouka Is Described by Brion Gysin to Genesis Beyer P-Orridge in Paris," *YouTube*, November 11, 2014, accessed April 12, 2018. https://www.youtube.com/watch?v=xDUIDQhOzOk.

28. Bockris, "Burroughs," email to author, April 9, 2017.

29. The Rolling Stones, "Undercover of the Night," accessed April 12, 2018. http://www.rollingstones.com/release/undercover/.

30. Bockris, "Burroughs," email to author, April 9, 2017.

Watch That Man

1. "Cut Up Technique—David Bowie," *YouTube*, October 27, 2013, accessed April 12, 2018. https://www.youtube.com/watch?v=m1InCrzGIPU.

2. Ibid.

3. Jung's own process of individuation was chronicled in *The Red Book*, a compendium of text and images composed/compiled between 1913 and 1930. Though *The Red Book* wasn't published in its entirety until 2009, an excerpt called "Seven Sermons to the Dead" was intermittently circulated by its author and is considered "a summary revelation of *The Red Book*." C. G. Jung, "VII Sermones Ad Mortuos" ("The Seven Sermons to the Dead [*Septem Sermones Ad Mortuos*]"), accessed April 17, 2018. http://www.gnosis.org/library/7Sermons.htm.

4. Burroughs, *Naked Lunch*, p. 172.

5. Neil McCormick, "1970s: Punk and Glitter, Grit and Glamour," *Telegraph*, September 4, 2015, accessed April 17, 2018. https://www.telegraph.co.uk/music/news/the-1970s-glamour-and-music-in-seventies/.

6. John Coulthart, "Looking for the Wild Boys," *Feuilleton*, December 1, 2012, accessed April 12, 2018. http://www.johncoulthart.com/feuilleton/2011/10/20/looking-for-the-wild-boys/.

7. Jon Savage, "When Bowie Met Burroughs," *The Guardian*, March 9, 2013, accessed April 17, 2018. https://www.theguardian.com/music/2013/mar/09/david-bowie-william-burroughs.

8. Gary Graff, "Bowie on Bowie: The Rock Icon on the Music Business, Being a Late Bloomer and His Daughter Making Him More Optimistic," *Billboard*, January 1, 2016, accessed April 12, 2018. https://www.billboard.com/articles/news/6836569/david-bowie-interview-1980s-through-2000s-life-career.

9. "David Bowie FAQ—Frequently Asked Questions," *Bowie Wonderworld*, accessed April 13, 2018. http://www.bowiewonderworld.com/faq.htm.

10. Craig Copetas, "Beat Godfather Meets Glitter Mainman: William Bur-

roughs Interviews David Bowie," *Rolling Stone*, February 28, 1974, accessed April 13, 2018. https://www.rollingstone.com/music/news/beat-godfather-meets-glit ter-mainman-19740228.

11. Nick Maslow, "'There Is No Definitive David Bowie': How the Late Music Legend Explained Creating His Iconic Persona to *People* in 1976," *People*, January 11, 2016, accessed April 13, 2018. http://people.com/celebrity/david-bowies -people-cover-story-from-1976/.

12. Paul Gorman, "Journalism: Interviewing David Bowie on Working with Eno Engaging with Visual Arts, 1995," *Paul Gorman Is*, January 18, 2013, accessed April 13, 2018. http://www.paulgormanis.com/?p=7510.

13. Michael W. Clune, *American Literature and the Free Market, 1945-2000* (Cambridge: Cambridge University Press, 2010), p. 79.

14. Jennifer Walden, *Art and Destruction* (Newcastle upon Tyne, UK: Cambridge Scholars, 2013), p. 63.

15. Dylan Jones, *David Bowie: The Oral History* (New York: Crown/Archetype, 2017). Kindle.

16. Matthew Braga, "The Verbasizer was David Bowie's 1995 Lyric Writing Mac App," *Motherboard*, January 11, 2016, accessed April 13, 2018. https:// motherboard.vice.com/en_us/article/xygxpn/the-verbasizer-was-david-bowies -1995-lyric-writing-mac-app.

17. *BBC News*, "How David Bowie Used 'Cut Ups' to Create Lyrics," *YouTube*, January 11, 2016, accessed April 13, 2018. https://www.youtube.com /watch?v=6nlW4EbxTD8.

18. Ibid.

19. Some of these experiments can be found in Burroughs and Gysin's *The Third Mind*, originally published in French by Viking Press in 1977, with an English edition appearing the following year.

20. Daniel Ferreira, "Verbasizer (David Bowie)," *7luas*, October 30, 2013, accessed April 13, 2018. http://www.7luas.com.br/all/research/researchblog /verbasizer-david-bowie-eng/.

21. Alan Yentob, "David Bowie Documentary 1998," *YouTube*, September 5, 2009, accessed April 13, 2018. https://www.youtube.com/watch?v=JNcMQe_ aRK0.

22. Ibid.

23. Martin Schneider, "Red Peppers, Milk, Cocaine: David Bowie-Themed Menu from the Big Bowie Exhibit in Chicago," *Dangerous Minds*, September 16, 2014, accessed April 17, 2018. https://dangerousminds.net/comments/red_ peppers_milk_cocaine_david_bowie-themed_menu.

24. "David Bowie—We Can Be Heroes," *The Foxley Docket*, June 2, 2017, accessed April 13, 2018. https://www.thefoxleydocket.com/luxury-news/david -bowie-heroes/.

25. "David Bowie Interview on Dick Cavett—1974," *YouTube*, January 11,

2016, accessed April 13, 2018. https://www.youtube.com/watch?v=RSSf3k 4UU64.

26. Jack Cummings, "I Went in Search of the 'Brown Note,' the Frequency That Makes You Shit Yourself," *Vice*, November 24, 2016, accessed April 17, 2018. https://www.vice.com/en_us/article/ppv35z/in-search-of-the-brown-noise.

27. Greg Myre, "How The U.S. Military Used Guns N' Roses to Make a Dictator Give Up," *NPR*, May 30, 2017, accessed April 17, 2018. https://www.npr.org /sections/thetwo-way/2017/05/30/530723028/how-the-u-s-military-used-guns -n-roses-to-make-a-dictator-give-up.

28. "US Special Forces Use Heavy Metal Music to Fight Taliban," *The Telegraph*, April 6, 2010, accessed April 13, 2018. http://www.telegraph.co.uk/news /worldnews/7558783/US-special-forces-use-heavy-metal-music-to-fight -Taliban.html.

29. The Intercept, "Leaked Documents Reveal Counterterrorism Tactics Used at Standing Rock to Defeat Pipeline Insurgencies," *The Intercept*, May 27, 2017, accessed April 13, 2018. https://theintercept.com/2017/05/27/leaked -documents-reveal-security-firms-counterterrorism-tactics-at-standing-rock -to-defeat-pipeline-insurgencies/.

30. Lily Hay Newman, "This Is the Sound Cannon Used against Protesters in Ferguson," *Slate*, August 14, 2014, accessed April 13, 2018. http://www.slate .com/blogs/future_tense/2014/08/14/lrad_long_range_acoustic_device_sound_ cannons_were_used_for_crowd_control.html.

31. Layla Quran, "The Mysterious Cuba 'Sonic Attacks' Are Still Puzzling Investigators," *PBS*, January 10, 2018, accessed April 13, 2018. https://www.pbs .org/newshour/politics/the-mysterious-cuba-sonic-attacks-are-still-puzzling -investigators.

32. "The Sound of Fear: The History of Noise as a Weapon," *FACT Magazine: Music News, New Music*, October 19, 2016, accessed April 13, 2018. http://www .factmag.com/2016/10/09/sound-fear-room40-boss-lawrence-english-history -noise-weapon/.

33. Copetas, "Beat Godfather."

34. Burroughs and Odier, *The Job*, p. 74.

35. Copetas, "Beat Godfather."

36. Jeffrey Morgan, "Inside William Burroughs," *Rock's Backpages* (1979), accessed April 13, 2018. https://www.rocksbackpages.com/Library/Article/inside -william-burroughs.

37. Peter R. Koenig, "The Laughing Gnostic—David Bowie and the Occult," *Ordo Templi Orientis Phenomenon* (1996), accessed April 17, 2018. http://www .parareligion.ch/bowie.htm.

38. "APIKORSUS," *Chaos Matrix*, (1986), accessed April 13, 2018. http:// www.chaosmatrix.org/library/chaos/texts/apikindx.html.

39. Annie Webb, "How Hermetic Initiates Used Magick to Study Reality,"

Ultraculture, July 5, 2017, accessed April 18, 2018. https://ultraculture.org/blog/2016/04/19/hermetic-initiates-magick-study-reality/.

40. Eric Olsen, "David Bowie Was No Stranger to the Occult," *America's Most Haunted*, January 12, 2016, accessed April 17, 2018. http://www.americas-most-haunted.com/2016/01/12/david-bowie-was-no-stranger-to-the-occult/.

41. Mikal Gilmore, "Cover Story Excerpt: David Bowie," *Rolling Stone*, January 18, 2012, accessed April 17, 2018. https://www.rollingstone.com/music/news/cover-story-excerpt-david-bowie-20120118.

42. Tara Isabella Burton, "Apocalypse Whatever," *Real Life*, December 13, 2016, accessed April 13, 2018. http://reallifemag.com/apocalypse-whatever/.

43. "David Bowie—Playboy Magazine," *The Uncool—The Official Site for Everything Cameron Crowe* (1976), accessed April 13, 2018. http://www.theuncool.com/journalism/david-bowie-playboy-magazine/.

44. "Features: Rock's Backpages: Classic David Bowie Interview: Adolf Hitler and the Need for a New Right," *The Quietus*, January 25, 2010, accessed April 13, 2018. http://thequietus.com/articles/03598-david-bowie-nme-interview-about-adolf-hitler-and-new-nazi-rock-movement.

45. Telephone interview by author, October 28, 2017.

46. Rod Meade Sperry, "That Time David Bowie Almost Became a Buddhist Monk—and What He Said (and Sang) about That Time," *Lion's Roar*, January 13, 2017, accessed April 18, 2018. https://www.lionsroar.com/that-time-david-bowie-almost-became-a-buddhist-monk/.

47. "Thurston Moore Reflects on David Bowie," *Pitchfork*, January 12, 2016, accessed April 18, 2018. https://pitchfork.com/news/62878-thurston-moore-reflects-on-david-bowie/.

48. William S. Burroughs and Victor Bockris, *With William Burroughs: A Report from the Bunker* (Open Road Media, 2016). Kindle.

49. Thomas Jerome Seabrook, *Bowie in Berlin: A New Career in a New Town* (London: Jawbone, 2008), p. 170.

50. Copetas, "Beat Godfather."

51. Morgan, *Literary Outlaw*, p. 632.

52. Lee Konstantinou, "William S. Burroughs' Wild Ride with Scientology," *Io9*, May 11, 2011, accessed April 18, 2018. http://io9.gizmodo.com/5800673/william-s-burroughss-wild-ride-with-scientology.

53. David S. Wills, *Scientologist! William S. Burroughs and the Weird Cult* (United Kingdom: Beatdom Books, 2013). Kindle.

54. "William Burroughs: Nothing Is True, Everything Is Permitted," *BBC Radio 4*, March 4, 2008, accessed April 18, 2018. http://www.bbc.co.uk/programmes/b0092bz5.

55. Burroughs, *Junkie* (New York: Ace Books, 1953).

56. Cover copy for Burroughs, Grauerholz, Miles, and Ballard, *Naked Lunch: The Restored Text* (London: Harper Perennial, 2010).

57. Daniel Bates, "Exclusive: How Lou Reed Was Given Electroshock Therapy Aged Just 17 Because of Mental Illness and His Bisexuality—at New York Psychiatric Hospital Described as 'Hell in Queens,'" *Daily Mail*, September 8, 2015, accessed May 23, 2018. http://www.dailymail.co.uk/news/article-3222881 /How-Lou-Reed-given-electroshock-therapy-aged-just-17-sexuality-New-York -psychiatric-hospital-described-hell-Queens.html.

58. Victor Bockris, *Transformer: The Complete Lou Reed Story* (London: HarperCollins, 2014), p. 14.

59. Lester Bangs, "Lou Reed v. Lester Bangs: A Classic Interview from the Vaults," *The Guardian*, November 8, 2011, accessed May 23, 2018. https://www .theguardian.com/music/2011/nov/08/lou-reed-lester-bangs-interview.

60. "David Bowie on Working with Lou Reed," *PBS*, accessed May 23, 2018. http://www.pbs.org/video/american-masters-david-bowie-working-lou-reed/.

61. Kristine McKenna, "Eno: Voyages in Time and Perception," *Musician* (October 1982).

62. Ben Beaumont-Thomas, "David Bowie: Lou Reed's Masterpiece Is Metallica Collaboration *Lulu*," *The Guardian*, April 20, 2015, accessed April 18, 2018. https://www.theguardian.com/music/2015/apr/20/david-bowie-lou-reed -masterpiece-metallica-lulu.

63. Stephen Davis, *Jim Morrison: Life, Death, Legend* (New York: Gotham Books, 2005). Kindle.

64. Bockris, *Transformer*.

65. Email interview by author, April 19, 2017.

66. Bockris, *Transformer*, Appendix B.

67. Email interview by author, April 19, 2017.

68. Ibid.

69. Ibid.

70. Ibid.

71. Bockris, *Transformer*, Appendix B.

72. Ibid.

73. Ibid.

74. Ibid.

75. Ibid.

76. Email interview by author, April 19, 2017.

Music and Other Dark Arts

1. "Jimmy Page 1957," *YouTube*, March 18, 2009, accessed April 29, 2018. https://youtube/iNViLFU6rdc.

2. Brad Tolinski, *Light and Shade: Conversations with Jimmy Page* (Virgin Books, 2013).

3. Ibid.

4. Master Musicians of JouJouka, performer, *Brian Jones Presents the Pipes of Pan at Joujouka*, Rolling Stones Records, 1971. Vinyl recording.

5. "Jimmy Page: 'Forget the Myths about Led Zeppelin,'" *Uncut*, May 12, 2015, accessed May 3, 2018. http://www.uncut.co.uk/features/jimmy-page-forget-the -myths-29362/3.

6. Burroughs and Gysin, *The Third Mind*.

7. Anger next tapped Manson Family stringer Bobby Beausoleil, who recorded the *Lucifer Rising* score in prison while serving a life sentence for the 1969 murder of music teacher Gary Hinman as the result of a drug deal gone awry.

8. Molly McBride Jacobson, "Boleskine House," *Atlas Obscura*, September 21, 2014, accessed May 03, 2018. https://www.atlasobscura.com/places/boleskine -house.

9. Greg Newkirk, "Did Aleister Crowley Accidentally Summon the Loch Ness Monster?," *Week In Weird*, June 15, 2016, accessed May 3, 2018. http:// weekinweird.com/2011/04/11/the-boleskine-house-loch-ness-other-stranger -monster/.

10. William S. Burroughs, "Rock Magic: Jimmy Page, Led Zeppelin, and a Search for the Elusive Stairway to Heaven," *Crawdaddy* (June 1975). https:// arthurmag.com/2007/12/05/willima-burroughs-onled-zeppelin/.

11. "Boleskine House, Legendary Residence of Jimmy Page and Aleister Crowley, Destroyed by Fire," *Daily Grail*, December 23, 2015, accessed May 14, 2018. https://www.dailygrail.com/2015/12/boleskine-house-legendary-residence-of -jimmy-page-and-aleister-crowley-destroyed-by-fire/.

12. Burroughs, "Rock Magic."

13. Ibid.

14. Jaan Uhelszki, "How Led Zeppelin *III* Was Their Most Misunderstood Album," *Loudersound*, October 5, 2016, accessed May 14, 2018. https://www.louder sound.com/features/how-iii-was-led-zeppelins-most-misunderstood-album.

15. Burroughs, *The Western Lands*, chap. 3.

16. C. Partridge, "Occulture Is Ordinary," in *Contemporary Esotericism*, ed. E. Asprem and K. Granholm (Abingdon, UK: Routledge, 2014), pp. 113–133.

17. Andrea Juno and V. Vale, *Re/Search #6/7: Industrial Culture Handbook* (San Francisco: Re/Search Publications, 1983), p. 11.

18. Simon Ford, *Wreckers of Civilisation: The Story of Coum Transmissions and Throbbing Gristle* (London: Black Dog, 1999), p. 15.

19. Telephone interview by author, May 2017.

20. Ibid.

21. "William S. Burroughs; Throbbing Gristle; Brion Gysin," *RE/Search* 4:5 (1982), p. 67.

22. The compilation has since been reissued on P-Orridge's current label, Dais.

23. Genesis P-Orridge, *Thee Psychick Bible: Thee Apocryphal Scriptures ov Genesis Breyer P-Orridge and Thee Third Mind ov Thee Temple ov Psychick Youth* (Port Townsend, WA: Feral House, 2010). Kindle.

24. Ibid.

25. Ibid.

26. Ibid.

27. Burroughs, "Playback from Eden to Watergate," *Harper's* (November 1973). http://harpers.org/archive/1973/11/playback-from-eden-to-watergate/.

28. Rich McCormick, "Odds Are We're Living in a Simulation, Says Elon Musk," *The Verge*, June 2, 2016, accessed May 3, 2018. https://www.theverge.com/2016/6/2/11837874/elon-musk-says-odds-living-in-simulation.

29. Dom Galeon, "The World's First Album Composed and Produced by an AI Has Been Unveiled," *Futurism*, August 21, 2017, accessed May 4, 2018. https://futurism.com/the-worlds-first-album-composed-and-produced-by-an-ai-has-been-unveiled/.

30. *Re/Search* 4:5 "William S. Burroughs," p. 69.

31. *FLicKeR*, directed by Nik Sheehan, performed by Marianne Faithfull, DJ Spooky, the Stooges, Iggy Pop, Lee Ranaldo, and Genesis P-Orridge (Canada: Makin' Movies, 2008). Film.

32. Ibid.

33. Ibid.

34. Ibid.

35. Ibid.

36. Ibid.

37. Ibid.

38. Perhaps the most significant litigation involving sampling was the 2005 case *Bridgeport Music, Inc. v. Dimension Films*, in which the judge ruled that any sample of a sound recording requires permission from the copyright owner.

39. John Zorn, *Arcana V: Music, Magic and Mysticism* (New York: Hips Road, 2010), p. 308.

40. Ibid., p. 309.

41. Ibid., p. 310.

42. Joseph Vecchio, "'I Was in a Position to Dismantle It'": Industrial Music Appropriations of William S. Burroughs," PhD diss., Texas State University, 2014.

43. Ibid.

44. Richard Metzger, *Book of Lies: The Disinformation Guide to Magick and the Occult* (New York: Disinformation, 2003). Kindle.

45. Ibid.

46. "Chaos Magic in a Nutshell," Specularium—Peter J. Carroll, July 24, 2014, accessed May 4, 2018. http://www.specularium.org/wizardry.

47. Matthew Levi Stevens, *The Magical Universe of William S. Burroughs* (London: Mandrake, 2014).

48. Metzger, *Book of Lies*.

49. Ibid.

50. Ibid.

51. Ibid.

52. Robert A. Sobieszek, *Ports of Entry: William S. Burroughs and the Arts* (Los Angeles: Museum of Art, 1996).

53. *Fist* (n.p.: 1992).

54. Edward S. Robinson, "Nothing Here Now but the Lost Recordings," RealityStudio. http://realitystudio.org/scholarship/nothing-here-now-but-the -lost-recordings/.

55. Joe Ambrose and A. D. Hitchin, *Cut Up!: An Anthology Inspired by the Cut-up Method of William S. Burroughs and Brion Gysin* (Swansea: Oneiros Books, 2014), p. 328.

56. Christopherson died in 2010; his partner Balance, six years prior. The pair leave behind a legacy of obscure and challenging music that tends to be appreciated by listeners who are also Burroughs enthusiasts.

57. David Keenan, *England's Hidden Reverse: A Secret History of the Esoteric Underground* (London: Strange Attractor, 2017).

58. Mike Barnes, "'Sleazy' Peter Christopherson Unedited," *The Wire* (August 2009), accessed May 14, 2018. https://www.thewire.co.uk/in-writing/interviews /p=14906.

59. Ibid.

60. Ibid.

61. Stevens, "Nothing Here Now But the Recordings."

62. P-Orridge, *Thee Psychick Bible*. Kindle.

63. Klint Finley, "Interview with James Grauerholz on William S. Burroughs and Magick," *Technoccult*, September 2, 2010, accessed May 04, 2018. http:// technoccult.net/archives/2010/09/02/interview-with-james-grauerholz-on -william-s-burroughs-and-magick/.

64. Telephone interview by author, August 2017.

Bunkers, Punkers, and Junkies

1. "Avant-Garde Unites Over Burroughs," *New York Times*, December 1, 1978, accessed May 14, 2018. https://archive.nytimes.com/www.nytimes.com/books /00/02/13/specials/burroughs-avant.html.

2. "Thurston Moore Curated William Burroughs Nova Convention Exhibition," *Fütüristika!*, September 5, 2014, accessed May 14, 2018. http://www.futuristika .org/thurston-moore-curated-william-burroughs-nova-convention-exhibition/.

3. *Burroughs: The Movie* bonus features.

4. "Thurston Moore Curated."

5. Telephone interview by author, August 2017.

6. "Here To Go," *YouTube*, May 4, 2011, accessed May 15, 2018. https://you tube.com/watch?v=Ibp-B4MSh8w.

7. Patti Smith, *The Nova Convention*, performed by Laurie Anderson, William Seward Burroughs, and John Cage (John Giorno, 1979). Vinyl recording.

8. Ibid.

9. Kevin EG Perry, "William Burroughs at 100: Thurston Moore on Seeing Him Watch Patti Smith at CBGB, His Response to Kurt Cobain's Suicide and 'Cut-up' Songwriting," *The Collected Works of Kevin EG Perry*, February 10, 2014, accessed May 14, 2018. https://kevinegperry.com/2014/02/05/william-s -burroughs-at-100-thurston-moore-on-seeing-him-watch-patti-smith-at-cbgb -his-response-to-kurt-cobains-suicide-and-cut-up-songwriting/.

10. Bockris, "Burroughs," email to author.

11. Telephone interview by author, February 3, 2017.

12. A type of coil-spring, extendable baton that can be used as an offensive or defensive weapon.

13. Bockris, "Burroughs," email to author.

14. Ibid.

15. Ibid.

16. Burroughs and Bockris, *With William Burroughs*, p. 225.

17. Ibid.

18. Ibid.

19. Ibid.

20. Strummer's visit took place at some point in 1980, shortly before Burroughs left New York City for Lawrence.

21. Patti Smith herself wrote about music; she quit in the middle of an interview with Eric Clapton when she realized she was more interested in telling him about her work than asking about his.

22. Victor Bockris, *Beat Punks: New York's Underground Culture from the Beat Generation to the Punk Explosion* (London: Da Capo, 2000). Kindle.

23. *Burroughs: A Man Within*. DVD.

24. Ibid.

25. Mish Barber-Way, "Hole's Patty Schemel Wrote the Realest Book About Being an Addict in a Band," *Pitchfork*, November 14, 2017, accessed May 15, 2018. https://pitchfork.com/thepitch/holes-patty-schemel-wrote-the-realest-book -about-being-an-addict-in-a-band/.

26. English punk was more sartorially focused than its US counterpart, but it was Americans, particularly Hell, who established punk's prototypical look and attitude.

27. Robin Lydenberg and Jennie Skerl, *William S. Burroughs at the Front: Critical Reception, 1959–1989* (Carbondale: Southern Illinois University Press, 1997), p. 146.

28. Ibid.

29. Richard Hell, *I Dreamed I Was a Very Clean Tramp: An Autobiography* (New York: Ecco, 2014). Kindle.

30. Ibid.

31. Burroughs and Bockris, *With William Burroughs*.

32. Bockris, "Burroughs," email to author.

33. D. Amorosi, "Seventh Heaven," *Philadelphia City Paper*, November 23, 1995, accessed May 15, 2018. http://www.oceanstar.com/patti/intervus/philly2 .htm.

34. Burroughs and Bockris, *With William Burroughs*.

35. *Burroughs: A Man Within*. DVD.

36. Victor Bockris and Roberta Bayley, *Patti Smith: An Unauthorized Biography* (New York: Simon and Schuster, 1999).

37. Ibid.

38. Ibid.

39. Ibid.

40. Ibid.

41. Ibid.

42. *Burroughs: The Movie*.

43. *Burroughs: A Man Within*. DVD.

44. Bockris and Bayley, *Patti Smith*.

45. Ibid.

46. Lisa Robinson, "Patti Smith: The High Priestess of Rock and Roll," *Hit Parader* (January 1976). http://www.oceanstar.com/patti/intervus/760100hp .htm.

47. Ibid.

48. Ibid.

49. Bockris and Bayley, *Patti Smith*.

50. Ibid.

51. Morgan, *Literary Outlaw*, p. 252.

52. Bockris and Bayley, *Patti Smith*.

53. Ibid.

54. Ibid.

55. Patti Smith, *Just Kids* (New York: Ecco, 2010), p. 17.

56. Ibid.

57. Ibid.

58. Bockris and Bayley, *Patti Smith*.

59. Victor Bockris, *Beat Punks: New York's Underground Culture from the Beat Generation to the Punk Explosion* (London: Da Capo, 2000). Kindle.

60. Simon Warner, *Text and Drugs and Rock 'N' Roll: The Beats and Rock Culture* (New York: Bloomsbury Academic, 2014). Kindle.

61. *Burroughs: A Man Within*. DVD.

62. Perry, "William Burroughs at 100."

63. Telephone interview by author, October 28, 2017.

64. Ibid.

65. Bockris, *Beat Punks*.

66. Bockris, "Burroughs," email to author, April 9, 2017.

67. Ibid.

Here to Go

1. "William S. Burroughs and Joy Division," *RealityStudio*, May 29, 2008, accessed May 15, 2018. http://realitystudio.org/biography/william-s-burroughs-and-joy-division/.

2. Ibid.

3. James Henke, "Jerry Garcia: The Rolling Stone Interview," *Rolling Stone*, October 31, 1991, accessed May 16, 2018. https://www.rollingstone.com/music/news/jerry-garcia-the-rolling-stone-interview-19911031.

4. Mary Eisenhart, "Jerry Garcia Interview," *YoYow*, November 12, 1987, accessed May 16, 2018. http://www.yoyow.com/marye/garcia2.html.

5. Rock Scully and David Dalton, *Living with the Dead: Twenty Years on the Bus with Garcia and the Grateful Dead* (New York: Cooper Square, 2001), p. 345.

6. Fred Goodman, "Jerry Garcia: The Rolling Stone Interview," *Rolling Stone*, November 30, 1989, accessed May 16, 2018. https://www.rollingstone.com/music/features/the-rolling-stone-interview-jerry-garcia-19891130.

7. Burroughs and Grauerholz, *Last Words*. Kindle.

8. Ibid.

9. Janet Maslin, "Review/Film; Drifting In and Out Of a Kafkaesque Reality," *New York Times*, December 27, 1991, accessed May 17, 2018. https://www.nytimes.com/1991/12/27/movies/review-film-drifting-in-and-out-of-a-kafkaesque-reality.html.

10. "John Oswald's 'burrows' Cutups," *RealityStudio*, June 27, 2006, accessed May 17, 2018. http://realitystudio.net/viewtopic.php?t=173.

11. "Grateful Dead Family Discography: Grayfolded."

12. Stevens, "A Report on The Final Academy," *Beatdom*, October 14, 2012, accessed May 16, 2018. www.beatdom.com/a-report-on-the-final-academy-then-now/.

13. Ibid.

14. Ibid.

15. Ibid.

16. Ibid.

17. Coulthart, "The Final Academy."

18. Joe Ambrose, "Final Academy," email to author.

19. *Words of Advice: William S. Burroughs On the Road*, directed by Lars Movin and Steen Møller Rasmussen, 2007. DVD.

20. Miles, "Call Me Burroughs." Kindle.

21. *Words of Advice*. DVD.

22. *Burroughs: A Man Within*. DVD.

23. Ibid.

24. Ibid.

25. Ibid.

26. Ibid.

27. Tav Falco, "Questions for Burroughs Book," email to author, September 23, 2017.

28. Bockris, *Beat Punks*.

29. Sara Rosen, "Ruby Ray: Punk Passage," *Missrosen*, June 30, 2010, accessed May 18, 2018. http://www.missrosen.com/ruby-ray-punk-passage/.

30. *Every Everything: The Music, Life and Times of Grant Hart*, directed by Gorman Bechard, performed by Grant Hart (US: What Were We Thinking Films, 2013).

31. Ibid.

32. Joshua Klein, "Grant Hart," *AV Club*, July 26, 2000, accessed May 18, 2018. https://www.avclub.com/grant-hart-1798208091.

33. *Every Everything*. Film.

34. Ibid.

35. John Giorno, "Giorno Poetry Systems—History," *Brainwashed*, accessed May 17, 2018. http://brainwashed.com/giorno/history.php.

36. Ibid.

37. Nate Freeman, "'Don't Wait For Anything': Dinner With John Giorno, and the Ghost of Burroughs," *Observer*, March 31, 2015, accessed May 18, 2018. http://observer.com/2015/03/dont-wait-for-anything-dinner-with-john-giorno -and-the-ghost-of-burroughs/.

38. Marc Campbell, "William Burroughs, Gus Van Sant and the Discipline of 'Do Easy,'" *DangerousMinds*, August 4, 2014, accessed May 18, 2018. https:// dangerousminds.net/comments/william_burroughs_gus_van_sant_and_the_ discipline_of_do_easy.

39. Ibid.

40. Ibid.

41. Van Sant would go on to direct a thinly veiled account of Kurt Cobain's suicide called *Last Days*, which arrived in theaters in 2005. Taking a page from Burroughs, we do not consider this a coincidence.

42. Paula Bernstein, "Gus Van Sant: On Working with William S. Burroughs

and the Evolution of Indie Film," *IndieWire*, May 28, 2016, accessed May 18, 2018. http://www.indiewire.com/2015/05/gus-van-sant-on-working-with-william-s -burroughs-and-the-evolution-of-indie-film-62460/.

43. *Words of Advice*. DVD.

44. Ibid.

45. Robert Wilson, "Interview," email message to author, January 25, 2018.

46. Ibid.

47. Spencer Kansa, "William Burroughs—Heavy Metal Guru," Beatdom, August 24, 2010, accessed May 18, 2018. http://www.beatdom.com/william -burroughs-heavy-metal-guru/.

48. "Devo Gets Down with William S. Burroughs," *Trouser Press* (February 1982).

49. David Kushner, "William Gibson on Life Inside and Outside the Internet," *Rolling Stone*, November 18, 2014, accessed May 18, 2018. https://www.rolling stone.com/culture/features/william-gibson-on-life-inside-and-outside-the -Internet-20141118.

50. Douglas Rushkoff, "William S. Burroughs and the Internet," email message to author, January 18, 2018.

51. James Jackson Toth, "Too Much Music: A Failed Experiment In Dedicated Listening," *NPR*, January 16, 2018, accessed May 18, 2018. https://www.npr.org/ sections/therecord/2018/01/16/578216674/too-much-music-a-failed-experi ment-in-dedicated-listening.

52. Gareth Branwyn, "Quote for Burroughs Book," email to author, January 22, 2018.

53. Tav Falco, "Questions for Burroughs Book," email to author, September 23, 2017.

54. Jamie Curcio, "Burroughs and Chaos Magick," email to author, January 17, 2018.

55. *Ghost Box*, accessed May 18, 2018. https://ghostbox.co.uk/.

56. "Burroughs' Statements at the 1962 International Writers' Conference," *RealityStudio*, February 21, 2008, accessed May 18, 2018. http://realitystudio.org /texts/burroughs-statements-at-the-1962-international-writers-conference/.

The Western Lands

1. William S. Burroughs interviewed by Jim McMenamin in *Across the Wounded Galaxies*, ed. Larry McCaffery (Champaign: University of Illinois Press, 1990), p. 51.

2. William S. Burroughs, *Painting and Guns* (Madras: Hanuman Books, 1992).

3. Kathryn Shattuck, "For Burroughs at 82, a Legion of Fans Under the Influ-

ence," *New York Times*, November 26, 1996, accessed May 21, 2018. http://www
.nytimes.com/1996/11/26/books/for-burroughs-at-82-a-legion-of-fans-under
-the-influence.html.

4. *Burroughs: The Movie* bonus features.

5. Dave Teeuwen, "Interview with Victor Bockris on William Burroughs,"
RealityStudio, May 27, 2010, accessed May 21, 2018. http://realitystudio.org
/interviews/interview-with-victor-bockris-on-william-burroughs/.

6. Ira Silverberg, *Everything Is Permitted: The Making of Naked Lunch* (New
York: Grove Weidenfeld, 1992), p. 15.

7. Burroughs interviewed by Kristine McKenna, September 13, 1990, in *Burroughs Live: Collected Interviews* (Los Angeles: Semiotext(e), 2000), p. 722.

8. Burroughs and Grauerholz, *Last Words*.

9. Miles, *Call Me Burroughs*, p. 623.

10. Perry, "William Burroughs at 100."

11. Ibid.

12. Kim Gordon, *Girl in a Band: A Memoir* (New York: Dey Street Books,
2015), p. 19.

13. Ibid.

14. Perry, "William Burroughs at 100."

15. Ibid.

16. "Thurston Moore Starts New Group Chelsea Light Moving," *The Wire*,
June 22, 2012, accessed May 21, 2018. https://www.thewire.co.uk/news/19179
/thurston-moore-starts-new-group-chelsea-light-moving.

17. Michael Nelson, "Chelsea Light Moving (Thurston Moore's New Band),"
Stereogum, June 22, 2012, accessed May 21, 2018. https://www.stereogum.com
/1073092/chelsea-light-moving-thurston-moores-new-band-burroughs/mp3s/.

18. "'Nova Convention: William Burroughs,'" interview with Thurston Moore,
Eva Prinz and James Hamilton" [in Spanish,] *YouTube*, May 15, 2017, accessed
May 21, 2018. https://www.youtube.com/watch?v=Bb0tNIRjsvk.

19. *Words of Advice*. DVD.

20. Al Jourgensen and Jon Wiederhorn, *Ministry: The Lost Gospels According
to Al Jourgensen* (Boston: Da Capo, 2014). Kindle.

21. Ibid.

22. Ibid.

23. Ibid.

24. Ibid.

25. Ibid.

26. Ibid.

27. Ibid.

28. Ibid.

29. Ibid.

30. Ibid.

31. Ibid.

32. The bicameral mind is a theory of evolutionary psychology advanced by Julian Jaynes that posits two distinct cognitive spheres, one of which produces command-based auditory hallucinations among developing humans, possibly interpreted in subsequent religious texts as the voice of God.

33. Miles, *Call Me Burroughs*, p. 608.

34. Burroughs and Grauerholz, *Last Words*.

35. Rania Aniftos, "A Timeline of Tom DeLonge's Connection With UFOs," *Billboard*, December 12, 2017, accessed May 21, 2018. https://www.billboard.com /articles/columns/rock/8071145/tom-delonge-ufo-timeline.

36. Helene Cooper, Ralph Blumenthal, and Leslie Kean, "Glowing Auras and 'Black Money': The Pentagon's Mysterious U.F.O. Program," *New York Times*, December 16, 2017, accessed May 21, 2018. https://www.nytimes.com/2017/12/16 /us/politics/pentagon-program-ufo-harry-reid.html.

37. Larry McCaffery (ed.), *Across the Wounded Galaxies: Interviews with Contemporary American Science Fiction Writers* (Champaign: University of Illinois Press, 1990). *Bulletin of Science, Technology and Society* 11, no. 1.

38. Burroughs and Odier, *The Job*, p. 45.

39. Burroughs, *The Western Lands*, p. 3.

40. Ibid.

41. Miles, *Call Me Burroughs*, p. 625.

42. Ibid.

43. Ibid.

44. *Words of Advice*. DVD.

45. Ibid.

Index